"*I Give you Authority* is a remarkable book on a subject tackled in a scripturally trustworthy manner. We have been in healing prayer ministry for over forty years, and in reading this book, we were challenged to grow in acceptance of spiritual authority in our own lives."

Francis and Judith MacNutt, Christian Healing Ministries

"Since it was first published in 1997, *I Give You Authority* has been the most thorough and comprehensive book on the authority of the believer. And now in revising and updating it, Chuck Kraft has made it even better! Read it and be equipped to take your authority in Christ."

Stephen Seamands, professor of Christian doctrine,
Asbury Theological Seminary

"In a world embarrased by the suggestion that Christians fully aware of the mission given them by God engage in spiritual warfare, Charles Kraft offers insights into the reasons why Christ gives His disciples authority over evil spirits, what he has learned about its exercise over a lifetime and how Christians are short-circuiting the Gospel when they do not attend to Satanic power in the world. His conclusions will be controversial, but there is no doubt that Professor Kraft shines light on issues that we ignore at our peril and leavens his words with the wisdom that comes only from experience and the illumination of the Spirit."

William R. Burrows, research professor of missiology,
Center for World Christianity

"It has been my experience that most Christians in the Western world live in either fear or ignorance about how to engage in spiritual warfare, and thereby give Satan an incalculable advantage over the people of God. In this book, Charles Kraft shares from his years of experience and his ministry with thousands of people as he demonstrates the incredible power and authority that has been given to all believers. This is a must-read for all believers."

Doug Hayward, Ph.D., professor of intercultural studies,
Biola University

I Give You
Authority

Other Books by Charles H. Kraft

Anthropology for Christian Witness

Appropriate Christianity

Behind Enemy Lines

Christianity in Culture

Christianity with Power

Communicating Jesus' Way
(formerly *Communicating the Gospel God's Way*)

Communication Theory for Christian Witness

Confronting Powerless Christianity

Deep Wounds, Deep Healing

Defeating Dark Angels

Two Hours to Freedom

The Rules of Engagement
(with David DeBord)

Worldview for Christian Witness

I Give You
Authority

Practicing the Authority Jesus Gave Us

Charles H. Kraft

Chosen

a division of Baker Publishing Group
Minneapolis, Minnesota

Published by Chosen Books
11400 Hampshire Avenue South
Bloomington, Minnesota 55438
www.chosenbooks.com

Chosen Books is a division of
Baker Publishing Group, Grand Rapids, Michigan

Printed in the United States of America

Library of Congress Cataloging-in-Publication Data

Kraft, Charles H.
   I give you authority : practicing the authority Jesus gave us / Charles H. Kraft. — Rev. ed.
     p. cm.
   Includes bibliographical references (p.   ) and indexes.
   ISBN 10: 0-8007-9524-5 (pbk. : alk. paper)
    1. Authority—Religious aspects—Christianity. I. Title.
BT88.K73 2012
262′.8—dc23   2011045035

Cover Design by Dan Pitts

13 14 15 16 17 18   8 7 6 5 4 3

Contents

Contents

Contents

Contents

Introduction

Walking in authority as Jesus did is crucial for every believer. The nature of Christians' authority is a central teaching in the New Testament; it was important to Jesus, and it is an important issue for all Christians to this day.

Indeed, it was the authority that Jesus displayed that bothered His enemies, for they kept asking, "What right do you have to do these things? Who gave you such right?" (Matthew 21:23). The people were fascinated with Jesus' authority to cast out demons. At the very beginning of His ministry, those watching Him deal with a demon remarked in amazement, "What is this? Is it some kind of new teaching? This man has authority to give orders to the evil spirits, and they obey him!" (Mark 1:27).

Jesus acted as if He owned the place!

Jesus acted as if He owned the place! He did not teach as the Pharisees taught, who tied their authority to famous teachers of years gone by with unrelenting fidelity. He spoke and acted like a person on a mission, coming to earth with the authority of God the Father. He was a Man both with authority and under the authority of the Father.

Then, of course, Jesus passed on this authority to His disciples—to the ragtag bunch of disrespected Galileans whom He had called and commissioned, saying, "As the Father sent me, so I send you"—thus giving them the authority to heal, cast out demons, even raise the dead (John 20:21) so that they could carry on Kingdom ministry after Jesus had gone.

The authority given us by our Master is what we are dealing with in this book. But before we tackle the substance of our authority in Christ, we must come to terms with two foundational issues: Scripture and experience.

The Bible, Our Tether

When I served as a missionary in Nigeria, I often saw horses and goats with one end of a rope tied around one back leg and the other end to a post driven into the ground. If the horse or goat moved as far as possible from the post and tried to walk, it would create a circle. Within that circle the horse or goat lived and grazed, but because the animal was tethered by the rope fixed to the post, it could not stray outside the circle's radius. The tether defined for the animal the range within which it could operate. Sometimes the rope was fairly long, giving the animal lots of room within which to graze. Sometimes the tether was short and the area small within which the animal could move.

I consider the inspiration of the Old Testament to be equal to that of the New Testament.

The point is that the length of the tether set the limits within which the animal had to function. For us the Bible is the tether that sets those limits. We learn about Christian authority by looking within Scripture for examples and teaching that we can follow. These set the parameters within which we are to work.

To learn about authority *in* Scripture, we submit ourselves to the authority *of* Scripture.

✄ The Authority of Scripture

I believe the Bible, consisting of the 66 canonical books accepted by Protestants, to be inspired by God Himself (2 Timothy 3:16). Nowhere does the Bible define what inspiration means, but it clearly points to God as the One who inspired it—the source of the inspiration—rather than to the humans who did the writing in partnership with God. This means that it is trustworthy and authoritative as the conveyer of God's truth.

The Bible is a casebook (see Kraft 2005b), recording the cases of people who interacted with God in the past and whose examples we are advised to follow or to avoid. Through the stories it tells, we are led to truth, sometimes presented in statements (e.g., the Ten Commandments, the Beatitudes), but more often through the examples of those whose stories are recorded in it. We are told negatively that we are not to follow the examples of those who disobeyed God (1 Corinthians 10:7–11) and positively that we should imitate the faithful, such as Jesus (John 13:15; 14:12), Paul (1 Corinthians 4:16; 11:1; Philippians 3:17) and the prophets (James 5:10).

It is the practice of some to, for the most part, ignore the Old Testament. I do not. I consider the inspiration of the Old Testament to be equal to that of the New Testament and most of the differences between them to be cultural rather than theological. Therefore I take instruction and examples from the Old Testament just as seriously as those from the New, except where they have been specifically superseded by New Testament teaching (e.g., animal sacrifices).

We derive teaching (doctrine) from the whole of Scripture, from both direct statements and the recorded descriptions of

God's people working in the authority He granted them. Though there are those who deny that we are to derive doctrine from historical passages, I consider such a position misguided. Rather, some of the most important teachings of Scripture lie in the ways God's servants demonstrate what life and ministry with God are supposed to be (which is to say, in the history). All of Scripture is there for our instruction and guidance.

Scripture is our guide and tether. So we seek to take seriously everything the Bible teaches, whether as specific directions or as general principles. This is our aim throughout the following chapters. It will involve interpretation of Scripture, and because all interpretation is thoroughly influenced by experience, we must acknowledge that differences of experience may lead to differences in interpretation.

Personal Experience

The way we interpret Scripture (and all else that goes on) is pervasively influenced by our experience. Jesus stated that as we obey Him, we will experience the truth (see John 8:31–32; the Greek meaning is that we will know through experience). The lessons in the following chapters come out of the interaction between my commitment to Scripture (and supremely to the Lord of Scripture) and my experiences working in the authority and power of Jesus.

My movement into what I now understand and practice in the realm of spiritual authority began in January 1982. That was when a course on healing was first offered in the School of World Mission (now the School of Intercultural Studies) at Fuller Theological Seminary, where I have been teaching since 1969.

At the time this course was taught, I had been a Christian for decades, from the time that I accepted Jesus as my personal Savior at a summer camp when I was twelve years old. Soon after my conversion I committed myself to becoming a missionary in Africa. I attended an evangelical, noncharismatic church and went first to an evangelical college (Wheaton) and on to an evangelical seminary (Ashland).

I considered myself a normal, strongly committed Christian. I also thought that charismatic and Pentecostal expressions of Christianity were too "far out" to be taken seriously. And yet I do remember wondering if there might not be something more to Christianity than I was experiencing. I had no idea what the missing element might be. Now, however, it is clear to me that I longed for the kind of authority and power that we see in the pages of the New Testament.

My wife and I worked as pioneer missionaries in northeastern Nigeria under an evangelical mission board in the late 1950s. It was there that, equipped as I was with good theological and anthropological preparation, I realized there was an area of Scripture that I could not handle: spiritual warfare. I had been taught well in church, college and seminary in the areas that evangelicals specialize in.

I realized there was an area of Scripture that I could not handle: spiritual warfare.

We studied scriptural truth that can be understood rationally and focused on the need for commitment to Christ. Emphases considered charismatic were never dealt with, however, unless it was to make fun of a branch of Christianity we considered weird and off balance.

In my Systematic Theology class in seminary, our textbook had a section titled "Satan and Demons." But we ran out of time before we got to that section. The professor said we would have to cover that material on our own, which, of course, we did not.

The Nigerian leaders, however, wanted to learn about how to handle evil spirits. I could deal with just about everything else in Scripture, but this one was beyond me, except to teach that Jesus was able to cast them out. I assumed that He was able to handle them because He was God. I had no idea that *I* had any authority over them, though I had heard stories of other missionaries (none in our particular field) who had encountered demons and successfully dealt with them. I believed that demons existed but considered myself very fortunate to never have met one. The Nigerians were gracious and did not press the issue; they knew I was not able to help them in this area.

With questions about demons deep in my subconscious, I found myself by the early 1980s firmly established in the most prestigious missions faculty in America. Neither colleagues nor students expected me to change radically from the solid evangelical approach to Christianity and its relationships to culture that I had been teaching for more than a decade. But when it was suggested to our faculty that we invite a pastor named John Wimber to teach a course titled Signs, Wonders and Church Growth, I remembered the embarrassment of not being able to answer those questions in Nigeria. So I strongly supported the offering of the course and even decided to attend.

A new phase of my life launched with the start of that course in January 1982. I began to see what it is like to assume that Jesus meant it when He said, "Those who believe in me will do what I do" (John 14:12). We saw many people healed before our very eyes because Wimber and his ministry team asserted the authority of Jesus over whatever problems people brought with them. And in due course I and others began to claim the same authority and experience similar results.

Now, three decades later, I have found meaning, excitement and spiritual enrichment beyond measure as I work in Jesus' authority to bring freedom to those who are hurting. Though the class Wimber taught focused on physical healing, I soon discovered that God has gifted me in dealing with the deeper emotional and spiritual areas that often underlie the physical problems. Since about 1984 I have been involved in what I call deep-level or inner healing. This ministry frequently brings me face-to-face with demons, since most of the three thousand or more ministry sessions I have led have involved demons.

With demons, even more than with emotional or physical problems, it becomes obvious that we are working both under and with Jesus' authority. Frequently I will ask a demon if he recognizes that I come in the authority of Jesus; the answer is always yes. And he has to submit to that authority since it is much greater than his. This authority, however, has many more dimensions than simply its usefulness in dealing with demons.

It is about this authority and its various dimensions that I write this book—an authority in the spiritual realm that many Christians (including myself, up to 1982) know little about. It is as if God has deposited a million dollars in a bank for us and we either do not realize it or cannot find the checkbook. Meanwhile the enemy, who has less authority than we have, goes about his business of disrupting God's plans and tormenting God's people, and we do not know what to do about it.

This book has been dedicated as a tool in God's hands to alert and instruct His people concerning the truths of this aspect of the Kingdom of God: our authority.

Bringing Tether and Experience Together

It seems to me that Scripture and Christian experience can be helpfully viewed in terms of three primary focuses: allegiance, truth and power. I will develop these later in chapter 18 (see also Kraft 2002).

For now, though, I will say that as I look back over my life, I see that before 1982 I had gone a long way in experiencing the allegiance and truth dimensions of Scripture. I had pledged allegiance to Jesus Christ and grown considerably in the depth and intensity of my relationship with and commitment to Him. In addition I would say that I had learned enough scriptural truth to have an authentic depth of understanding of what the Christian life is all about.

But I knew very little about the power dimension of Christianity. I knew the power of love and the power of faith, but I was almost totally ignorant of the power that Jesus and the apostles demonstrated in opposition to Satan, a power often spoken about and demonstrated in Scripture. I would say I had two-thirds of Scripture fairly right. But this other dimension of Scripture was foreign to me. By moving into spiritual authority and power, I feel I have become more biblical than I was previously.

There is, however, a major problem stemming from the fact that many of the situations we face in contemporary life are neither exemplified nor discussed in Scripture. We and the churches we form have developed a number of techniques to fill in the blanks that are left open by the silence of Scripture, and as far as the allegiance and truth categories go, we have gotten quite used to them. We endorse evangelistic rallies in which appeals are made for commitment, educational techniques such as schools and Sunday schools that train people in the truths of Scripture and a variety of other approaches not specifically endorsed by Scripture.

We feel that these approaches are within the tether of Scripture. But because of our unfamiliarity and discomfort with the power area, questions are often raised concerning whether techniques some Christians use are scriptural or not. Frequently it seems that as we ask God for specific guidance in situations involving spiritual authority and power, we find ourselves doing things that cannot be supported by any biblical "chapter and verse."

In the pages that follow—as in my own ministry—we are trying to work within the limits imposed by Scripture. We try to be careful not to claim as the voice of God any direction that goes outside scriptural guidelines. As in the allegiance and truth areas, though, there seems to be a lot of room within the scriptural tether for God to lead us creatively. Scripture itself gives us plenty of evidence that God can and will lead both directly (e.g., through words of knowledge or even, sometimes, audibly) and creatively.

I would like to acknowledge the assistance of a number of people who have helped me in the writing of this volume. Most of them are also ministry associates, so my gratitude to them goes much deeper than for the help they have been to me in writing.

Special thanks to Sam Fraser, Ellyn Kearney, Jim Wilder, Bill Dancy, Mike Crow, Tom Harang, Gary and Betsy Runkle-Edens and Mark White. And extra-special thanks to Jane Campbell, faithful, conscientious and encouraging editorial director of Chosen Books.

1

God's Authority Challenged

❧ Before Creation

"In the beginning, God . . ." God was already there when history began—supreme in His power, in total authority over all that existed. With Him were angels and perhaps other heavenly beings that He had created. These lived under His authority and did His bidding.

Certain of these angels seem to have had authority delegated to them. We read of the archangel Michael who is said to have been assigned at a later date to protect Israel (Daniel 12:1). And Gabriel, who describes himself as one who "stands in the presence of God," seems to have been given authority to interpret God's revelations to humans (Luke 1:19; Daniel 8:15–27; 9:20–27).

Then there was the angel named Lucifer. He was certainly one of the archangels, perhaps the highest of them. We are not told what his assignment was, only that he rebelled. As Isaiah puts it, "You were determined to climb up to heaven and to place your throne above the highest stars. You thought you would sit like a king. . . . You said you would climb to the tops of the clouds and be like the Almighty" (Isaiah 14:13–14).

We do not know why this being that we know as Satan sacrificed his position as second in command to fight his Master. Perhaps, though, the thing that tipped him in that direction was the rumor that God planned to create a new being, one that would carry God's own image, who would therefore displace Lucifer as second in authority over the universe. My theory is that this plan of God angered him beyond his ability to remain obedient to God. So he rebelled and set up his own kingdom.

Whatever the reason, when Lucifer rebelled he became an enemy of God. But he left the presence of God with a considerable amount of authority and power. We do not know just how much Lucifer was able to keep of the authority and power he had as an archangel; perhaps God allowed him to retain as much as he had had when he served God.

No matter the amount, Lucifer seems to have a significant ability to disrupt the plans of God and His creatures. This situation has resulted in one of the great ironies of history—a being who uses the very power God allows him to oppose the God who gave it to him. But this irony is paralleled by another: the fact that God has done the same thing with humans. God has set certain limitations on Himself by giving to humans and, apparently, to angels a certain amount of autonomy that we can use, if we choose, even to oppose the One who gives it to us.

> *We do not know just how much Lucifer was able to keep of the authority and power he had as an archangel.*

Creation

At the right time, then, God created the earth and all that He put in it, culminating His creation with His masterpiece: human beings. Having provided a lovely garden for them to live in, God made Adam and then Eve, placing them high above all other created beings. God made them in His image, to resemble Him, act like Him and have power over all creation (Genesis 1:26). He then commanded them to have many children who would bring the earth under their control (Genesis 1:28). As the psalmist says, "You made them inferior only to yourself [literally 'a little lower than God']; you crowned them with glory and honor. You appointed them rulers over everything you made; you placed them over all creation" (Psalm 8:5–6).

So authority of several kinds was given to Adam and Eve: authority to carry the image of God, authority to create children in God's image and authority over all creation. And all would have gone well with God over all, humans under Him and angels serving them both if God's enemy, Lucifer, had not succeeded in enticing Adam to misuse his authority by giving it all away. But, as we know all too well, Adam fell for Satan's deceit. God's enemy led Eve to doubt the truth of what God had said and offered her the possibility of knowing as God knows (Genesis 3:4–5). Foolishly, Eve and then Adam agreed to doubt and then to disobey God, in the process becoming obedient to Satan.

By obeying Lucifer, then, Adam gave away the authority over creation that God had given him. All that was under Adam's authority fell when he fell. His disobedience brought a curse on God's creation and gave Satan authority over all that God had given Adam and Eve. Satan had a right, therefore, in his discussion with Jesus to claim that the power and wealth of the world "has all been handed over to me, and I can give it to anyone I choose" (Luke 4:6).

The Fall did something to our status in the universe. Though we had been created above the angels, including Satan, we now fell below him—a delightful turn of events for Satan, since it restored him to second place in the universe until he lost it all at the crucifixion. We may summarize the relative places of created beings as follows:

Before Creation Genesis 1:1	Just After Creation Psalm 8:5	After the Fall Luke 4:6; Hebrews 2:7, 9	After the Crucifixion Colossians 2:15
1. God	1. God	1. God	1. God
2. Archangels	2. Humans	2. Satan	2. Humans
3. Angels	3. Archangels (Including Satan)	3. Humans	3. Satan
	4. Angels	4. Angels	4. Angels

From the day of the Fall up to now there has been war between two kingdoms. Satan uses the authority given him by God to oppose God. As mentioned earlier, Satan apparently had been given a certain amount of authority as an archangel of God, and this authority was not taken from him when he fell. We can be thankful, however, that after the crucifixion and resurrection of Jesus, the relative positions of humans, angels and Satan changed once again.

✎ Redemption

Because of the events described in the fourth column above, the bad news became good news. God Himself worked out a plan to redeem us and, in doing so, to restore us to our rightful position in the universe. Into the third situation above, Jesus came as a human being, dwelling in our post-Fall human context "for a little while lower than the angels" (Hebrews 2:7, 9). As a man, having laid aside His deity, He then retraced Adam's footsteps up to the point of temptation—facing temptation after temptation—and succeeded in obedience where Adam failed.

Jesus' life was a continual exhibition of the obedience in which humans were intended to live. We were made to function in dependence on and obedience to God, and things have not been right since our ancestor chose not to depend and obey. But Jesus came as Adam came, innocent of sin, and committed Himself to win the battle Adam lost and to show us the way things were intended to be.

Jesus came under an agreement with God the Father never to use His divine abilities while on earth. According to Philippians 2:6–8, Jesus, though fully God, encapsulated that part of Himself and chose to function totally as a human, modeling what true humanity was intended to be (see Wagner 1988, 113–32 for an excellent discussion of this point). He did no mighty works before the Holy Spirit came upon Him at His baptism.

Having won the battle as a human being, Jesus then gave us the same Holy Spirit who guided and empowered Him.

Indeed, He lived such an ordinary life before that time that the people of His hometown, Nazareth, were startled when He began asserting the Holy Spirit's authority in ministry (Matthew 13:54–57).

Jesus' obedience took Him even to the cross, and through that to the empty tomb. Thus He prevailed over Satan from behind enemy lines—He was victorious as a man for both humans and God. When the Father resurrected Jesus, a cosmic battle was won and the usurper was defeated and deposed from second place in the universe.

Having won the battle as a human being, Jesus then gave us the same Holy Spirit who guided and empowered Him. This makes it possible for us ordinary humans, as we follow Jesus' example of obedience to and intimacy with the Father, to return to the original place of authority for which we were created.

Jesus went behind enemy lines to defeat the enemy and to begin establishing His own kingdom in the middle of enemy territory. As He set about establishing His kingdom, He assumed the authority (the "glory") He had with the Father before the creation of the world (John 17:5). And because this was occurring behind enemy lines, warfare—spiritual warfare aimed at taking back God's world from the usurper—was inevitable.

He then recruited us to continue the operation in Satan's territory. So the context in which we operate as soldiers in Jesus' army is a context of spiritual warfare. It is on a battlefield that we assume our authority. And it is the enemy of our General, Jesus, that we challenge when we exercise that authority. Every time we assert our authority we are cutting into the domain of the imposter king who extorted it from our ancestor Adam. And, according to Romans 16:20, it is God's desire that we press on with Jesus until that enemy is crushed under *our* feet.

Our redemption both restores humanity to the possibility of the relationship God intended when He created Adam and Eve and empowers us for victory over the evil one within the territory he stole from us. Redemption enables both our relationship with God and our victory over Satan. And the authority and power that come with the relationship enable us to participate in present victories over the usurper.

How Much Authority Does Satan Have Now?

Even now, we live in a world under the authority of the enemy—for, as John says, "the whole world is under the rule of the Evil One" (1 John 5:19). So we wonder, how much authority does Satan have? Can he do anything he wants to, or are there restrictions? What about differences between non-Christians and Christians? Can he hurt Christians, or only non-Christians?

First of all, we know from Scripture what Satan wants to do: John states that "the thief [Satan] comes only in order to steal, kill, and destroy" (John 10:10). And to that end he does whatever he can within the parameters of his authority. According to Hebrews 2:14, this authority may include the ability to bring about death—though still within the limits God sets for him.

Knowing what Satan intends for us while recognizing that there are many people still alive in the world, however, suggests that much of the time Satan does not get his way. The reason Satan cannot destroy those still alive must be because they are, at least for the present, protected by a greater power, the power of God. I believe that all who are alive, whether Christian or non-Christian, are alive because they are protected by God.

Some seem to have greater protection than others, however. In the first chapter of Job, we read of Satan complaining that God has "always protected [Job] and his family and everything he owns" (Job 1:10), thus keeping enemy forces from doing to him what they wanted. And God agrees to relax His protection, allowing Satan to do anything but take Job's life.

From Job's story we learn at least two things about authority. The first is that Satan's authority is limited by God—in some cases at least, very strictly limited. Job seems to have been granted special protection beyond that available to many others. Thus, in Job's case and probably in many other cases through history to this day, God set even stricter limits than normal on Satan. The second thing we learn is that, under certain circumstances, God grants greater authority to Satan than is ordinarily his. Satan requested permission to launch a special attack on Job and was granted it.

This is reminiscent of the apostle Paul's thorn, of which he wrote to the Corinthians. Whether Satan requested that God grant him the right to attack Paul, we cannot know. But we do know that God allowed "a messenger from Satan" (2 Corinthians 12:7, NLT) to afflict Paul in order to keep him from becoming puffed up with pride. It is not impossible that this also happened to King Saul, about whom it is recorded that an evil spirit from

God troubled him (1 Samuel 16:14–16, 23; 18:10; 19:9). We know that God was fed up with Saul, and therefore He may very well have given Satan extra permission to harass him.

Another possible area of satanic authority is weather. Did Satan gain authority over weather at the Fall, or does he gain authority in each instance by special permission? Take, for example, the storm that sprang up while Jesus and His disciples were crossing the Sea of Galilee (Matthew 8:23–27; Mark 4:35–41; Luke 8:22–25). It is not clear from the gospels what Satan's attempt to kill Jesus in the storm indicates about the source of his authority over weather, but I suspect that God controls weather and sometimes gives Satan special permission to interfere in the normal operation of things.

From other Scriptures we learn a third principle concerning how much authority Satan has. Exodus 1:8 describes the ascension of an Egyptian king who felt no obligation to keep the agreement of his predecessors to treat the Israelites kindly. As long as the kings had kept this agreement, Satan could do nothing to the Israelites, for Israel had Pharaoh's protection. But as soon as a king was willing to lay aside that agreement, the enemy gained the ability to take advantage of the diminished protection and to afflict them.

It becomes clear from this that if Satan is to be able to exercise the authority he wants to exercise, he needs *human* cooperation, a human partner. At the time of Jesus' birth, for example, it was Herod's agreement to carry out Satan's plan that enabled the enemy to slaughter the babies of Bethlehem. This and other examples suggest that the amount of authority Satan can exercise in any given situation may be correlated to the amount of human cooperation he receives.

I recently heard of a man who had a very ill son. In his concern for that son, he vowed that he would be willing to give up his life if his son would thereby be healed. Sometime after he made this vow, he and his son were walking together and were struck by lightning. The father was killed, but at that same moment, the son apparently was healed—at least, the doctors could find no trace of the disease in him after that event. I assume that God did not cause the father to be killed; but vows transmit power, and they work according to the rules of the universe (see Kraft 2000). Though God could have countered the vow, He allowed it to work, resulting in death for the father and healing for the son. Satan could only have the authority to empower that vow with God's permission.

Another problematic area of Satan's authority concerns death. Hebrews 2:14 speaks of Satan as the one who "*has* [present tense] the power over death" (emphasis mine). Does this mean that Satan is the agent of death all the time or some of the time? Or are we being misled by the tense of the verb? I cannot answer this question, and my speculations are not satisfying.

❧ Implications of Satanic Authority for Christians

On several occasions I have heard people ask something like this: "Can you tell me why I had fewer problems in life before I became a Christian than I have had since I came to Him?"

My answer is usually something like this: "If you were the enemy, who would you attack? Your friends, who are on your side and doing your bidding? Or your enemies—those committed to Jesus—who could hurt you?"

Another question people often ask me is, "If I get into spiritual warfare, will I and my family be in danger?" The answer is yes. Then I usually ask them how they prefer to *lose* a battle—running, hiding or fighting? For we are at war whether we like it or not. And in war one side hardly ever wins all the battles. If we are not fighting—if we are simply standing around, running away from the reality of the war or trying to hide from it—we are being

29

defeated. I submit, then, that if I am going to lose some battles, I would rather lose while fighting than in any other way. If we are fighting, though we may lose some of the time, we will often win.

The point is that Satan has real authority to harass and even attack us, just as he attacked Jesus, the apostle Paul and all the other apostles. He is our enemy who, as the apostle Peter wrote to a Christian audience, roams around "like a roaring lion, looking for someone to devour" (1 Peter 5:8). Since we are at war, then, we should expect harassment and attack.

For example, in 1 Thessalonians 2:18, Paul speaks of Satan being the one who prevented him from traveling back to Thessalonica to visit the church there. And, in 2 Corinthians 12:7, Paul calls his thorn in the flesh "Satan's messenger to beat me and keep me from being proud," even though it was clear to him that God Himself had allowed the problem. And Satan was undoubtedly behind the imprisonments, whippings, stoning, shipwrecks and multiple dangers that Paul lists in 2 Corinthians 11:23–27.

Apparently Satan even has authority to blind people's minds to the truths of God. With respect to unbelievers, Paul writes,

> They do not believe, because their minds have been kept in the dark by the evil god of this world. He keeps them from seeing the light shining on them, the light that comes from the Good News about the glory of Christ.
>
> 2 Corinthians 4:4

I am afraid that Satan is also able to blind certain Christians, leading some away from Christ and making it impossible for some of those to return. I believe Hebrews 6:4–6 speaks of such people, stating that it is simply impossible to bring back to faith those who have once been believers but then abandoned Christ.

For many other Christians, the enemy seems to be able to render them completely ineffective. It is as if they came to Christ and almost immediately got locked up in camps for prisoners of war, headed for heaven but never to be a threat to the enemy. Satan definitely has the authority to hinder God's people and their organizations, whether directly or indirectly through people who knowingly or unknowingly serve him.

But does God not protect us? Does He not send angels to look after us? Indeed He does. If He did not, none of us would be here, since the aim of the enemy is to kill and destroy us. (Often when we deal with demons, they will make us aware of the fact that God's angels are helping us. Realizing this, one of my former ministry team members asked a demon how many angels were present. The demon answered that the room was filled with them.) If angels are always present to protect us, why do bad things often happen to Christians? I am afraid that I do not know the answer to this question. I assume, though, that we have the right to ask for more angels to protect us whenever we find ourselves in dangerous places. It is my practice to constantly keep myself aware, though in a calm frame of mind, that I am living in enemy territory. Though God is supreme and constantly grants me a great deal of protection, since I do not know all that is going on in the spiritual realm, I regularly ask for more protection. For example, I always ask for extra protection when I am driving or riding in a car, when I am walking on sidewalks and crosswalks, when I am traveling by plane and at any other time and place that seems dangerous.

Misunderstanding the Enemy's Authority

The activity of Satan in the world is so obvious to many that they assume he has more authority and power than he actually does. Others, of course, ignore or deny his existence and blame all troubles on human beings or our environment. As C. S. Lewis has pointed out, either of these extremes is dangerous. And both positions leave us with misunderstandings of the enemy's authority and power.

For those who believe Satan is alive and active, most know in their heads that the power of God is greater than that of Satan. But the "box score" of good and evil seems to indicate that Satan is winning. So, for those who simply look at surface-level phenomena, it looks like there is a big Satan and a small God.

Unfortunately many Christians fall into this category and, without meaning to, give more honor to Satan than he is due. Even in Pentecostal and charismatic circles, where the power of both God and Satan is a frequent topic, one recurring result is to raise the level of fear of the enemy beyond what it should be. Stories of violence as people are being delivered from demons, for example, often focus people's attention on what the enemy did even more than on what God did. Seldom in such circles is it recognized either that most of what demons do is bluff rather than power or that by taking authority over the strongholds within a person first, the power of demons can be greatly reduced before they are challenged (see my book *Defeating Dark Angels* [1992] for a complete treatment of this approach). In this way, I and my colleagues in ministry have been able to perform literally thousands of deliverances without violence.

Another unfortunate aspect of our Christian experience that seems to credit Satan with more power and authority than he has is the fault of irresponsible translators, who, in translating the New Testament into English, made liberal use of the term "demon possessed." We find numerous uses of this term or its corollary, "demoniac," in the King James Version, the New King James Version, the American Standard Version, the New American Standard Bible, the Revised Standard Version, the New Revised Standard Version and the New International Version (see, for example, Matthew 4:24; 8:16; 8:28, 33; 9:32; 12:22; Mark 1:32. See also John 7:20; 8:48, 52; 10:20; Acts 19:13 in the New International Version). There is absolutely no warrant for the translation "demon possessed"; each of the Greek terms so translated means simply "to have a demon" (see the rendering of the above verses in the Good News Translation). When a translation gives the impression that someone who harbors a demon is "possessed" by that demon, people get a distorted view of Satan's authority, because that term exaggerates the amount of authority the enemy has. And, I am sure, it puts a smile on his face.

The true situation is that no one is totally controlled by a demon 100 percent of the time, which is what is implied by the term "possessed." Even in the case of people who come under demonic influence willingly (such as shamans who call upon spirits to possess them for various purposes), the possession lasts only for a short time. Though I and my ministry associates have found that having a demon, or *demonization*, is very common, comparatively few people who are involuntarily inhabited by demons are taken over to the extent implied by the term *demon possession*. And the vast majority of those who have demons are seldom, if ever, under the total control of the demons. Even the man of Gerasenes who had a demon (Mark 5:1–20), the most severe case of having a demon in the New Testament, had enough free will to run to meet Jesus and fall on his knees in worship (verse 6). The demons would not have had him do that even though they had control over his behavior at other times.

In reality, the devil has very little, if any, power or authority other than that granted him by those who obey him or by their ancestors. Even most of those who harbor demons are able, often with difficulty, to thwart much of what the demons try to do. As Nigel Wright says, "The vitality of the devil is parasitic and his strength substantially drawn from humanity. . . . The power that the devil has in himself is far less than we might imagine and far more dependent on that which mankind gives him" (Wright 1990, 48).

Because of this fact, James can assume that it is possible for humans to "resist the Devil," resulting in his (eventual) fleeing from us (James 4:7). As Walter Wink points out, the devil of James 4:7 "is not the devil of popular fantasy, that virtually omnipotent enemy of our race. This devil knows his place!" Wink goes on to quote Ignatius Loyola to the effect that this enemy by nature is given to flight as soon as someone spiritual stands up against him, courageously doing just the opposite of what Satan has tempted him or her to do (Wink 1986, 21).

On the other hand, it is just as dangerous to misunderstand the presence and power of Satan by ignoring or denying his existence as it is to overemphasize his power. This is the fallacy that millions of Western Christians have fallen into. We have allowed the enemy to do his work unchecked by ignoring him. Many sincere Christians even deny his existence, preferring to see the evil of the world totally as a result of humans and/or human structures. They think Jesus was simply accommodating Himself to the ideas of His day and to His culture by referring to psychological problems and other unexplained phenomena as demons and by personifying evil and naming it Satan.

> *We have allowed the enemy to do his work unchecked by ignoring him.*

Soldiers who are on the battlefield but are not fighting cannot expect to win. This is one reason why so many Christians are living defeated lives. Such inactive soldiers do, however, win occasionally—when they do the right thing unconsciously. Fortunately, some who ignore the enemy do win at least some of the battles by following certain spiritual rules, even though they know nothing of the impact of their behavior in the spirit world. When they love God with all their heart, soul and mind and their neighbors as themselves (Matthew 22:37–39), Christians wage spiritual warfare whether or not they know it. Likewise when they pray, worship, forgive, spend time in God's Word and do deeds of mercy. But though occasional battles may be won even by bystanders, it takes active soldiers to win the war. If we do not assert our authority over Satan, he will assert his authority over us.

Misunderstanding the position of the devil relative to that of the children of God is a misunderstanding of who we are and the authority we are given in our position. Unlike Satan, we bear the image of God and have been both redeemed by God and made co-inheritors with Jesus of the riches of our Father God (Romans 8:17; Galatians 4:7). We carry by virtue of our position and the fact that God the Holy Spirit lives within us infinitely more power and authority than the whole satanic kingdom. This we must understand as we probe the various dimensions of spiritual authority.

❧ Seeing through Spiritual Warfare Lenses

Many people object to this "two kingdoms in conflict" teaching. They do not like this interpretation of Scripture, feeling that it gives the enemy too much attention and does not put enough focus on God's great plan of redemption. Some of them also are bothered by the teaching that we are as affected as this approach contends by the actions of our original parents. This does not seem fair, they say, since we were not there to have our say or to place our vote.

In answer to such positions, I point out that God has rules (see chapter 5), such as the one that has established a mystical bonding between members of the same family and, indeed, between all of us as members of the human race. This means that there is a spiritual inheritance as well as a biological inheritance, enabling the sin of our first parents to be passed down to all of their descendents, with spiritual bondages and strongholds passed from generation to generation within families.

With regard to spiritual warfare, some objectors claim that most of the Bible does not speak overtly to this theme. My answer is that in a sense they are right, especially when the Bible is interpreted naturalistically rather than supernaturalistically. Then I remind them about the opening three chapters of Genesis, which clearly introduce a spiritual and cosmic conflict between Satan and God, with humans as the intended prize. I can also point to the book of Revelation, with its focus on the climax of this same struggle. Those who are willing to listen will usually open up to this perspective when I point to glimpses of the interactions between God and Satan that are provided by Job, Daniel, the gospels and Acts.

Though not every page and verse of the Bible speak to this spiritual warfare theme, a good bit of Scripture does. And, whether or not we understand or agree with it, the apostle Paul reminds us that "we are not fighting against human beings but against the wicked spiritual forces in the heavenly world, the rulers, authorities, and cosmic powers of this dark age" (Ephesians 6:12).

The themes in this chapter capped by these words from Paul should help us view the entire biblical revelation *through spiritual warfare lenses.* When we begin to do so, both Scripture and the authority issues in focus here take on new significance. War between the two kingdoms is the essential backdrop from which to interpret the Bible and to discover what spiritual authority is all about. With this background, then, let us turn to a discussion of the way the authority God gives is transmitted and several other basic issues concerning it.

2

Jesus' Credit Card

Dad, would you put my name on your credit card?" This request came from my son Rick, who was driving off to college fifteen hundred miles away in an old car. He was concerned lest the car break down and he not have the money to get it back on the road. "You wouldn't want me to be stranded somewhere without being able to pay the bill, would you?" he continued. "I promise I won't misuse it."

His reasoning made sense to his mother and me, though we were a bit apprehensive about whether he would keep his word not to misuse the card. We had known this kid for seventeen years and were not at all sure we could trust him. But he is *our son*, our own flesh and blood. And since we were very much in favor of his going to college, we knew that, in addition to paying his tuition, our granting him the use of a credit card made sense. Our names would appear first on the card as the ones with ultimate responsibility. But Rick's name would appear immediately under our names, giving him authority to spend whatever the credit card company would allow us by way of credit.

When my son's name was added to our credit card, he gained all the financial authority that *our* name would bring. At that time, our son's name carried no authority, since he had no credit with any financial institution. But with my name and my wife's name to back him, he would have the resources to handle almost any emergency that might confront him far from home.

We made it clear to Rick how we expected him to use the authority we were giving him. He was young and might well have misused it. But he knew that he needed to keep on good terms with us, his parents, lest his privilege be revoked. To his credit, he never abused the privilege; and now that he is a well-off attorney, we would be glad to have our names on his credit card!

Jesus' Authority under the Father

When Jesus came to earth, it was as if He carried a credit card from His Father with the Father's name at the top and His own name under it. Like my son, *Jesus came with all the authority His Father's name would bring.* He had full authority to spend whatever was in the Father's account, so long as He kept on good terms with the Father and spent it for purposes of which the Father approved. Jesus knew both that He had His Father's authority and that His right to use it was contingent on His maintaining intimacy with His Father.

As He stated in John 5:30, "I can do nothing on my own authority . . . I am not trying to do what I want, but only what he who sent me wants." Earlier He had said that "the Son can do nothing on his own; he does only what he sees his Father doing" (John 5:19). And with reference to His teaching, He said, "I do nothing on my own authority, but I say only what the Father has instructed me to say" (John 8:28; see also John 7:16–18).

Jesus was a man under authority. He worked according to the guidelines He and the Father had agreed to before He came to earth. The major guideline, as we noted in the last chapter, was that *He would never use the power and rights of His divinity while on earth* (Philippians 2:6–8). He agreed to work totally under the authority of the Father while being empowered by the Holy Spirit. Following the Father's instructions, Jesus did nothing miraculous until after His baptism.

This commitment to His Father's will was put to the test when Satan directly challenged Jesus' authority by tempting Him. The devil showed Jesus "all the kingdoms of the world," saying, "I will give you all this power and all this wealth. . . . It has all been handed over to me, and I can give it to anyone I choose" (Luke 4:5–6). The power he offered was the authority he had won from Adam. Satan, to whom Jesus later

Jesus' power came from being filled with the Holy Spirit, not from His own "Godness."

referred as "the ruler of this world" (John 14:30), was offering our Lord an easy way to the authority the Father planned to give Him through His death and resurrection (Philippians 2:9–11). Jesus held firm and kept His agreement with the Father.

Jesus' power came from being filled with the Holy Spirit, not from His own "Godness." The source of His authority, then, was His intimacy with the Father. He spent hours alone with the Father in prayer, keeping in close contact with Him and cultivating that most precious relationship. In this way He kept His will lined up with the Father's, seeing to it that He always obeyed Him and that He did nothing except with the Father's agreement. And on at least two occasions, the Father stated His pleasure with Jesus, saying, "This is my own dear Son, with whom I am pleased" (Matthew 3:17; 17:5).

As Jesus ministered, His ears were always open to the voice of the Father. He was always listening for what the Father wanted to do. Because He listened, He could take authority confidently, knowing He was acting in God's purposes. Jesus' intimacy with the Father enabled Him both to maintain His authority and to get God's instructions for what the Father wanted Him to do each day.

Authority Both Surprising and Threatening

It was the authority in which Jesus worked that most surprised the people of His day and that was most questioned by the Jewish leaders. Jesus experienced a fairly normal childhood and young adulthood, during which the people of His hometown apparently noticed little that gave any indication of what He would become. This is clear from the fact that they were amazed when He started to do miraculous things and teach with authority. "Where did he get such wisdom? they asked. And what about his miracles? Isn't he [merely] the carpenter's son?" (Matthew 13:54–55; see also Mark 6:1–6). In amazement they acknowledged that He did not teach like the teachers of the Law; "Instead, he taught with authority" (Matthew 7:29; Mark 1:22). The people would not have asked these questions had they seen any indication during Jesus' growing up of what He would become.

At about age thirty, Jesus went to John to be initiated (through baptism) into John's faith renewal movement (Luke 3:21–22), after which things took quite a different turn. The Holy Spirit came on Jesus at His baptism, and He started to minister in authority and power beyond anyone's expectations or understanding. He began to heal and cast out demons, causing amazement among the people: "What kind of words are these? With authority and power this man gives orders to the evil spirits, and they come out!" (Luke 4:36).

Seeing demons cast out was not new to these people, for the Pharisees had ways of getting at least some people free from demons. Jesus acknowledged this when, in countering their claim that He worked in the power of Beelzebul, He asked by what power "do your followers drive [the demons] out?" (Luke 11:19). The people had not, however, seen the Pharisees approach demons in the authoritative way Jesus worked—and they had not, of course, seen the demons respond as if they had no option but to obey.

Though the people were amazed, the leaders were threatened by Jesus' authoritative way of going about His ministry. In spite of the fact that He did things no one else could do, they refused to believe He had come from God. So they challenged His authority, asking, "What right do you have to do these things? Who gave you such right?" (Mark 11:28; see Luke 20:2).

It was the religious leaders who questioned His right to help people, heal them and free them from the clutches of Satan. How ironic! Those appointed to serve God and demonstrate His care for His chosen people were opposing the One who was doing what they were supposed to be doing. The reason is that the Pharisees felt their own power and authority threatened by Jesus. The extent to which this perceived threat dominated them is seen in John 12:19, in which they exclaim, "You see, we are not succeeding at all! Look, the whole world is following him!"

So the scribes, Pharisees and other Jewish leaders, instead of recognizing in Jesus the God they claimed to serve, played into Satan's hands and opposed Him. Thus they used their authority to "lock the door to the Kingdom of heaven in people's faces" (Matthew 23:13)—they neither entered in themselves nor allowed others to do so.

They were not the only ones to mistake the source of Jesus' authority, for we see a further confrontation between His authority and that of Rome as represented by Pilate. This Roman official asserted his claim to authority over Jesus as he attempted to get Jesus to defend Himself, saying, "Remember, I have the authority to set you free and also to have you crucified" (John 19:10). In response Jesus pointed to the real source of Pilate's authority: "You have authority over me only because it was given to you by God" (verse 11).

Authority Passed to Us

As One under authority yet exercising the authority of God, Jesus did a most amazing thing after His resurrection: He passed on the authority in which He worked to His followers. These were Galileans, people without respect in Jewish society; but they had spent time with Jesus, and He trusted them even though they were continually letting Him down.

The disciples had worked in Jesus' authority while He was on earth; during His ministry, Jesus sent them out to heal and cast out demons in "power and authority" (Luke 9:1; see Luke 10:9, 17). He promised them that when He left, He would send them the Holy Spirit—the One who had empowered Him—to enable them to do all He had done and more (John 14:12). So, just before departing, He instructed them to wait in Jerusalem "for the gift I told you about, the gift my Father promised . . . the Holy Spirit" (Acts 1:4–5). And He commissioned them to carry out certain tasks: "Go, then, to all peoples everywhere and make them my disciples: baptize them in the name of the Father, the Son, and the Holy Spirit, and teach them to obey everything I have commanded you" (Matthew 28:19–20).

This Great Commission is prefaced by this statement: "I have been given all authority in heaven and on earth" (Matthew 28:18). The commissioning of Jesus' followers, which gives them authority to teach and minister, is founded on the authority of Jesus. Jesus' disciples are then to teach their disciples, and their disciples to teach their disciples, and so on.

Thus Jesus' final command to us, as well as our commission to represent Him, are grounded in the authority He won through obedience to the Father. His command—that we bring all peoples into a discipleship relationship with Him, initiating them into the family of God and teaching them to obey everything Jesus commanded—is founded on the incredible authority given Him by His Father.

The Great Commission implies, I believe, that Jesus' authority will underlie ours as we obey.

✣ Knowing Who We Are

Both Jesus and my son Rick knew who they were in relation to the one granting them authority. If we are to operate properly in Jesus' authority, we, too, need to understand who we are in the universe. We need to understand our identity.

It was *our* son who asked to have his name put on our credit card, not someone else's. Our relationship with Rick is very special, and this made it possible for him to ask such a favor with confidence, knowing we would grant his request because of who he is to us. As our son, he has certain rights stemming from his relationship with us. He could come to us without fear of being rejected, knowing and trusting both our relationship and our positive attitude toward him. He was (and is) proud to bear our name and be identified with us. And we are proud to have him bear our name and be identified with him.

Through years of working in inner healing and deliverance, I have become convinced that the enemy's primary area of attack is our self-image. *He does not want us to discover who we are.* I minister to victimized, abused and defeated people whose lives are often characterized by severe hopelessness or depression. Yet they are often brimming with hidden talents and untapped spiritual gifts given to them by God from the time they were conceived. The enemy, knowing what these gifts and talents are, has done his best to keep these people in the dark about their abilities and their relationship to God. In so doing he has destroyed or nearly destroyed their awareness of who they are intended to be. My aim is to get them cleaned up from their emotional problems and any demons they may be carrying, and to bring them to a new understanding of who

God made them to be. What a joy it is to watch people come to know who they are!

If we are to live and minister effectively for Christ, we need to know who we are and what it means to be who we are. As Dean Sherman writes in *Spiritual Warfare for Every Christian* (1990), "If we are unsure of ourselves, it is because we do not yet know who we are, or in whose authority we operate."

So let me answer this all-important question with these eight points:

1. *We were intended for second place.* We are created "only a little lower than God" (Psalm 8:5, NLT), in the image of God Himself (Genesis 1:26). Our position at Creation (as we saw in the last chapter) was far above all created beings, including the angels—in second place in the universe. We must never forget this, for the enemy will not be content until he has blotted it out of our minds.

2. *We are redeemed.* Although in Adam we gave it all away, God has stepped in and redeemed us. Through the Fall we dropped to a position below the angel Satan. But God did not leave things that way; He made it possible through Jesus, the second Adam (1 Corinthians 15:45–47), for us to be reestablished in our rightful position just under God, on the basis of our faith. I think it is significant that God did this for us but not for the angels. We—not the angels nor any other part of God's creation—are His masterpieces. And only we have been offered redemption.

3. *We are children of God.* For those of us who have committed ourselves to Christ, John writes, "See how much the Father has loved us! His love is so great that we are called God's children—and so, in fact, we are" (1 John 3:1). As God's beloved children, we even inherit the glory of God with Christ (Romans 8:17; Galatians 4:7). God has adopted us, even chosen us (Ephesians 1:4), much as a childless couple chooses and adopts a child into their family. By His choice we are part of God's family, restored through redemption to our original position above Satan. And the universe, including Satan's hosts, have to recognize this fact.

4. *We have the Holy Spirit.* As family members, God gives us the Holy Spirit to live within us. Thus we get to carry infinitely more power than all in the satanic kingdom put together! Within us lives God Himself, the Creator and Sustainer of the universe and the creator of all the angels, including Satan. When we realize this, in our own eyes we become different people in relation to the enemy and the universe. For we know this really is our Father's world, even though Satan has control of it for the present (1 John 5:19).

It was difficult for the disciples to understand why Jesus needed to go away so that the Holy Spirit could come (John 16:7). The disciples (and we) may wonder how anything could be better than Jesus' presence. But I believe Jesus was pointing to the time when the Holy Spirit would not simply be *with* them but *in* them (John 14:17).

For up to the coming of the Holy Spirit in Acts 2, the relationship between the followers of Jesus and the Holy Spirit seemed to be an external one. Jesus was with them, and on occasion He guided them, gave them authority and empowered them (see, for example, Luke 9:1–6). But from the time that the Holy Spirit descended on each of them, as recorded in Acts 2, God Himself has come to live *in* us, bringing with Him power (Acts 1:8), gifting (1 Corinthians 12:1 and following), fruit (Galatians 5:22–23) and *the very presence of God permanently from within.*

5. *We are united with God.* Our position has been further dignified by the fact that in Jesus, God has united with us for eternity. He could not have united with an angel or animal, only with one who bears His image. So God in Jesus joined Himself to us, forever becoming the union between Creator and creature. In His ascension Jesus never went back to simply being God; He is *still one of us* and will be for eternity! And because of this, we get to share with Him the inheritance reserved for the siblings of the King.

6. *We are children of the King.* This is our true identity, giving us special rights and privileges with our famous Father. We have, among other things, special permission as His princes

and princesses to come into the King's presence at any time. Someone has written a book about life with a famous grandfather entitled *I Called Him Grand Dad*. Though many would have given their right arms to spend time with this person's famous grandfather, it was the grandson, the author of the book, who got to come into that man's presence at any time, without an appointment.

That is the way it is between us and God. The awesome Creator of the universe—the One whose name strikes fear into the hearts of those who have offended Him—this God, this fearsome One, is our Father. We need have no fear in His presence, as Isaiah did (Isaiah 6:5), or uncertainty over whether the King will extend His favor to us, as Esther did (Esther 4:11).

> *This God, this fearsome One, is our Father.*

We have been invited to come boldly and confidently into His presence (Hebrews 4:16), running even into His throne room, knowing we are welcome because we are His children. And we call Him *Abba*, our dad (Romans 8:15; Galatians 4:6). To exercise our authority properly, we need to know experientially just who we are and—as my son did when he asked to be added to my credit card—just who our Father is.

Allowing this truth to penetrate the deepest parts of me has transformed me, destroying my negative self-image and abolishing destructive mind-sets. I have lived most of my life with an attitude akin to Charlie Brown's or Murphy's Law, an attitude that says, "It's normal for things to go wrong, so if anything goes right, it must be a mistake." With this attitude, I felt God must have made a mistake by linking up with me. What freedom I have found by allowing myself to accept and bask in the truth of what God thinks of me! And what confidence in operating in the authority and power He has entrusted to us!

We are saved by God's grace (Ephesians 2:8). We are also adopted, given position and empowered by that grace. All this is incredible, totally beyond anything we deserve. Yet God Himself has chosen to arrange things this way. So we stand in the universe as the adopted children of God Himself, given all the rights and privileges of family members, including the right to operate in the power and authority of the Maker and Sustainer of the universe.

7. *We are entrusted with divine authority.* By God's grace, He actually trusts us! Something within me says, *He should have known better than to entrust His work to us.* But Jesus *does* trust us, just as He forgave and trusted the adulteress (John 8:1–11), forgave, reinstated and trusted Peter (John 21:15–19) and trusted His disciples enough to turn the Kingdom over to them. When Jesus left the earth, He entrusted us with the Holy Spirit, predicting that we who believe in Him "will do what I do—yes, they will do even greater things" (John 14:12). Jesus trusted the disciples and us so much that He calls us His friends—those entrusted with "everything I heard from my Father" (John 15:15). It is therefore our Kingdom as well as His (Luke 12:32; 22:29–30). Knowing who we are enables us to work in unison with the Lord, tapping into the riches of our position in Christ.

Back when genuine kings and queens ruled a country, their rule was absolute. Princes and princesses had authority as well, and all the subjects of the kingdom had to yield to their authority. In the spiritual realm we carry the same authority as God's princes and princesses. When we understand our identity as royalty and use the power of Jesus' name appropriately, the spiritual realm has to obey. We have "every spiritual blessing in the heavenly world" available to us (Ephesians 1:3). If only we could grasp how much God wants us to appropriate the authority and power that rightly belongs to us, based on our position in Christ! The satanic kingdom trembles to think what that would mean.

The position God has given us is awesome. We are in such an elevated place that the angels watch us curiously (1 Corinthians 4:9; 1 Peter 1:12) and serve us (Hebrews 1:14). At some point we will even judge them (1 Corinthians 6:3). Again, God did not esteem the angels enough to redeem the ones who followed Satan; *He redeemed only us.* What grace and love! What a privilege is ours to belong to God's family! We must never forget who we are, whether we feel like that is who we are or not.

8. *We are inseparable from our spiritual authority.* Our authority is recognized by God and by the enemy world as *flowing from our very beings.* As Michael Crow (1996) has written, spiritual authority

> is the activity of God which occurs in and through a person's life, not simply because of his or her position or competency. It is the operation of the Spirit of God which emanates out of a leader's personality, gifting, character and intimacy before God, and influences others toward a similar commitment to the purposes of God.

> As Christians we have no choice as to whether or not we possess this authority. It is part of the package given to us with the Holy Spirit. Our only choice is whether we learn how to use this authority and whether we actually make use of it.

✤ What If We Do Not Use the Credit Card?

What if Rick's car had developed an engine problem on his way to college? He could have ignored it, at least for a little while, and perhaps ruined the engine. His passenger would likely have said, "Let's get it fixed. We have your parents' credit card to cover the cost."

We are inseparable from our spiritual authority.

Suppose, though, that Rick had said something like, "I don't want to use their credit card. I just don't feel right about claiming my parents' authority to fix my car." Or suppose Rick had lost the card, had it stolen or simply forgotten that he had it. Though he would have had full authority to use the card, he would have been unable because he did not know where it was. Or suppose he had never asked for the card and did not know that he could have had one.

I believe that most of our church people fit into one or another of these categories. Many Christians either forget they have God's authority or for some reason refuse to use it. Perhaps they refuse to use their authority because they are afraid they will use it wrongly and find themselves defeated when they are attacked by the enemy. Whatever the reason, I pray that the principles in this book will contribute to getting more of God's people operating in the authority that God has given us.

3

Our Authority under Jesus

We have seen that, on what was probably Jesus' last day before His ascension, He stated, "I have been given all authority in heaven and on earth" (Matthew 28:18). On the basis of that authority, He commissioned His followers with authority to make disciples of "all peoples everywhere" and promised to be with them "to the end of the age" (verses 19–20).

What a great day when He was able to claim "all authority"! It meant He had fulfilled His mission, successfully completing the task assigned Him by His Father. He had refrained from claiming this authority during His pre-resurrection time on earth since He had agreed with the Father to work only under His authority. But now the Father had chosen to turn over all heavenly and earthly authority to His Son in repayment for Jesus' obedience. As He did so, "God raised him to the highest place above and gave him the name that is greater than any other name" (Philippians 2:9) and restored to Him the authority humanity had lost through Adam.

One of Jesus' first uses of that authority was to give us the Holy Spirit, as He had promised in John 16:7. In anticipation of this empowerment of His followers, Jesus had told them, "As the Father sent me, so I send you" (John 20:21), and, "Those who believe in me will do what I do—yes, they will do even greater things, because I am going to the Father" (John 14:12). This means we get the credit card! But now it has Jesus' name, the name above all names, on the top, with our names under it.

With the credit card, we go into the world with Jesus' authority to spend whatever is in His account, so long as it is for purposes of which He approves. And He says, "I will do whatever you ask for in my name" (John 14:13), meaning, "I will back up with My authority whatever you say and do that is in accord with My will and the Father's purposes."

So we are to imitate our Master, enabled by the same power of the Holy Spirit under whom He worked and exercising the authority He has given us to use that power. As Jesus obeyed the Father, receiving the Holy Spirit and launching into ministry, so we are to obey Jesus' command by being filled with the same Holy Spirit who empowered our Lord (Luke 24:49; Acts 1:4–5, 8). Then we, too, can be launched into a ministry of love, power and authority like His and actually do what He did—and even more.

Many Christians think they have no right to even think such a thing. "After all," they say, "He was God and we are not. He had the power and authority of God; we are merely human." But it is clear from Scripture that Jesus laid aside His divine prerogatives to become human. Though in some mysterious way He continued to be fully God, He compartmentalized His deity and never used it while on earth. So He, like us, lived in a state of powerlessness, except for what the Father entrusted to Him (John 5:19).

One thing God promises is the right to use our authority to bring about whatever is in accord with His will (1 John 5:14–15). Our task is to get our wills lined up with the will of Jesus and the Father, and on that basis to exercise the authority they have given us. This comes for us, as it did with Jesus, from spending time in prayer and fellowship with God in private, listening to Him to get His instructions and to line up our wills with His. Then we receive from God the necessary power and authority for the specific task ahead of us. Our aim in our relationship with God should be nothing short of total intimacy; again, Jesus is our model.

When we seek to heal or release people from demons, there is no doubt that God has given us enough power to accomplish what is needed. But we must ask ourselves, *Is this what the Father wants?* Jesus' success rate in ministry was 100 percent, since He always lined up His will with that of His Father. He obeyed continually and in that obedience attained perfection. What we are able to do in His name may be considerably less than He could do. The difference, I believe, lies in our ability to hear and follow the Father's will.

Fortunately we already know certain things about the Father's will. We know He wants people to be blessed, to be free from satanic captivity (Luke 4:18), to be joyful and to experience love. Jesus never left people with their problems. He never said what some pastors say: "Hang on to your problem, because God wants to teach you patience through it." So to release a given person from illness, brokenness or demonization is likely to be in line with God's purposes; we can minister confidently in such a way as to expect God to work in at least these key areas. Whether He desires to relieve a person of a particular disability at precisely this time is not as easy to determine; we must pray to find out.

For me the biggest challenge in ministering to others is not in the area of power but in the area of intimacy in my relationship with the Father—a relationship that is essential for coordinating my will with His. Apart from an intimate relationship with God and an ear tuned to what He desires, our own authority taking can be powerless. What seems to put the power in our authority taking, as it did with Jesus, is intimacy and hearing God.

I Give You Authority

Together these enable believers to do (as Jesus did) the works we see our Father doing. Discerning God's purposes packs our authority with God's power.

During ministry, prayer is crucial; throughout any given ministry session we are to be in prayer continually for guidance. But the ministry time itself is not a time for *asking God for something we have not yet received*; it is a time for *exercising authority He has already given us*. We are to minister as Jesus did, with and in authority. Jesus commanded things to happen as if He were in charge. He spoke to diseases, to demons, even to people as One who knew both who He was and the authority He had been given. This is our privilege and mandate as those who carry His name.

When Jesus sent out the Twelve (Luke 9) and the Seventy-Two (Luke 10), He "gave them power and authority to drive out all demons and to cure diseases" (Luke 9:1; see also Luke 10:17). Some contend that this empowerment was just for the disciples, but I believe the Master intended for His followers to teach their followers this authority taking, along with the other things He included when He said, "Teach

We are to exercise our authority in the same areas in which Jesus ministered.

them to obey *everything* I have commanded you" (Matthew 28:20). And again, Jesus' promise in John 14:12 (NLT) holds that "*anyone* who believes in me will do the same works I have done."

On this basis we are to exercise our authority in the same areas in which Jesus ministered—in sickness, death, blessing, deliverance from demons, granting forgiveness (John 20:23), teaching and, above all, loving. To equip us for these tasks, when Jesus ascended to heaven, He "gave gifts to his people" (Ephesians 4:8, NLT). And the extent of our authority in any given area, as we will discuss in chapter 10, is calibrated to our gifting.

✣ Authority Prayer

When we are speaking to God, we usually call what we are doing *prayer*. Jesus believed in prayer and practiced it frequently. But prayer, at least in the usual sense of the word, was not His central activity when He was healing people or delivering them from demons.

There are at least six kinds of activity we may call prayer. The most common of these, the one we usually think of first, is what I will call *asking prayer*. In this kind of prayer, we ask for what we would like or need, as Jesus invited us to do in John 16:24: "Until now you have not asked for anything in my name; ask and you will receive, so that your happiness may be complete."

Another familiar kind of praying is *confession prayer*. We pray to confess and receive forgiveness, for we are told that "if we confess our sins to God, he will keep his promise and do what is right: he will forgive us our sins and purify us from all our wrongdoing" (1 John 1:9).

A third kind of prayer is *thanksgiving prayer*, in which we express our gratitude to God without requesting anything from Him. We do this verbally, of course, but we also give thanks using music when we worship.

Then there is *intercession*, an intense kind of praying in which we lay hold of God's faithfulness and promises in regard to something that concerns us greatly. Some with the gift of intercession agonize over a given situation, much like a woman going through labor to bring a child into the world.

The two kinds of prayer most relevant to the present discussion are what I will call *intimacy prayer* and *authority prayer*. The first of these is the most basic of all kinds of prayer: It involves simply being in God's presence. We have already spoken of the need for intimacy with God if we are to exercise the authority He expects of us. Jesus modeled this kind of prayer by going up a mountain or out into the wilderness to be alone with the Father, and during these times He was refreshed and enabled to meet the challenges of the day. It was also at these times that He received His instructions from the Father as to what He should do next. Jesus could then teach and minister with authority.

And what about authority prayer? Although we often use the expression *praying for healing* and might refer to this activity as *authority prayer*, I do not believe this is a form of prayer. It is rather the activity appropriate immediately *after* prayer when we are ministering to someone.

Jesus certainly prayed before ministering (John 11:41–42) to get His directions from the Father. Sometimes He prayed all night. But while ministering He did not ask the Father to do the job, as I have heard many ask when they want someone healed or delivered. With His Father's authority He simply spoke and it was done, because He submitted to the Father's will and always obeyed Him. He knew who He was and what His authority was, so He had no need while ministering to pray in the "asking" sense.

Jesus took the authority the Father had given Him and acted on His Father's behalf. He usually *commanded* the person to be well (Luke 4:39; 5:13; implied in Luke 7:6–10), or the spirit to leave (Luke 4:35), or the winds and waves to be still (Luke 8:24), or the person being healed to do something in faith (Luke 5:24; 6:10; 7:14). Sometimes He touched the person (Luke 5:13). Other times people touched Jesus and were healed (Luke 8:44; Matthew 14:36).

Yes, Jesus prayed before He did His deeds. But what He did *during* them should not be called prayer. So referring to the part we play in God's healing ministry as *praying for healing* may be misleading. We are to imitate Jesus and take authority as He did. When Jesus said that whoever believes in Him will do what He did, I believe He meant to include the *way* He did things in *what*

He did. Like Him, we are not to ask God to do the works; rather we line up our wills with His and talk not *to* the Father but *on His behalf*, speaking authoritatively to correct the situation.

An overview of this perspective on prayer might be described as follows:

We are to pursue intimacy with God (as Jesus did).

1. Flowing from this intimacy, we are expected to
   - ask
   - confess
   - praise and give thanks
   - intercede
2. Through this intimacy we hear God and receive His instructions.
   - On the basis of these instructions, we operate in the authority God gives to His servants.

Exercising the Authority We Have Been Given

In this section we will review areas (treated in more detail later in the book) in which we are to assert the authority we have been given.

When we assert authority over children or animals, we typically do it vocally. We command what we expect to happen. It is important that we realize, in exercising spiritual authority, that *the spirit world is always listening.* We can speak what we expect to happen to the listening spirit world and know we are heard. A useful way of asserting our authority is simply to say something like this: "I speak protection (or blessing, healing, etc.) in the name of Jesus Christ."

Asserting our authority vocally is easiest with demons, for they can answer back. But when we command illness to stop or weather to change, it is much less obvious that our words have been heard, especially when the change we have commanded does not take place immediately. Among the reasons for the apparent lack of response could be that we have not really heard from God, or it is not yet God's timing for the change to take place, or we do not have the right amount of authority to effect this change, or the problem may not be under the control of enemy spirits.

The spirit world cannot turn a deaf ear, however, to the commands of God's servants. Just as we know God hears us when we speak to Him (1 John 5:15), so we can be sure that the entire invisible world is listening when we direct our words its way. Any command we utter, therefore, that relates to the activity of enemy spirits will be heard loud and clear by them. And if our command is in accord with what God wants to do, it will be done.

When our wills line up with God's, we can and should assert our authority in at least three areas: to protect, to prevent and to attack.

To Protect

With regard to protection, we have no need to fear or be the least insecure. As the psalmist states, "The Lord will not abandon his people; he will not desert those who belong to him. . . . The Lord defends me; my God protects me" (Psalm 94:14, 22). If the Lord were not protecting us from the enemy, we would all be goners. It is clear what the enemy wants to do: "steal, kill, and destroy" (John 10:10). It is because of the high level of protection God grants us as His children that the enemy cannot carry out his will.

So we need not be insecure with regard to God's protecting activity. He is always guarding us at a high level. Yet there are things going on in the universe that we may be quite unaware of; for example, whether God loosened His protection of us as He did when He allowed Satan to attack Job. And there are rules in the universe (see chapter 8) of which we might be unaware that could allow the enemy to get at us from time to time. Just before His arrest Jesus advised His disciples to increase their protection by praying so that they "will not fall into temptation" (Luke 22:40). And to guard them in the end times, He instructed them to "be on watch and pray always that you will have the strength to go safely through" the end-time troubles (Luke 21:36).

So, on the one hand we can assume a high level of protection. But on the other hand we need to be alert to vulnerabilities that require more prayer—which includes, I believe, taking more authority for protection. For there may be areas in our lives that are not healed (even if we are not aware of them) that give the

The spirit world cannot turn a deaf ear to the commands of God's servants.

enemy a right to interfere in our lives. If so, we need to claim as much protection as possible, saying simply, "I claim protection in Jesus' name."

By learning more of what is going on in the spirit world and more about who we are, I believe it is possible to gain more protection than God grants automatically. For in spite of whatever is going on, there is good news! We have the authority to counter the enemy's devices. We simply need to be aware constantly of who we are and the fact that Satan is less powerful than we are (having the Holy Spirit within us). He can have only the rights that we do not challenge. But it is up to us to ferret out all the authority he has been given and to cancel it.

The world is a dangerous place, and I am sure I do not know all the rules that could result in problems for myself and those dear to me. So, without being fanatic or fearful, I claim God's special protection regularly as I go about my daily activities. Much of this is experimental, since I am not always sure whether I need more protection than I would receive if I did not claim more.

I call on God's protection and safety, for example, whenever I am driving, by saying something like this: "I claim safety and protection, in the name of Jesus Christ, as I drive." I also claim protection over myself when I am in a potentially dangerous place. One such place I sometimes go is the health food store, since some of these stores are run by people who follow New Age spirituality. Knowing my authority, I simply say, "I claim the protection of Jesus Christ over any enemy power that may operate in this place" before I go in. If I forget to say this and notice later that something strange seems to be going on, I cancel any rights the enemy may have gained over me in that place.

I claim God's protection regularly over our home and family. And when I am on the road and staying at a motel, I claim Jesus' protection and the breaking of enemy power over the room I am staying in—although I often forget to do this, and on only a few occasions did it seem to matter. At such times, when there seemed to be some hindering power in the motel room, I claimed God's presence and protection after the fact, and things changed.

To Prevent

Much of the discussion on asserting authority to protect also applies to using it to prevent things from happening. Often we can see something about to happen and, by taking authority over the situation, prevent it.

On several occasions teachers have described for me the change that has taken place in the behavior of their students after the teachers asserted their spiritual authority over the classroom. They have learned to go into the room before the children arrive and claim it for Jesus Christ. Once I even heard about a person who, concerned over the dangerous way children were running around a motel swimming pool, took authority over the pool area and found that the children's behavior improved.

One of the most effective preventive strategies I have learned to use is to assert spiritual authority over arguments. When I see a potential disagreement coming, I say, "If this is the enemy, stop it!" I am seldom sure in such situations that it actually is the enemy. But enough potential problems have not happened when I have used this strategy that I have come to believe in it. On several occasions, when I saw an argument with my wife coming, I said these words under my breath, and our mood changed immediately.

On learning about this aspect of authority several years ago, a young woman, then a student of mine, decided to experiment with it. Her sister was coming to visit that evening, which usually meant some kind of difficulty or argument. Just prior to her sister's arrival, my student took authority over her sister, the place of meeting, their time together and whatever passed between them. For the very first time in their recent relationship, the sisters spent an enjoyable evening together with no problems and no arguments.

Regarding my family, I regularly state to the enemies in the spirit world, "If you want to attack my wife, children, their spouses or our grandchildren, *you must go through me*, because I am the gateway into this family. But on the authority of Jesus Christ, you will not get through me." I believe this activity has had a lot to do with the prevention of attacks on our family. Later I will give further illustrations of people who have seen situations change by using this preventive strategy.

Another area in which we can prevent enemy activity is in dealing with artifacts purchased in pagan cultures or in New Age or Native American contexts. In many societies such items are dedicated routinely to evil spirits, often as they are made. When dedicated objects are in our possession, they give the enemy rights. But these rights can be taken away when we claim the power of Christ to break Satan's power over the item.

My practice is to verbally break the enemy power over anything I buy in a "suspicious" place (which includes medicines or food supplements bought at health food stores in addition to decorative items), and then to bless the item with the power of God so it becomes a source of blessing rather than of danger. I make one exception to this cleansing rule: If something has no purpose other than a religious or occultic one, I destroy it after praying over it. A few years ago I was asked to help a friend deal with his Freemasonry books and paraphernalia. He had turned to Christ and knew those objects carried satanic power. So we took authority over them to break all enemy power, burned whatever was burnable and threw the rest in the trash.

To Attack

Finally, we should assert our authority to attack. When we minister healing or deliverance to people, we are attacking the enemy's grip on them.

Because much in the following chapters has to do with attacking the enemy, joining with Jesus to take away the enemy's rights in people and places, we will not deal with this subject thoroughly here. Suffice it to say that since Satan is "the ruler of this world" (John 14:30), we are attacking him whenever we assert the authority given us to hinder his plans. Thus, preventing and protecting are also forms of attack. Our task in any use of this authority is to capture as much as possible of what the enemy has asserted his authority over.

Even witnessing for Jesus is a form of attack. The result, I believe, depends on the will of the person we are witnessing to. But people have reported to me that things changed dramatically when they claimed the authority of Jesus to break through the blinding of 2 Corinthians 4:4, where it is recorded that "the evil god of this world" keeps people's minds darkened so they cannot respond to the Gospel. Believers are especially able to assert our spiritual authority to bring about change in those over whom we have human authority (for example, our children, other family members and our students). As those who belong to Christ, we have the right to claim our authority to open them up to the light of God.

I am often asked if our authority to attack works at a distance. If we look at the account of Jesus healing the Roman officer's "very dear" servant (Luke 7:1–10; Matthew 8:5–13), I have to answer yes, although some of the specifics of that situation probably indicate that certain conditions have to be met in order for authority to be exercised effectively at a distance. The first thing to note was that Jesus had heard from the Father that He was to heal the servant, for He was already on His way to minister to him. Second, a great amount of faith was exercised by the Roman officer, probably paralleled by great willingness and faith on the part of his servant. Third, the officer showed profound understanding of the spirit world and Jesus' position in relation to it.

We might infer, then, that when we find willingness and faith on the part of the recipient and a go-ahead from the Father, the enemy can be attacked successfully even at a distance. I do not know if ministering over the telephone counts as attacking at a distance, but I have often ministered effectively over the phone, both in deep-level healing and in casting out demons.

ᓀ Authority to Bless and Curse

We will deal with blessing and cursing again in chapter 14, but they are such an important aspect of our authority that I will begin to treat them here.

If we look to Jesus' behavior after the resurrection as an example (John 20:19, 26), He blessed people regularly when He came into their presence with the lovely Hebrew greeting

Shalom, "peace." He commanded His followers to bless people's households in the same way when He sent them out to minister (Luke 10:5).

From Jesus' instructions in Luke 10 we learn that we are to bless freely, before we even know how our recipients will react. Not everyone will accept us (verses 6, 10–11); when this happens, we are justified in taking back our blessing (verse 6), since the person who declares a blessing "owns" that blessing. Indeed, if we are rejected, we can go further and publicly shake the dust of the unreceptive town off our feet (verse 11).

We are not authorized, however, to curse those who reject or offend us, although with the authority to use words to bless others comes the authority to curse. Instead we are commanded to bless and pray for others, even those who curse us (Luke 6:28; Romans 12:14; 1 Corinthians 4:12). One exception to this kind of blessing, according to 2 John 9–11, is that we are not to bless heretics—"anyone who does not stay with the teaching of Christ, but goes beyond it." A heretic, says John, "does not have God. . . . Do not welcome them in your homes; do not even say, Peace be with you. For anyone who wishes them peace becomes their partner in the evil things they do."

The authority to bless and curse is an incredible endowment. God empowers our words, so we need to watch them and use them only as He directs. I doubt He wants us to use them indiscriminately to bless everyone. We should therefore listen to Him, blessing only those He tells us to bless. It is from listening to Him, furthermore, that we hear what we are to bless them with.

Things happen when we bless. I have heard many people remark that they felt a pleasant charge like electricity flow through them when I spoke a blessing over them. I believe it was the spiritual healer Agnes Sanford who reported an experience in an elevator in which she silently blessed a woman who was complaining about everything. By the time the woman got off the elevator, she had become positive about the day and about life in general! I have had similar experiences with people to whom I have ministered.

The protection we discussed in the previous section can be brought about by blessing whatever it is we seek to protect. Besides protecting cars, computers, homes and family members, I have been experimenting with blessing myself with protection from disease and accident. I think it has been working.

Blessings can be passed along when we take authority over places and things that are then used by others. The power of God through blessing apparently extends even to influencing people who use objects that have been blessed. This happens (as I suggested) when teachers take authority over their classrooms. It also happens when we bless churches, sacred objects, our homes, specific rooms within our homes, the furniture on which people sit, our offices or other workplaces, computers and other objects people use. The blessing carries over to the people who use the items or places.

I know of a pastor who accepted a temporary assignment to a church that was badly split. He told me he did not know what to do to bring the people back together again. Then in prayer an idea came to him. He went to the church each Saturday evening for several weeks and systematically blessed each seat and the person who regularly sat in it. Within a few weeks the people were turning away from their bickering, and the division in the church was healed.

We should take seriously the blessing of our food before we eat. Those of us who regularly say "grace" before meals should not simply do so as a matter of routine. We have the authority to empower food and drink to bring blessing to those who eat and drink it.

A scriptural example of these things is the use of Paul's handkerchiefs and aprons to bring healing and deliverance (Acts

19:12). There was no magic in these items; the power of God through the blessing of being close to the man of God brought about miraculous things. People have told me about situations that changed when they blessed letters and sent them to people. I am not sure what rules govern this type of blessing, but it cannot hurt to experiment with using our authority to bless things used by or given to others. We can bless places and buildings with freedom from enemy activity and with protection against any plans he might have for them in the future.

We can bless places and buildings with freedom from enemy activity.

I was told that one lady was learning about the power of blessing and decided to try it on her unbelieving husband. So she began blessing his toothbrush. In about two weeks her husband turned to Christ! When she reported this to some of her friends, some of them asked if such a blessing would work on other things, such as their husbands' underwear! I suspect that kind of strategy is dependent on the openness of those receiving the blessing to the work of God in their lives.

Things also happen when we curse by directing negative words toward people or objects. Many who have spoken such negative words toward themselves have found themselves, or parts of themselves, cursed. Frequently people who are sexually abused, for example, curse their sexual organs or their ability to enjoy sex. Directing spiritual power toward oneself in this way is likely to develop into disease in one's sexual organs or dysfunction in one's sexual experience.

Many people curse their bodies or their whole selves during their teenage years. They are not satisfied with the way their bodies develop and say things like, "I hate my hips/face/breasts." (see chapter 14 for more on self-cursing.) I have seen dramatic changes in people who have asserted their authority to renounce the curses they put on themselves or parts of themselves. Once they have renounced the curses, I usually ask them to begin blessing those parts of themselves that are now freed from the curses. We can do this with the authority God gives us.

A helpful use of cursing is in praying for people who are ill. Often I curse the germs and viruses (never the people) that are causing the illness. Frequently things change, probably due at least in part to the cursing of the germs and viruses. Since we do several other things when we minister to people, however, it is impossible to know just what role the cursing of germs and viruses plays in our healing experiences.

Authority to Bind and Loose

In Matthew 16:19, just after Peter's great acknowledgment of Jesus as the Messiah, and again in Matthew 18:18, the Lord makes an amazing statement: "What you prohibit on earth will be prohibited in heaven, and what you permit on earth will be permitted in heaven." When Jesus first said this to Peter, He used the singular *you*. But when He repeated it in Matthew 18, He used the plural *you*, extending this authority to the whole group and to all His followers down through the centuries.

Older translations use the word *bind* rather than *prohibit* or *forbid* and *loose* rather than *permit* or *allow*. Whatever terms are used, the focus is on the close relationship between what happens on earth and what goes on in heaven. Jesus' statement seems to confer great authority on us to do *something*. Just what that something is, though, is hard to figure out with any degree of certainty.

The Aramaic terms that underlie the Greek words were used technically to relate to the excommunication and reinstatement of people. The original hearers, in the view of Herman C. Waetjen (1984), would probably have assumed that Jesus was giving His followers "the authority to exclude from, as well as to reinstate in, the community of believers." This is an incredible authority to have. But the question is, did Jesus intend something broader than simply including or excluding people from the Christian community?

Many people speak of "binding Satan" and often say things like "I bind you, Satan," when they want to stop something he seems to be doing. Some who speak like that, I am afraid, regard these words as almost magical, as if by their simple utterance, the enemy will be stopped. We do have authority over Satan, but it is questionable whether the utterance of religious words is what Jesus had in mind when He spoke of binding and loosing. So I prefer to say to demons, "Stop it!" or "I forbid you to do that!" to make the point in more understandable terms.

But there is probably a relationship between Jesus' statements in Matthew 16:19 and 18:18 and this one in John 20:23: "If you forgive people's sins, they are forgiven; if you do not forgive them, they are not forgiven." If so, one of the things we have authority to do that is honored in heaven is to forgive. We will explore this further in chapter 15.

In whatever sense we take binding and loosing, Jesus has given us great authority. This authority is wielded ordinarily through words, whether they be words of commitment, vows, blessing/ cursing, accepting/rejecting or forgiving/not forgiving. It is important that we use this authority, as Jesus used His, with wisdom.

If Only We Realized the Power We Carry!

Our authority gives us the ability to use the power God gives us through the indwelling of the Holy Spirit. Most of us, however, seem only vaguely aware of how much power that is. We would do well to consider that when the Holy Spirit dwells within us, we are invested with the power of God Himself, and with the full authority of Jesus to use it. What a tragedy that many of God's choice people, although given both His power and the authority of His credit card, either do not realize what is theirs or else refuse to exercise those rights!

A friend told me once about an acquaintance who had been converted to Christianity out of a New Age group. While in bondage to Satan, this woman had the ability to "see" the amount of spiritual power different people carry with them, and she could pick out the Christians in a group "a mile away" by simply noting the amount of power they carried. Although she knew Christians wield more power than New Agers, she also knew that most Christians have no idea what to do with that power. So the Christians were no threat, except the occasional one who knew how to use the power of Christ. She and her fellow New Agers tried to keep well away from such people. How different their experience might have been, the convert remarked, if the Christians they met had only realized how much power they carried and had exercised their God-given authority to use it.

So that we ourselves may better realize our own God-given authority, let's turn to a discussion of the nature of that authority.

4

What Is This Authority?

✄ Educating the Sons of Sceva

There were apparently a number of people in New Testament days who went around casting out demons. Like anyone in a deliverance ministry, they were always open to learning new techniques. They probably attempted to coax out the demons, as was the custom among the Pharisees in Jesus' day. They heard, however, that some were having success driving out demons by using the name of Jesus, a prophet about whom a man named Paul spoke.

So they decided to try this new approach. We are not told how many used the new approach nor how often they were successful with it. The impression given in Acts 19:13–16 is that there were a number of these deliverance specialists. And it appears that the new approach worked for a certain period of time.

But seven of these men, all sons of a Jewish high priest named Sceva, tried the technique on the wrong demon! For we are told that a demon they tried to cast out would not buy their approach. He was, evidently, a very powerful demon, and he knew who had authority over him and who did not. So he responded to their command to leave by saying, "I know Jesus, and I know about Paul; but you—who are you?" (verse 15). The man carrying the demon then proceeded to beat up all seven brothers, attacking them "with such violence that he overpowered them all." In response, these seasoned deliverance specialists "ran away from his house, wounded and with their clothes torn off" (verse 16), never to try that approach again!

There is a big difference between having the authority of Jesus and not having it. These men did not have it—an authority the demon knew of and respected. We do. That should change things for us.

Why did they not have the authority they needed? They used the right words, the right formula, the right name. But the power was not in the formula; it was not even in the words they used to claim the authority of Jesus and Paul. *The power is in a relationship with Jesus*, a relationship these men did not have. And the demons had no obligation to obey those who, though they knew the right words to say, had no relationship with the One who could empower the words.

✎ Defining Authority

Jesus said, "I have been given all authority in heaven and on earth" (Matthew 28:18) and "I have given you [the disciples] authority, so that you can . . . overcome all the power of the Enemy" (Luke 10:19). Earlier, as He sent the disciples out "to preach the Kingdom of God and to heal the sick," He defined this authority as the "power and authority to drive out all demons and to cure diseases" (Luke 9:1–2). If Jesus meant this to apply to us also, and I believe with all my heart that He did, what we are dealing with is truly an awesome privilege and responsibility.

The concept of authority is closely connected with the concept of power in Scripture. The Greek words are *dunamis* (power) and *exousia* (authority). According to Luke 9:1, Jesus gave both to His followers.

Dunamis occurs some 118 times in the New Testament. Paul uses the word frequently, as do the writers of the first three gospels. It is the normal word for power, might, strength or force and is often used in the plural to refer to miracles ("wonders"), as in the phrase *signs and wonders* (Acts 2:22; 2 Corinthians 12:12; Hebrews 2:4). It is also used to refer to supernatural beings, the "powers," as in Romans 8:38; 1 Corinthians 15:24; Ephesians 1:21; 1 Peter 3:22.

The power of God is ordinarily referred to as *dunamis*, as is the power Jesus gives us (Luke 9:1). Earthly power, whether of rulers, armies or weather, was also labeled *dunamis*. So the English word *power* is usually an adequate translation of this word. Contrary to many simplistic references in sermons, it has nothing to do with dynamite, though the word *dynamite* in English is derived from this Greek word.

Exousia, though often referring to power, focuses on the right to use power rather than on the power itself. This word occurs 108 times in the New Testament, always related to people. It is a personal right, conferred either because of status or by delegation to assert power, whether in the legal, political, social or moral domains, and whether in the human world or in the spiritual realm.

> *Jesus gave His followers the Holy Spirit, the source of His power, and advised them to keep close to Him.*

In the New Testament, both power (*dunamis*) and authority (*exousia*) flow from the work of Christ, first as He employed them and then as He empowers His followers to do His works. Jesus received His power from the Holy Spirit and His authority from maintaining His intimacy with the Father. At the end of His ministry, then, He gave His followers the Holy Spirit (Luke 24:49), the source of His power, and advised them to keep close to Him (John 15:1–17).

Thus, the authority we participate in is that modeled by Jesus Himself, grounded, as it was with Jesus, in the same power of the Holy Spirit. As Jesus said concerning our power and authority, "Those who believe in me will do what I do—yes, they will do even greater things, because I am going to the Father" (John 14:12).

Our authority, then, is the God-given right to receive and use God's power that flows from the indwelling Holy Spirit.

What Our Authority Is Not

Perhaps, if we are to properly understand what our authority is, we need to consider what it is not. We need to know that the basis of our authority is our position in Christ. It is certainly not our feelings. We may not always *feel* authoritative any more than we always feel married or even accepted by God. Our feelings are just not good indicators of the truth.

A missionary I will call Lisa is a case in point. Lisa and her husband were students at Fuller's School of World Mission, where I taught, and were learning a lot about spiritual warfare. When Lisa came for ministry, one of her main concerns was that she was unable to exercise her spiritual authority in Christ. She felt that every other Christian was worthy of the privilege except her. She was believing a lie, and her feelings supported the lie. As Lisa began to practice using her authority, however, she learned just how crippled she had been by the lie. To escape her dilemma, she began choosing to defy her feelings and to believe the truth. She found that by first accepting and choosing to believe the truth of her authority and then by acting on it she was as worthy as anyone. Lisa has now become a powerful spiritual warrior and a real threat to the enemy's kingdom.

Our authority, then, is not a matter of feeling or emotions. Nor should we see Christian authority as a kind of gifting or personality type. We may regard certain persons as "persons of authority" because they have authoritative positions. Though the Christian's authority is truly a gift, it is given to *everyone* in God's family and is not related to status or personality. Several of the members of my ministry teams over the years have had rather meek and mild personalities, and one has a major physical disability. It is exciting to see how obediently demons respond to their authority. On the other hand, those who attempt to command demons purely on the basis of their own personal authority, like the sons of Sceva, do not get very far.

Our spiritual authority is rooted in our position as members of God's family. And it is ours whether or not we feel it or have a special gift, status or personality type. Though there is a relationship between gifting and the authority to minister in any given area, as we will see in chapter 10, that relationship is a secondary one. All Christians have the right both to pray and to challenge enemy forces in Jesus' name. This is authority. It has been legally won for us by Jesus through His victory on the cross and from the tomb, where "Jesus took from the devil the legal right to the balance of power on this planet" (Sherman 1990, 118).

But it is a scary thing to have the authority of God to use His power. It is like handling live electric wires; carelessness could result in great damage. Indeed, the amount of spiritual abuse occurring in churches today should serve as a warning to all of us to be careful lest we misuse the authority that has been delegated to us. Perhaps the following considerations will help.

1. We Do Not Own It

First and foremost, *the authority should not be seen as something that belongs to us.* It is entrusted to us by God, and *we are*

75

to manage it. Our first responsibility, then, is to be faithful to our Master in the way we use what He has trusted us with. For "a person who is put in charge as a manager must be faithful" (1 Corinthians 4:2, NLT). We are therefore to treat this authority as something precious, something God has trusted us to manage, something loaned to us by the One to whom we have committed ourselves. We dare not consider it a right or legacy with which we can do anything we want.

2. We Must Use It Rightly

Since we are stewards or managers of something that we do not really own, *we need to be careful to use the authority for the purposes for which it was given to us.* Fortunately, we have Jesus as our model. We can see that we are not to use it to show off or simply to enhance our own reputation, for such use of authority and power was refused by Jesus (Matthew 12:38–39; 16:1, 4; Mark 8:11–12; Luke 11:16). When someone is in need, however, especially if that person is being tormented by the enemy, we are to show the same kind of compassion that motivated our Master.

3. We Must Not Presume

Thirdly, we must be constantly on our guard and *fight any tendency toward presumption.* There are several dimensions to this tendency.

For one thing, we must be careful never to assume that our authority gives us the right to command God to do our will. This is one of the errors Satan made when he put God to the test (Matthew 4:7) by seeking to control when Jesus would do miraculous things. Though God in His mercy sometimes gives us our way, we should be careful not to try to "force His hand." As usual, it is Jesus who showed us how it should be done. For He did nothing on His own authority, but said and did only what the Father instructed Him to do (John 8:28; see also 5:19).

I am afraid we fall into this error when we try to bargain with God over someone's healing, saying, "This person has done so much for You, he surely deserves to be healed," or "It would be such a great testimony to all the unbelievers for this person to be healed." Even worse are those who teach that we should simply "name" what we want and "claim" it. Such people are, perhaps without realizing it, leading us to believe that we can coerce God into doing our will. "God wants us to be happy," they say. "If, therefore, we simply exercise our faith by picturing what we want and claiming it, He will give it to us—if our faith is strong enough." If we do not receive our desire, it is because we do not have enough faith, or else there is sin in our lives. This is not a proper use of authority; it is presumption and deceit. And this kind of teaching leaves a lot of people confused about the nature of God, feeling guilty about their lack of faith.

We must be careful never to assume that our authority gives us the right to command God to do our will.

A friend of mine who has had to use a wheelchair all her life told me of an event that happened to her at a church picnic. During the prayer and worship time, a very athletic young man came to her to ask if he could pray with her. Of course, she accepted. Much to her surprise and dismay, the young man prayed for a few seconds and then attempted to yank her out of her chair. When she was not healed, he turned to her and asked, "Where's your faith, sister?" Later on, a pastor suggested she should have replied, "Not in you, brother!" Faith is not refusing to accept or believe reality. It is pressing on with God despite a reality that is sometimes not of our choosing.

Another presumptuous way of trying to get God to do our will is to first make our plans and then expect God to bless them. I am afraid I make this mistake often. I am used to being in charge and have long had the habit of working things out pretty well on my own before I think to consult God. I am trying to work my way out of this habit into consulting God first. But it is easy to assume that we know in advance exactly what God wants to do and to quickly apply our authority to it. In this way we abuse the privilege God gives us of working with Him in His authority.

A related presumption is to think that we alone know the mind of God on any given issue and, therefore, can assert His authority without reference to what others are thinking. This error easily leads us to use our authority to promote any personal agenda that we have. We may have ambitions for some position or prominence and assert the authority God has given us for selfish ends. But just as prophecy is not to be interpreted individualistically (2 Peter 1:20), so any plans for the use of authority should be made in consultation with others who hear God's voice, especially if that authority will be applied in a church or community setting.

Then there is the presumption that leads to wrong timing. We may discern quite correctly what God wants but run ahead of Him, using our authority to implement something or tackle a problem before the time is ripe. God tends to work slowly. We tend to be impatient, even to the point of wanting to "force God's hand" too soon. We must resist this presumption.

Too frequently there is the presumption that leads to defiance and/or rebellion. Unfortunately, some who once committed themselves to God now, like Satan, use the authority God gives them to resist Him. King Saul, who could not wait for the prophet Samuel to arrive to offer the appropriate sacrifice (1 Samuel 13:7–11) and who later took the attitude before another battle that "There's no time to consult the Lord!" (1 Samuel 14:19), is an example of this. God, however, is very patient and often allows even those who are disobedient to Him to continue to operate in His authority, at least for a time.

4. We Are Not Indispensable

A fourth misuse of authority *results in spiritual pride.* It is important to not get so focused on the results of ministry, many of which are truly spectacular, that we begin to feel we are especially gifted or, worse, indispensable to God. If we fall into these errors, spiritual pride develops and takes over. We then lose our ability to love and serve as Jesus wants us to. Our relationship to the Giver of our authority must always take priority over the results. When first the Twelve and then the Seventy-Two, whom Jesus gave power and authority over demons and to heal diseases (Luke 9 and 10), returned to Him, they came rejoicing, astonished at the results of their authority (Luke 10:17). They marveled at what they had been able to do in spiritual power. But Jesus quickly put the issue of spiritual authority back into perspective for them by reminding them that their relationship to God is most important, not the ability to do spectacular things. In His words, "Don't be glad because the evil spirits obey you; rather be glad because your names are written in heaven" (verse 20).

Let these misuses of God-given authority serve as warnings to be careful to use it rightly—in submission and obedience to our Lord. We must always remember that our authority is not a license to do whatever we want to do whenever we want to do it. Our motivation for using God's authority needs to be as pure as possible. We must not be seeking our own gratification but rather the glory of God. We must be seeking to fit in with God's purposes when we take His authority so that through faith our wills are aligned with His will. Then when there is success, we can rejoice both over what God has done and about the fact that we were submissive and obedient.

✣ Accountability to God

A critical concern in the exercise of power is our *accountability*. In the Kingdom of God, the one with authority is accountable to God to discover and follow His will rather than to simply implement the person's own desires. As Nee (1972, 116) has well put it:

> For one to be in authority does not depend on his having ideas and thoughts; rather does it hinge on knowing the will of God. The measure of one's knowledge of God's will is the measure of his delegated authority. God establishes a person to be His delegated authority entirely on the basis of that person's knowledge of God's will. It has nothing at all to do with having many ideas, strong opinions, or noble thoughts. Indeed, such persons who are strong in themselves are greatly to be feared in the church.

Conformity to the will of the One who grants the authority is, then, a major requirement. Indeed, whenever we assert the authority given us, it is up to God whether or not He will carry it out. But as 1 John 5:14 tells us, "We are sure that he hears us if we ask him for anything that is according to his will." We are to use the authority delegated to us to *represent* God and His will, not to substitute our desires for His (Nee 1972, 118).

As Nee points out, *ours is a delegated authority—delegated by God*. We are simply stewards of what God has entrusted us with. We are never to assume that our authority comes from any quality or worth inherent in us.

Whether we have a greater or lesser degree of authority, we are all of equal value to God. A husband's authority over his wife, for example, is based not on any greater value of a man (there is none) but solely on the fact that God has delegated authority in this way. Likewise with the authority of parents over children or of Christians over non-Christians. The authority

He delegates to each of us may yet differ, for it is not something that is inherently ours, that we possess. It is something granted to us for the purpose of representing the God who gave it to us (Nee 1972, 116).

Accountability in Obedience

Since this is a delegated authority, it is crucial that we exercise it in obedience. We should be conscious at all times that big mistakes have been made in this domain and try not to make any more. The sin of Adam, the one that gave away human authority over creation, was the sin of disobedience. Thus it was only through obedience that Jesus, the second Adam (1 Corinthians 15:45, 47), won back our right to assert authority over the universe.

Practicing obedience to the One under whose authority we operate teaches us how to exercise the authority He delegates to us. As we obey, we become more like Him both in character and in our relationships with those under our authority. We learn, for example, to focus on Him, the Giver of authority and power (as well as all other gifts of the Spirit), not on the gifts themselves. Assuming obedience and submission to God, then, we take a stand for the same things that the One we obey stands for.

> *As we obey, we become more like Him.*

Accountability to Other Believers

In addition to our accountability to God, we need also to relate to mature, dedicated people who will hold us accountable. We have seen over and over in public life what happens when people in authority are not accountable to others in the way they exercise authority. The founders of the United States set up its government with three branches so that, theoretically, with its system of checks and balances, no one branch has more influence than another. Temptations to misuse our authority exist in abundance in the exercise of spiritual authority. It is important, therefore, to make sure that there are safeguards to prevent this from happening.

We must constantly solicit the help of others to monitor our submission and obedience to God in the way we exercise our authority. It is important that each Christian belong to a group of respected, mature Christians who can give feedback in the wisdom of God. Too often those in Christian ministry allow themselves to get isolated from those who can advise and, if necessary, correct them. We tend to be "lone rangers," consulting only ourselves. But God wants us to function as a body, not as isolated body parts.

One of the best decisions I have made was to agree with several (between five and ten) other men to meet weekly for fellowship and counsel. We have different gifts but the common purpose to live for and serve our Master as faithfully as possible. To this end, we seek to hold each other accountable both in personal matters and in ministry. We need, with the help of such a group, to regularly conduct "reality checks" on ourselves by comparing what we are doing to the ways in which Jesus carried out His activities.

Examining the Fruit

An important but often slower measure of accountability is the fruit a ministry produces. Jesus said that if we are connected to the vine, we will bear much fruit (John 15:5). If the authority we exercise results in people being helped, healed and freed and gets them growing in the Lord, it should be continued. If there are constantly negative results, if people are damaged or if the name of the Lord is dishonored, the activity should definitely be discontinued. One's accountability group needs to be vigilant and bold in alerting that person to any negative fruit.

The nature of our authority demands that we keep ourselves aligned with the character of the One who grants us our authority in His name. We are accountable to be true to the nature and character of God. One common pitfall is to behave as if we can wear our authority like a lawman wears his or her badge and command authority because of the power it represents. Just as we hear about police abusing their authority, so this happens in the Christian realm as well.

Authority is an awesome responsibility and privilege. The power of that authority can be used to bear much fruit. It can also be mishandled and used to abuse. To remain submissive and obedient to the One who grants authority, we need to understand the character of God so that we do not overstep the boundaries that are set up. As we have said before, our authority is Him. It is not ours, except as He allows us to use it.

Healthy Fear

Another incentive to accountability is a healthy fear. Fear can keep us accountable. Though fear of the enemy can be crippling, a healthy fear of misusing our authority can be very freeing. Knowing how easy it is to overstep our boundaries and to misuse the authority God has granted us should raise within us a constructive kind of fear.

It is said that if we fear God, we do not need to fear anything else. Let the fear of displeasing God keep us accountable and able to work in freedom. It was this fear that guided Joshua and kept him faithful while he was conquering the Promised Land. He was told by God to be determined and confident (Joshua 1:7). Because he feared to disobey, then, Joshua could exercise his God-given authority fearlessly.

5

Power Wrapped in Love

As always, the model that we imitate is Jesus. With all the power of the Holy Spirit within His authority, He was remarkably controlled in His use of that power. He only used His power in a context of love. In fact, He used His power specifically to show His love.

So the first rule in exercising the authority God has given us is to operate in His authority *lovingly*. Those with authority are constantly tempted to behave harshly. This is not God's way. Jesus, though working in great authority, also recognized that He was under authority. Being under authority, then, He was responsible for doing His Father's works *in His Father's way*. Our responsibility is likewise to exhibit the character of Jesus as we assert the authority He gives us. We are to manifest the fruits of the Spirit (Galatians 5:22–23) as we operate in the gifts of the Spirit, and we are to wrap all authority in love.

Throughout Scripture, we see God as very concerned for those who are in difficult circumstances, such as these groups of people:

orphans (Deuteronomy 24:17; 27:19; Psalm 10:18; 146:9; Isaiah 1:17; Jeremiah 22:3; Zechariah 7:10; James 1:27)

widows (Deuteronomy 14:29; 24:19; 27:19; Psalm 68:5; 146:9; Isaiah 1:17; Jeremiah 22:3; Zechariah 7:10; James 1:27)

the poor (Exodus 23:6; Deuteronomy 15:11; Psalm 35:10; 82:3; Isaiah 11:4; Zechariah 7:10)

the oppressed (Psalm 10:18; Isaiah 1:17)

God wants His power to be used for the sake of the powerless. This is why God was so angry with David for stealing Bathsheba from her husband. David, with all the power of his kingship and all of the wives his position entitled him to, used that power to defraud Uriah of his only wife.

With this God-ordained concept of how power is to be used, Jesus resisted the constant temptation to do power demonstrations on demand or to show off. When asked to prove Himself by displaying His power, He refused. He would not use His power even to prove Himself to the skeptics (Matthew 12:38–39; 16:4; Mark 8:11–12; Luke 23:8–9). But when He saw someone in need, it is recorded over and over again that His heart was "filled with pity" for them, or, as the older translations have it, He was "moved with compassion" (Matthew 9:36; 14:14; 15:32; 20:34; Mark 1:41; 6:34; Luke 7:13).

Likewise, His heart was full of compassion when He encountered demonization. But, though He could have made a big deal of delivering people from the power of the enemy, He chose to do it quietly. Jesus even shut the demons down when they tried to broadcast who He was (Mark 1:25; Luke 4:35), thus using His authority to keep control over when, what and who would reveal who Jesus was. In all of this, then, Jesus used His authority and power to show God's love. Jesus always wrapped His power in His love.

We must never lose sight of the fact that the authority God gives us is to be used only for His purposes and in His way. Obedience and submission to Him imply this. It is agonizing to see the apparent pride of some who conduct "miracle healing campaigns" or even local church healing services. They often seem to be more concerned to parade their own gifts than to honor the Giver of those gifts. Something I do not understand is the graciousness of God in allowing even those who seem to be misusing their gifts to continue to operate in them.

I was watching such a healer on TV one evening (though I cannot stand to do it very often) and thought, *How different this must be from the way Jesus did things!* This man was a showman, his every move timed for dramatic effect. He strutted. He swaggered as he moved from place to place on the stage to touch the people who had been brought to him. They usually fell backward as he touched or blew on them, a behavior he fully expected and milked for dramatic effect. He lifted his head, touched his forehead and closed his eyes dramatically as he spoke his words of knowledge—as if he were dragging them out of the Master's mind.

Though God in His love and mercy uses this man and often brings blessing and healing through him, I doubt that He approves of the way he goes about ministry. The man's performance made me angry because he was making a public spectacle out of the right that Jesus has given us to assert authority over the results of illness and accident. Since such showing off is so unlike our Lord, I feel this man was using his authority irresponsibly. My own conviction is that *we are to demonstrate the character of Jesus in the way we use His authority.*

It is interesting that the only characteristic Jesus mentioned as designating a true disciple was love. Though spirituality, intimacy, righteousness, authority, power and a number of other things are important marks of a disciple, it is love that is the distinguishing characteristic. We are, therefore, to imitate Jesus by living lives of love. And all that we do with the authority and power God gives us is to be wrapped in love.

My rule is, if it is not loving, it is not Jesus' way, even if it is spectacular. Anything we do that is unloving is not of God, even if it is powerful. The gifts of the Spirit (1 Corinthians 12:8–11; 28–31) are to be accompanied by the fruits of the Spirit (Galatians 5:22–23), especially love. I contend that people such as those mentioned above, though they are marvelously gifted, abuse other people even while they are trying to help them. This is not God's way of doing things, and it is not to be our way. The first rule for each of us as we minister in the authority God has given us is *to wrap God's power in God's love, like Jesus did.* Only if what we do is truly loving is it truly healing.

We are to demonstrate the character of Jesus in the way we use His authority.

Other Ways to Exercise Authority

In addition to being accountable to God and others and bathing all use of authority in love, there are four other ways in which we are to exercise the authority we have been given.

First, *we are to exercise this authority in humility.* I find the fact that God trusts us with His power and authority deeply humbling. Indeed, I have found nothing so humbling in my life as the experience of using the authority granted me by God to constantly do things I know I cannot do. As Nee says, "The nearer one is to the Lord, the clearer he sees his own faults" (1972, 119), as well as his limitations. When we take authority to bring healing, if the Holy Spirit does not come to bring it about, nothing happens. The fact that He comes so regularly, in spite of our weakness, unworthiness, sinfulness and just plain inadequacy, produces deep humility in anyone who thinks deeply about what is going on.

Secondly, *we need to exercise this delegated authority in the same kind of security that characterized Jesus.* We can be as secure as Jesus was because, like Him, we know who we are, who God is and what the source of our authority is. On this basis, we can be free from insisting that others listen to us or submit to us. As Nee has said, "The more God entrusts to us, the more liberty we grant to people" (1972, 121).

Secure husbands are intent on enabling their wives to live in freedom. Pity the wife that has an insecure, authority-abusing husband who is threatened by freedom. Secure parents allow their children a lot of room to grow. Secure pastors and other leaders exercise their authority by encouraging freedom and growth, not by restricting it. Jesus was secure enough to reinstate Peter after his denials and to trust him with His sheep (John 21:15–17).

In the third place, *truly God-ordained authority always emanates from service.* Since Jesus is our model, His commitment to serving is the example we are to follow in the exercise of the authority He gives. As Richard Foster has said in *Celebration of Discipline,*

> The most radical social teaching of Jesus was His total reversal of the contemporary notion of greatness. Leadership is found in becoming the servant of all. Power is discovered in submission. The foremost symbol of this radical servanthood is the cross. . . . Christ not only died a cross-death, He lived a cross-life. . . . He lived the cross-life when He took a towel and washed the feet of His disciples. . . . Jesus' life was the cross-life of submission and service. . . . The cross-life of Jesus undermined all social orders based on power and self-interest. . . . The cross-life is the life of voluntary submission. The cross-life is the life of freely accepted servanthood (1978, 101–102).

We are taught in Ephesians 5:23, 25 that a husband is to exercise his authority over his wife by giving himself for her, just as Jesus gave Himself for the Church. Jesus, our model for how to exercise authority, stated that He "did not come to be served; he came to serve and to give his life to redeem many people" (Mark 10:45). Authority is to be exercised in service.

All of this adds up to maturity. The Christian is to exercise his or her authority in as mature a fashion as possible. Though maturity is often difficult to define, any person who operates in love, humility, accountability, obedience, security and service, taking seriously his/her stewardship, would qualify as mature. The proper practice of the authority with which God entrusts us requires nothing less.

✥ When and Where Are We to Exercise Authority?

Again, Jesus has showed us the way. As we have pointed out, He did no mighty works on demand. When He was approached by one or more needy persons, however, Scripture often notes that He felt compassion or pity, and He always healed them (Luke 5:12; 6:9–10; 7:13–15; 9:13; 18:35–43).

Most of Jesus' healings seemed to be public (Luke 4:40; 5:18–20; 7:13–15; 8:43–48; 9:42–43; 18:35–43; 22:50–51), though sometimes He seems to have worked in private or semiprivate settings (Luke 5:12–14; 8:26–39). When crowds converged on Him, there is no record of Him turning them away. Usually it says that He healed many or all of them (Luke 4:40; 5:15; 6:19; 7:21; 9:11). Sometimes He went to a home (Luke 4:38–39; 8:51–56; 14:1–4), at other times He healed in the Temple or in a synagogue (Matthew 21:14; Luke 4:33–35; 6:6–10; 13:10–13) and once it is recorded that He healed at long distance (Luke 7:2–10). Though there was much to do, Jesus never seemed to get frantic or even hurried.

An interesting thing about Jesus' use of His authority is that He seldom went looking for people to minister to. Perhaps this was because He did not have to. They knew He could heal and sought Him out. We do, however, know of one time when Jesus sought out someone to minister to. John 5:2–9 records the story of the man who had been lying beside the pool of Bethzatha for 38 years, seeking healing. The Master, undoubtedly on specific instructions from the Father, went to the pool specifically to seek and heal one person from what may have been hundreds at the poolside.

The message for us seems to be that if we are to follow Jesus' example, we should be prepared to minister in power and authority at any time and at any place and to anyone. Though we, like Jesus, should rarely, if ever, set out to find people to heal, we should be open to pray with anyone who comes our way. To get started, so that people know we are able and willing to minister in power and authority, we may have to keep our eyes open for those who need prayer. Americans today, even Christians, are so reticent to seek God's power for healing that I found it important, especially when I was taking my first steps in a healing ministry, to ask people who were suffering from

We should be prepared to minister in power and authority at any time and at any place and to anyone.

some ailment if they would like to be prayed for. After a prayer, even the disappearance of such comparatively minor things as colds or headaches makes quite an impression. And once it gets known that you are one whom God uses to heal, people will come to you.

So use your authority everywhere. Our job is to be faithful to the One who has called us to do His works. It is up to God to bring results.

✧ Spiritual Authority and Human Authority

I believe that all authority is from God, whether it is granted directly by God or indirectly through human means. And our primary concern here will be for authority granted directly by God. It is, however, important to survey the various forms of human authority and the ways in which spiritual authority is (or should be) expressed in relation to them. For there are distinctions to be made both in how any given authority is granted and how that authority is exercised.

First, there is what we might call *status authority*. Positions such as head of family, head of church, head of state and even teacher (James 3:1) carry with them God-given authority commensurate with the responsibility borne by those in such positions for carrying out their duties. In addition, we often grant authority to people who have wealth, schooling or high status, such as those who have gained prominence in business, education, science, athletics, music, theater, media, politics and the like. For better or worse, we grant such people the authority to set standards and influence us in a multitude of ways. A certain amount of authority and responsibility is *given automatically by God to those in such positions*.

In addition, Genesis 1:28 seems to indicate that every human has been given a certain authority over creation. Though we tend to think of these kinds of authority in human terms, I believe they all have a spiritual dimension as well. And this dimension springs from the fact that each position is given by God as well as by humans.

Second, though we are conscious of these forms of status authority, there is a more direct form of spiritual authority that is, as Richard Foster says, "God-ordained and God-sustained" (1978, 108). I will call this *personal intimacy authority*. This kind of authority may or may not bear any relationship to the authority granted by human society or institutions. Personal intimacy authority is direct from God and unrelated to status. Foster elaborates,

> When people begin to move into the spiritual realm they see that Jesus is teaching a concept of authority that runs completely counter to the thinking of the systems of this world. They come to perceive that authority does not reside in positions, or degrees, or titles, or tenure, or *any* outward symbol. The way of Christ is in another direction altogether: the way of spiritual authority. Spiritual authority is God-ordained and God-sustained. Human institutions may acknowledge this authority or they may not; it makes no difference. The person with spiritual authority may have an outward position of authority or may not; again, it makes no difference. Spiritual authority is marked by both compassion and power. Those who walk in the Spirit can identify it immediately. They know without question that submission is due the word that has been given in spiritual authority (1978, 108).

Unfortunately, many who are in positions of human status authority do not have much, if any, personal intimacy authority. It is tragic for a church, a theological institution or even a nation or a family if the person with human authority is one without real intimacy authority. Pastoral training institutions regularly graduate people who have learned to function in the classroom but have not been led close enough to Christ to gain either the intimacy authority or the personal capabilities to adequately function in church leadership. Countless churches and other Christian organizations are being led by people operating solely in human status authority.

But concerning God, it is *fellowship with Him* that is crucial. We need to be in constant *communion* with Him (Nee 1972, 119). There is an important intimacy requirement for those who carry another's authority. And there is a close connection between what I have called intimacy prayer, defined as spending time alone with God as Jesus frequently did, and authority prayer, defined as speaking in power and authority to bring about healing or deliverance. Operating in both intimacy and authority, Jesus traveled around Palestine doing the "will of the one who sent [Him]" (John 4:34). We, like Jesus, need to learn during times of intimacy with Him what God wants us to do with His authority, and then we must go out as Jesus did to exercise that authority in the world.

A third important consideration in any discussion of the relationship between human and spiritual authority is the need to *distinguish between the authority inherent in the position and the presence or absence of this special God-given authority* that Foster is describing. As indicated above, I believe that the head of a home and the head of a church are automatically given a kind of spiritual authority by God as an inherent part of their status. This is what young David was recognizing when he refused to attack King Saul, saying, "I must not harm him in the least, because he is the king chosen by the Lord!" (1 Samuel 24:6). Saul had the God-ordained authority of the position as long as he was in that position, even though his behavior showed that he neither deserved the position nor retained the special spiritual authority that comes from closeness to God. He continued to have status authority but not the personal intimacy authority that servants of God are meant to experience. David, on the other hand, before he became king had personal intimacy authority without the status authority of the position of king.

Personal intimacy authority comes from spending time with Jesus. The only requisite is to be in an intimate relationship with the Source of authority. This is the relationship Jesus spoke of in John 15:5 when He said, "I am the vine, and you are the branches. Those who remain in me, and I in them, will bear much fruit; for you can do nothing without me." As we stay connected to the Lord we both gain the authority that personal intimacy brings and learn to use that authority in the right manner. With regard to the latter, as Foster points out, the spiritual authority that Jesus demonstrated "was an authority not found in a position or a title but in a towel" (1978, 111), the towel He used when He washed His disciples' feet. The intimacy with the Father that gave Jesus this authority was matched by His use of the authority to serve, not to be served (Matthew 20:28).

The Paradox of Submission

Any discussion of spiritual authority needs to continually deal with submission. As we have indicated, the authority is not really ours. It is God's, and we gain the right to use it through submission to Him. That submission, then, paradoxically subjects us to one of the "upside-down" rules of the Kingdom: *serve to lead.*

One of the "upside-down" rules of the Kingdom: serve to lead.

In the spiritual realm, submission puts one under the authority of the spirit being to whom we submit. We receive, therefore, whatever that being's character dictates. If we submit to Satan or a human serving him, the result of the submission is captivity. If, however, the one we submit to is God, our submission results in freedom, since it is of the character of God to set people free. What seems like a contradiction, then, is not, if it is to the Freedom-Giver that we submit.

The apostle Paul learned this lesson well, probably from Jesus. For he states, "I am a free man, nobody's slave" (1 Corinthians 9:19), yet he represents himself in Romans 1:1 as a bondservant of Jesus Christ. This chosen designation reminds us of the statement made about Jesus in Philippians 2:7, where it is declared that Jesus "gave up all he had, and took the nature of a servant" in order to carry out the will of His Father.

By yielding to God we actually become liberated. Submission to God does not lead to bondage; it leads to freedom, spiritual freedom. Nor is submission about humiliation, though submission is based on humility. We are expected, then, to use our freedom to clothe ourselves with humility (1 Peter 5:5) and thus to fight the pride that can floor us. For "'God opposes the proud but shows favor to the humble.' Humble yourselves, therefore, under God's mighty hand, that he may lift you up in due time" (1 Peter 5:5–6, NIV). True biblical submission is only humiliating if it is done in pride. Surrender without grace is bondage. In humility, then, God gives us the grace that enables us to submit. *Surrender with grace is empowerment.*

✎ The Ten Commandments of Spiritual Authority

Dr. J. Robert Clinton, senior professor of leadership in Fuller's School of Intercultural Studies, has, in two books on Christian leadership, helpfully summarized and elaborated on much of what I have been presenting here. He calls his summary "The Ten Commandments of Spiritual Authority."

Throughout his books and teaching, Clinton connects the development of a Christian leader with an increase in spiritual authority. As Christian leaders mature, Clinton contends in *Leadership Emergence Theory* (1989), they find a distinct increase in their use of spiritual authority replacing mere human authority as "the primary authority used in leadership influence."

Clinton also points out that spiritual authority can be developed and exercised only in an experiential context. It is neither given nor achieved by "armchair" Christians. It comes, rather, "from a life and a ministry which demonstrates the presence of God. . . . A leader with spiritual authority knows God and His ways and demonstrates this in life."

Furthermore, in an important addition to what we have discussed so far, Clinton asserts that spiritual authority is always a *by-product*, never something to be sought for its own sake. In *The Making of a Leader* (1988) he writes, "A leader does not seek spiritual authority; a leader seeks to know God." As we grow in our experience with and obedience to the living God, the only true source of spiritual authority, we find our own spiritual authority growing right alongside.

With this introduction to Clinton's emphases, I present my version of his ten basic principles, the Ten Commandments of Spiritual Authority:

1. The ultimate source of authority is God. It is He who provides this "power base" to undergird ministry.

2. This authority is delegated by God. We are only channels for it, not owners of it.

3. We are responsible to God for how we exercise the authority He gives us.

4. True Christian leaders will recognize God's authority whenever it is manifested in life situations, whether through themselves or through others.

5. Persons in authority are subject directly to God, not indirectly through other authority figures.

6. Refusal to obey others in authority over us is actually rebellion against God, not just against the human instruments of that authority (Romans 13:2).

7. If we are rightly subject to God's authority, we will seek and recognize other spiritual authority and be willing to be subject to it.

8. We are never to exercise spiritual authority merely for our own benefit.

9. If we are truly working in spiritual authority, we do not need to insist that others obey us. That is their responsibility before God.

10. God Himself can be depended on to defend our spiritual authority. We do not need to assert it in such a way that we are defending ourselves.

Let these "commandments" or principles serve to summarize and amplify what we have been trying to say in this chapter. Now we can go on to a discussion of responsible versus irresponsible uses of the authority God has given us.

6

Using Our Authority Responsibly

✣ The Irresponsibility of Not Using Our Authority

What if our master, in anticipation of a journey, gives us the equivalent of 5,000 days' wages—or even 2,000 or 1,000—and tells us to use it on his behalf while he is away (Matthew 25:14–15)? The money is like the power God gives us. His command to use it wisely is the authority. What are we to do?

We know from the parable that two of the servants did the right thing with the money they had been given. They put it to use and were commended by the master when he returned for handling it well and doubling the amount given to each of them. But one servant simply buried his money, refusing to use it because he feared the shrewdness of the master. And he was condemned for not handling rightly what he had been put in charge of. He was afraid to risk. The master, therefore, took the money from him, called him lazy (verse 26) and had him cast out into "the darkness" (verse 30).

This was pretty harsh treatment for what might seem to us to be a fairly small mistake. Apparently, though, God does not take it kindly when we do not use what He has given us. Jesus had a lot to say about stewardship. He often spoke, as He did in this parable, of the custom among wealthy people of going away and leaving someone else in charge of their goods. In Luke 12:41–48 He speaks of a servant who runs the household while his master is away and is happy and rewarded if he has been found faithful when the master returns or sad and punished if he has done an incompetent job. At one point Jesus even seems to be praising a dishonest servant because he has been shrewd in using his authority to collect from his master's debtors (Luke 16:1–8).

In these and other stories Jesus advocated what Paul states in 1 Corinthians 4:2: "The one thing required of such servants is that they be faithful to their master." Peter adds, "Each one, as a good manager of God's different gifts, must use for the good of others the special gift he has received from God" (1 Peter 4:10).

Think of the gifting He has invested in each one of us. Think also of the authority and power—the authority of the Father and the power of the Holy Spirit—that He has put within us. What happens if we refuse to use these gifts? Does the message of this parable apply to us? I believe it does. And I am frightened lest I be found to be like the lazy servant.

We can take these gifts and ignore those around us who are hurting. We can even ignore our families. Those of us in leadership positions can ignore our students, our parishioners, our employees. We, whom God intended to be conduits of His love and power to such people, can easily become blockers of that love and power if we do not take the authority we have been given to use the credit card on their behalf.

As Dean Sherman helpfully points out,

> With our authority comes the responsibility to use it for God's purposes. If we don't rebuke the devil, he will not be rebuked. If we don't drive him back, he will not leave. It is up to us.

Satan knows of our authority, but hopes we will stay ignorant. We must be as convinced of our authority as the devil
is (Sherman 1990, 123).

Sherman goes on to illustrate irresponsibility by describing
a scenario in which policemen given legal authority to protect
people and apprehend those who are breaking the law simply sing
and declare their authority—as we often do in church—instead
of actually exercising it, while allowing perpetrators to get away
with their crimes. He writes,

> This may seem ridiculous, yet that is often an accurate picture
> of what we do. We talk about our authority. We sing about it.
> We even proclaim it loudly. But we don't exercise it. We must
> recognize that there is a difference between having authority
> and exercising it (Sherman 1990, 123–24).

As we will see in a later chapter, we who are heads of families
have the responsibility to use our authority to free and protect
those under our care. Those of us who have authority in churches
have the responsibility to use our authority to free and protect
the flock that has been entrusted to us. Those of us in adminis-
trative positions have the same kind of responsibility for those
under us in whatever organization we serve.

We have the authority and the responsibility to rid ourselves,
our homes, our families, our workplaces, our churches of demonic intruders and influences. Are we doing this? The point
is that we are to be faithful and true to our Master in how we
make use of what He has given us. We are not to simply sit back
and drift into glory. We have a responsibility to use the gifts,
including the gift of authority, that the Master has given us.

Furthermore, we have the responsibility to get to know
what the rules are for using our authority in the spirit realm.
As with physical laws, such as the law of gravity, our ignorance

of spiritual laws does not keep them from affecting us. Whether we understand what the enemy is doing or not, he will keep doing it until we take the authority God has given us and stop him. This book is an attempt to help us know what we should be doing with this great gift, the gift of authority.

✂ Misuse of Authority

Responsible use of authority is one of the biggest issues in our society today. Almost daily we hear of politicians, law enforcement officials, CEOs of large corporations, and even popular Christian leaders who have blatantly misused authority. This is bad enough when it is secular authority that is being misused. It is, however, absolutely tragic when we observe spiritual authority being misused.

Misuse of authority is one of the things that God risked when He gave us both authority and freedom. For we can use our freedom to misuse our spiritual authority. For example, parents can use their authority to dominate their children and thus stamp out their freedom and creativity. A pastor can use his authority to gain perks and prestige for himself rather than to help his people. He can even use a church to enhance his own social position in a community or a denomination. Christian healers can use their authority to produce spectacles, with themselves at the center, so that God is hardly noticed, no matter how often they give credit to Him. Or we, like Adam, can simply use our spiritual authority and our freedom to sin. So Paul warns us against using our freedom as a license to sin (Romans 6:1–2).

It is easy to misuse authority, whether human or spiritual. Let's look at six ways authority is misused in the spiritual realm.

1. When People Given Authority Are Exalted

Authority is misused whenever it exalts the receiver of the authority rather than the Lord, the Source and Giver of the authority. Unfortunately, many who have been exalted by God turn aside from His ways and misuse the authority they have been given, turning that authority into counterfeit. King Saul in Old Testament times is a very obvious case. Even though Saul's was a legitimately given authority, he misused it even to the extent that he attempted to kill God's chosen one, David (1 Samuel 18–21), to whom God had given the authority that had been Saul's.

Pilate has been mentioned as one who was in authority; he correctly understood that he had authority granted from Rome. What he did not see was that beyond that Rome-given authority lay the authority he had been given by God, an authority that he badly misused. All authority comes ultimately from God, and we are therefore accountable to Him for what we do with it, whether we acknowledge it or not.

Authority is misused whenever it exalts the receiver of the authority rather than the Lord.

At least two of the apostles, James and John, tried to exert their authority to gain position for themselves (Mark 10:35–45). As Jesus said, it is not to be this way in the Kingdom. Our authority is only rightly used when we imitate Jesus by serving others.

2. When Those without Power Are Hurt

Authority is misused and God is angered when those with authority use it to hurt those without power. Throughout the Bible, statements are made concerning how those in power are to treat those without.

The story of David and Bathsheba is a case in point. Though David was guilty of both adultery and murder, it was the misuse of his authority and power as king that the prophet Nathan brought to light in his parable (2 Samuel 12:1–15). In Malachi 3:5 God speaks the harshest condemnation against "those who cheat employees out of their wages, and those who take advantage of widows, orphans, and foreigners." And it was the Jewish religious leaders' misuse of their authority and power that aroused Jesus' wrath. For example, He condemns the teachers of the Law for "tak[ing] advantage of widows and rob[bing] them of their homes" and then making long, pious prayers (Mark 12:40).

Those of us in positions of power are especially vulnerable to the possibility of misusing our authority. As James says, we should not all want to be teachers (or other leaders) since "teachers will be judged with greater strictness than others" (James 3:1). When you are a leader, it is easy to step on other people's toes without noticing it. We need to train ourselves to be careful in the way we use our authority and especially sharp in noticing reactions that may indicate that we have hurt someone or encroached on their territory.

In this regard it is very easy to misuse words. Several years ago a student of mine who had gotten to know me well asked one day, "Have you ever noticed how you put people down in class when you answer their questions?" I, of course, denied that this was happening. She simply said, "Watch yourself." So I started to notice how I answered students' questions. To my surprise I discovered that she was right. I had been misusing my authority as a teacher by responding cleverly to student questions in such a way as to intimidate them. Out of my own insecurities I had been using their questions to parade my knowledge, in contrast to theirs. Most of their questions I had heard before and, therefore, had had opportunity to develop clever answers to them. So sometimes, anticipating what the question would be, I would not even wait for the student to finish the question before I would give my answer. In this way I was able to show my own intelligence, but only at the expense of those over whom I had authority. I now work hard in these situations to use my authority lovingly rather than to serve my own selfish ends.

Unfortunately, many in positions of authority seem to specialize in using their words to oppress and intimidate. They are accomplished at putting people down, weakening their self-images and contributing to shame and guilt. This use of words is especially damaging when used on the young by authority figures such as parents, teachers or employers—or those in Christian leadership. Even pastors and others in Christian ministry can be guilty of verbal oppression. All authority comes from God (Romans 13:1–2) and is therefore ultimately spiritual. Such misuse is, therefore, likely to result in spiritual damage.

In addition, as pointed out in chapter 3, words can be used to curse (James 3:9–10). This is a particularly heinous use of authority, but one that is easy to fall into when we are angry or hurt. Saying, "Damn so-and-so," "I wish so-and-so were dead," or even "I hate so-and-so," needs to be taken very seriously here on earth. The number of times in ministry that we need to break such curses to bring freedom to people indicates that they are taken seriously in the enemy spirit world. We must heed James' warnings concerning how we use our tongues.

3. When Scripture Is Mishandled

Authority is misused when pastors misuse scriptural passages in such a way that people feel unnecessarily condemned. There are, of course, things that we need to condemn if we are to be biblical. When, however, a verse such as Philippians 3:13 (speaking about forgetting those things that are behind) is used to imply that God commands us to simply forget our past hurts, great damage can be done. In context, that verse has nothing to do with past hurts. Paul is advising us to put behind us past *victories* so that we can win the race we are now running. When someone who is hurting badly from past abuse hears such a verse thus misused, that person goes away further abused, wondering why he or she cannot simply forget as the preacher advised. How is that person to know that God does not want such hurts to simply be swept under the rug? God wants instead for people to openly face such wounds and to forgive in order to enter God's freedom. His way is to face problems and to go straight through them—as with sin, so with emotional and spiritual problems. With regard to sin, God says, "Admit it, face it, give it to Me and I will forgive you." With regard to emotional and spiritual problems, He says the same thing: "Admit it, face it, give it to Me and you get to go free." God does not heal us when we try to stuff the problem.

The preacher in this scenario misused his authority by misrepresenting God and hurting his hearers. I am afraid we will be judged harshly by God for such misuse.

4. When People Are Led Away from God

Authority is misused when it is wielded by religious or political leaders to lead people away from God. In Scripture we see over and over again the leaders of Israel abandoning the true God to follow false gods. In 1 Kings 16–22 we read of King Ahab and his wicked wife Jezebel who, with hundreds of priests, led the people of Israel in worshiping the Baal gods. The true prophet Elijah was given authority by God to confront these prophets and to destroy 850 of them (1 Kings 18).

At a later time, God led His prophet Jeremiah to speak harshly against false prophets for prophesying lies. He also speaks against the wicked priests who ruled "by their own authority" (Jeremiah 5:31, NIV). These prophets attempted to represent God and to work in His authority without ever hearing from Him. God said, "I did not send them, nor did I give them any orders or speak one word to them. The visions they talk about have not come from me; their predictions are worthless things that they have imagined" (Jeremiah 14:14; see also 23:18).

I am afraid we have such leaders today as well. There are many who claim to be hearing from and speaking for God who really are counterfeits of the real thing. Some who lead major denominations in the United States fit into this category, especially in their permissive attitudes toward homosexuality and/ or abortion, not to mention theological issues. But they "obey lying spirits and follow the teachings of demons" (1 Timothy 4:1). They often stand for untenable positions with regard to foundational truths of biblical Christian faith, using the authority of their offices to mislead people. We need to use our authority to warn people about such false leaders.

5. When God's Work Is Opposed

Authority is misused when it stands against God's authentic working. Often we see persecution in Scripture of those who work in God's authority and power. As Jesus said in His lament over Jerusalem, those in authority misused it to "kill the prophets, [and] stone the messengers God has sent" (Luke 13:34). And, of course, Jesus Himself was the recipient of persecution and death at the hands of those who used their human authority to serve the enemy. The authority Pilate claimed, even though coming ultimately from God (John 19:10–11), was being used for Satan's purposes rather than the purpose for which it was intended.

Authority is misused when it stands against God's authentic working.

I just heard of a publisher who has broken the contract of a friend of mine for reasons that seem to fit into this category. As near as I can tell, my friend is listening carefully to God and following Him closely; the publisher, however, holds a different position on certain issues and is, I believe, using his authority to block the authentic working of God. I fear this kind of misuse of authority is common in contemporary Christian circles.

6. *When Authority Is Counterfeited*

A misuse that is a bit more difficult to explain is the counter-feiting of authority in animism and magic. *Animism* is the term used by missiologists to label the majority religion of the world. Most of the tribal peoples plus most of those who claim to follow a world religion are really animists. A common form of animism involves belief in a high god who is good and benevolent toward humans and, therefore, can safely be ignored most of the time. But between this god and us there are a multitude of dangerous spirits or gods who must be kept happy if life is to go smoothly. Animists spend lots of time, energy and money attempting to satisfy and manipulate these spirits. They think that by doing or saying certain things, they can control supernatural beings. So, much of their effort is put into doing or saying these things to magically bring about the desired end.

Animistic thinking is both very prominent and condemned among the Old Testament peoples and even among the Israelites. All of the idolatry that God so condemns was animistic. Among many Old Testament examples is the likelihood that God was trying to break an animistic reverence for Moses' rod when He commanded him to speak to the rock rather than to strike it to get water (Numbers 20:7–12). Whenever Israel accepted the be-lief that the true God was a god of the mountains and the Baal gods were in control on the plains (see 1 Kings 20:23–25), they were submitting to an animistic system and lowering the true God to the level of the territorial gods. By lowering Him to that level, they could subject Him to the same type of manipulation that non-Jews practiced toward their animistic gods. This belief system did not disappear in the New Testament, either; in Jesus' day we see animistic and magical attitudes toward the temple (see, for example, Matthew 23:16–21) and the keeping of the Sabbath.

Authority is counterfeit when animistic and magical ideas lie behind it, rather than commitment and obedience to the true

God. Today those practicing animism expect automatic results that coerce God into doing our will by using "sacred" phrases or "sacred" objects. Among the phrases used are "the blood of Christ," words concerning binding and loosing, special words used repetitively in prayer (including the word "just" preceding a request) and certain Scriptures with the expectation that these words will "work" to bring about the desired result. Among the objects used magically are crosses, anointing oil and the Bible.

When people regard such words and objects as *containing* power rather than *conveying* the power of God, they are manifesting a magical attitude toward them. This can be seen when someone speaks of "the power of the Word/Bible" as if it *contained* power, rather than recognizing that as important as the Bible is, it is a *means* that God uses and not a *container* of the power of God. The power is in God, not in the Bible, though He regularly flows His power through the Bible. For many conservative Christians the functioning Trinity is the Father, Son and Bible; they (or we) are unconsciously betraying an animistic attitude. In a different vein of Christianity, when Christians who follow "name it, claim it" theology choose something they want (even healing) and think that when they simply claim it, God is obligated to do it for them, they are practicing animism, not Christianity.

For more on the differences between animism and true Christianity, read my article "Christian Animism or God-Given Authority" in the book *Spiritual Power and Missions* (1995).

To use responsibly the authority God gives us means to not misuse it. If, further, we are to be responsible in our use of the authority God has given us, we would do well to become aware of any misuses on the part of others. Scripture shows that, as Christians, we have a multitude of responsibilities to God, others and ourselves. We are, therefore, to use our spiritual authority responsibly in carrying out all such obligations and the privileges that come with them. But the fact that there are frequent misuses makes it important for us to seek the advice of those with gifts of spiritual discernment when evaluating ministries that purport to come from God.

What Jesus' Disciples Failed to Learn

Jesus was very patient with the Twelve as He taught them what life in the Kingdom is all about. He took them everywhere He went so they got to watch and listen as He carried out His Father's will. As He walked, talked and carried out His ministry, they learned how to be like Him. He taught them by word and by deed.

Jesus' primary teaching method was demonstration. He not only spoke as He expected them to learn to speak, He showed them what their ministries were to be like. Since He expected them to heal and cast out demons, He showed them how to do that. In both His healing ministry and His teaching, He demonstrated how to use the authority the Father had given Him and that He had passed on to them. The next step was for the Twelve to launch out and use that authority.

But they did not learn easily. As usual, they were up sometimes and down at others. After they had been watching Jesus for quite a while, they found themselves in the teeth of a storm on Lake Galilee. They woke the Master to rescue them, and He did. But He rebuked them for their lack of faith (Luke 8:25). Could it be that Jesus expected the disciples to use the authority He had already given them to calm the storm? If so, they failed the test.

The next time, though, in Luke 9:1–6 and again in 10:1–12, Jesus sent His followers out to minister on their own after giving them power and authority "to drive out all demons and to cure diseases" (Luke 9:1). Apparently they did this quite well and got a real taste of what this God-given authority was all about. They had discovered the authority in Jesus' name and marveled that "even the demons obeyed us when we gave them a command in your name!" (Luke 10:17).

When the apostles returned to Him after the sending out in Luke 9, they next faced a hungry crowd of five thousand or more and had only a small boy's lunch to work with. The apostles were wringing their hands in concern for the people's physical needs, so Jesus told them to "give them something to eat" (Luke 9:13). That is, "Be creative. Use your authority to produce the food to feed them." It must have been truly puzzling for Jesus' friends to hear that He expected them to take care of the situation, for they were just learning what this authority business was all about. So they hesitated and Jesus did the job, though in the disciples' hands!

In the same chapter, it is recorded that Jesus and His followers headed for Jerusalem via Samaria, where some Samaritans refused to give them lodging (verses 51–55). So James and John, angered over this affront, asked Jesus for permission to "call fire down from heaven to destroy them" (verse 54). Finally they got the idea that they had been given great authority. But now they wanted to use it in a wrong way—to hurt rather than to help! Jesus refused to allow this and rebuked them for their desire to use their authority irresponsibly.

The same temptation exists today. And, I am afraid, many in positions of authority in Christian institutions and many who simply function in the spiritual authority God has given them misuse that authority. When God's people misuse their authority, God does not always take the ability to use His authority away from them. The Pharisees, for example, had status that gave them power and authority both in the human social context and spiritually. Note what Jesus says concerning the need to grant them the honor due their position (Matthew 23:3), while He is quick to caution against imitating their behavior.

Though the demons were not fooled by the sons of Sceva when they tried to exert an authority that was not theirs, humans seem to be fooled quite often. But even at the risk of our being fooled, Jesus forbids us to "pull up the weeds," lest in so doing we pull up some of the wheat also (Matthew 13:29).

✆ Jesus Does Not Like It When We Wake Him

If I have a secretary and I ask her to go to, say, an office supply store to purchase some supplies for my office, I expect her to do it. Suppose she has been working for me for some time and knows what we need to make our office work. In addition, I have taken her with me on previous trips to buy supplies, so I am sure she knows the ropes. I trust her and have given her the money (or my credit card) so that the materials can be paid for.

Suppose then that I find out the next day that she has not carried out my request. Nor does she do it the next day, or the next. I might reprimand her. I might even fire her. But if she continues to not do what I have requested, I will do it myself.

I believe this is what happened in the boat the day the disciples and Jesus encountered the storm. I mentioned earlier that I believe Jesus expected His followers to calm the storm themselves (Luke 8:22–25). He did not appreciate it when they woke Him up. And later He expected them to feed the five thousand (Luke 9:10–17). How disappointed Jesus must have been to have to do it Himself!

An important part of responsibility is to not neglect it. I wonder how often we have neglected the authority Jesus has given us by not applying His power to illness, weather, poverty or other life situations that He expects us, as His agents, to deal with? I wonder how many people Jesus heals directly because we do not participate? Worse yet, how many go unhealed because we who have been commissioned to operate in Jesus' authority and power have neglected our responsibility?

7

More on Using Authority

✿ The Apostle Paul on Authority

In the passage beginning with 2 Corinthians 10:8 and concluding with 2 Corinthians 13:10, the apostle Paul, while defending his own authority, demonstrates how leaders should exercise their authority. In the verses that cap this passage he speaks of "the authority that the Lord has given me—authority to build you up, not to tear you down." In short, Paul seeks to exercise considerable authority with a large amount of gentleness and love.

Missionary D. Michael Crow, in his doctoral work at the Fuller Theological Seminary School of Intercultural Studies, has found fifteen characteristics of spiritual authority articulated by Paul in the passage enclosed between the above verses. I find these so helpful that, with Crow's permission, I list them here, worded as I understand them. Before listing them, though, we should note two things about the way Paul goes about his argument.

First, at the beginning (10:1–2) and end (13:10) of his statement, Paul implies his right to be harsh with the Corinthians but his desire to be gentle, kind and loving. Though the issue at hand involves a serious challenge to his apostolic authority, Paul chooses to exercise that authority in love and gentleness.

Second, Paul grounds his discussion in a context of spiritual warfare. I believe he is affirming what I suggest in the next chapter—that every human event, even a disciplinary problem, has an important spiritual dimension. For Paul says in 2 Corinthians 10:3–5 that although "we live in the world . . . we do not fight from worldly motives." Nor are our weapons worldly ones. They are "God's powerful weapons, which we use to destroy strongholds . . . false arguments . . . [and] every proud obstacle that is raised against the knowledge of God." So "we take every thought captive and make it obey Christ."

Thus Paul shows us the basis for spiritual authority (Spirit-led motives) and some of the goals we aim for in our assertion of that authority.

1. Spiritual authority has a territorial dimension. Paul asserts his authority in 2 Corinthians 10:12–18 over an area he believes God has assigned him—an area that includes Corinth.

2. Spiritual authority flows from a burden to see a love relationship between those served and Christ (11:1–6).

3. Spiritual authority is grounded in a substantial knowledge of God and His activities in the human sphere (11:6).

4. Spiritual authority must operate without being tied to payment. Paul exercises his spiritual authority as a servant without charging the Corinthians (11:7–12) or anyone else.

5. Spiritual authority involves an uncompromising opposition to charlatans—those who masquerade as true Christian leaders but who teach lies (11:13–15).

6. Spiritual authority serves even to the extent of readily sacrificing and suffering (11:16–33). Paul, in exercising the authority God gave him, has endured incredible hardship on behalf of those he has ministered to, mostly at the hands of those who oppose him.

7. Spiritual authority involves direct revelation from God (12:1–6). Paul was taken up to "the highest heaven" and heard things there "which cannot be put into words, things that human lips may not speak."

8. Spiritual authority is exercised in weakness and ordinariness, even with God-allowed satanic reminders to keep us humble. In 12:6–10 Paul speaks of his weaknesses and of the "painful physical ailment" (verse 7), or "thorn in the flesh" (KJV), that God has allowed "as Satan's messenger to beat me and keep me from being proud."

9. Spiritual authority is authenticated through the operation of spiritual gifts (12:12). Paul points to signs and wonders as proving his apostolic authority.

10. Spiritual authority is ready and able to rebuke and discipline those who persist in disobedience (13:1–2).

11. Spiritual authority can be tested by checking the presence and activity of Christ in those who have responded to the message presented by the one who claims that authority (13:5–6).

12. Implied in the passage is the fact that spiritual authority is not contingent on a given personality type.

13. Neither is spiritual authority contingent on one's ability to preach or communicate in other ways. Spiritual authority precedes these abilities, acting as a life-giver to these means but not restricted by whether or not one is a gifted communicator.

14. True spiritual authority affirms rather than puts down others, encouraging them to operate in all the gifting and authority God has given them.

15. Spiritual authority can be exercised in a multitude of unique ways. Rather than being something we merely "do," it is to be grounded in and exercised out of a person's very being.

We see in Paul's teaching, then, several characteristics of the one who would use spiritual authority responsibly. And we note that these all apply to the way Jesus exercised His authority.

One way to test whether or not our exercising authority is on track is checking to see how well we measure up to these characteristics.

✒ The Place of Experimentation

We have imprecise guidelines for much of this territory. That is, we do not always know how to go about using our authority responsibly in life situations that are not addressed in Scripture. Even when situations are addressed in Scripture, we often experience twists and turns that we do not see dealt with there. (Many such twists and turns occur when dealing with demonization.)

In such cases I recommend experimentation. My rule of thumb is, *If in doubt, experiment.* This is the only way I know to discover what works and what does not. It is responsible, I think, to experiment. Otherwise, how will we discover what Jesus promised the Holy Spirit would teach us (John 16:13)?

It was as an experiment that I first began saying, "If this is the enemy, stop it!" when something seemed to be going wrong, either in general circumstances or in relationships. I mentioned that this command is often effective when interpersonal conflict seems imminent. It has also worked sometimes (not always) when a baby starts to cry in church or when the students in class seem distracted. It seldom works, however, when I am caught in traffic on the Los Angeles freeway system! But once I spoke this command after a flight my wife and I were scheduled to fly on was canceled, at which point we saw a major improvement in a difficult situation. Did that change come about by chance? Perhaps. But maybe it was another of many experiences I have had in which the enemy's attempts to disrupt my life were thwarted when I claimed the authority Jesus has given me.

It was likewise as an experiment that I began suggesting to the head of a family that he (or she, in the case of a single parent) assert his protective authority over the family by saying to the satanic powers, "I am the head of this family, so if you want my wife or children, you will have to go through me." For many this action has brought release from attacks on family members.

One man reported that after he asserted this authority, his fearful three-year-old daughter changed immediately and has been a happy little girl ever since. A couple whose ten-year-old boy was being picked on unmercifully by his schoolmates did the same thing. That very day the youngster came home from school reporting happily that the children who had been taunting him had all changed now and become his friends.

I have experimented a lot in dealing with demons and found that most of the experiments work. I have learned, for example, that during a session it helps, in keeping track of the demons, to lock each group in a spiritual "box" until all are collected and it is time to send them to Jesus. This practice started as an experiment several years ago when we were in the middle of a deliverance session at the end of class one day. The members of the class had to go home, and I wanted to pick up at the same place the next morning when class reconvened. So without knowing how (or if) it would work, I commanded the demons into a box overnight. As we started working on them the next day, I asked them where they were. They said angrily, "Right in the box where you put us!" From this I learned of our authority to lock them up—an authority I have been able to use to good advantage over the years. Similarly I learned by experimenting that we can cut off the demonic communication system (see chapter 11).

More Prerequisites to Authority

If we are to work effectively in Jesus' authority, there are certain prerequisites. We have already considered several of these, including the need for intimacy with our Master, the obedience requirement, the recognition that we are at war and the importance of knowing who we are in Christ. In this section I discuss some additional requirements.

Ask for the Release of the Holy Spirit

It is necessary to start where Jesus started—with the baptism or filling of the Holy Spirit (Luke 3:22). We have noted that Jesus did no signs and wonders before His baptism. Then, when He ascended to heaven, He told His disciples to wait to go out to minister for Him until the same Holy Spirit who had empowered Him came upon them and empowered them (Luke 24:49; Acts 1:4–5). They, like Jesus, were to do no signs and wonders, or witness to God's loving concern for humans, until they were under the complete control of the Holy Spirit.

Some distinguish between the baptism of the Holy Spirit and the filling of the Holy Spirit. The only distinction I make is to regard the baptism as the first infilling. We receive the Holy Spirit when we accept Jesus as Savior and Lord (Romans 8:2, 4, 9, 15–16). At that time we have the potential for being filled with Him. We can, however, hinder the Spirit's full release within us. So most people need at some later time to ask Him to take over in His fullness, as the disciples did on the Day of Pentecost (Acts 2:1–4).

> *It is necessary to start where Jesus started—with the baptism or filling of the Holy Spirit.*

From my perspective, *a filling is more like the release of the Spirit who already resides in us than like the pouring into us of something from outside.* Such release can and should take place many times as we live and minister with and for our Lord. Thus, I can agree with those who say there is one baptism but many fillings or releases. And I believe it is appropriate to ask God for a new infilling or release of the Holy Spirit daily, because we leak!

The need to be filled with the Holy Spirit (though the concept is often abused) is scriptural. Jesus needed it; so do we. What the fullness of the Holy Spirit brings is power (Acts 1:8) and gifting—the power and gifting we need to go with our authority as Jesus' disciples. And it is our privilege to receive the fullness of the Holy Spirit simply by asking for Him to fill us (Luke 11:13). There is no required ritual, place, time or level of emotion in order for the fullness of the Holy Spirit to be released.

We should dissociate ourselves, therefore, from all unbalanced, unscriptural forms of belief and practice with regard to the filling of the Holy Spirit. Becoming Spirit-filled does not require us to become more emotional or fall under the power of the Spirit, though many find that when they experience these things they grow in their ability to feel and express emotion, especially in worship. Nor should such release result in arrogant, unloving behavior toward those who have not had such experiences and, therefore, do not seem to be Spirit-filled. Such behavior is not what Jesus intends.

Being Spirit-filled does not make us any better than we were before, nor does it assure us that what we sense as prophetic utterances or words of knowledge will always be right. And it certainly does not give us any right to boast or act haughtily. Indeed, it should make us more humble, more loving and in every other way more Christlike. As for tongues, although those in Scripture who were filled with the Spirit often began to speak in tongues (Acts 19:6), Paul says not everyone has this gift (1 Corinthians 12:30), and he suggests in 1 Corinthians 14 that the gift of tongues, as valuable as it is, is the least of all the gifts.

For some, the release of the Spirit comes with the laying on of hands. It is good to seek it this way, but this is not the only option. For to others the gift is given directly by God in private, as God's quiet response to our request for His filling. However received, this gift, like all others that come from God, is given as an expression of His love, mercy and grace apart from our merit. We do not qualify for it by our righteousness, goodness or achievements, but by our openness and yieldedness to God.

In addition to the empowerment and gifting that the release of the Holy Spirit brings, another major purpose is for us to overflow with the fruits of the Spirit: "love, joy, peace, patience, kindness, goodness, faithfulness, humility, and self-control" (Galatians 5:22–23). Overflowing, not containing, is what we are to do. I like the story of a little fellow who commented on the filling of the Holy Spirit: "I'm not big enough to hold much, but I can overflow a lot!" Let's receive the Holy Spirit until we overflow, and then continue to overflow a lot.

Tend to Your Spiritual Condition

A second important requirement is that a person working in Jesus' authority tend to his or her spiritual condition. God is usually generous to those He has gifted, even if they do not keep close to Him, but the enemy keeps track and may challenge a person's authority during a ministry session. Though this has never happened to me (yet), some have told me that demons they were trying to evict started listing their sins for all to hear, hoping to embarrass them enough to get them to quit! If this should happen to you, simply remind the demon that your sins are all under the blood of Christ. Then there are those whom the enemy has been able to keep from even engaging in ministry through accusations concerning their spiritual condition or through fear that their sins would be made public.

Many, on the other hand, who have not been in good shape spiritually but have been faithful in ministry anyway have been so humbled by God's graciousness to them that they have cleaned up their acts. This was true of a man I will call Chet who was in an adulterous relationship when he started to minister deliverance. He was so blown away by the fact that God would use even him in such authority and power that he confessed his sin and got right with God, his wife and everyone else concerned.

Likewise with a woman I will call Donna. She went with us on a ministry trip in spite of the fact that she believed firmly God could not use her in a healing ministry because she was not right spiritually. She came to me to confess her problem only after God had used her powerfully. Puzzled, she could not reconcile her spiritual condition—and the constant, accusing voice of the enemy—with what God was doing through her. She discovered an important principle: that the authority and power of the Holy Spirit, received when one is filled with Him, remains even when one's intimacy with God is impeded by sin. In response to the grace and mercy of God flowing to and through Donna, she repented and got right with Him.

He is merciful to those of His children who fall frequently while learning to walk.

Just as we do not kick toddlers when they fall down while learning to walk, so God is patient with us, reaching down a hand to help us up, knowing that eventually we will learn (Isaiah 42:3; Matthew 12:20). He reads our hearts and makes a clear distinction between making mistakes, even at times willful ones, and confirmed rebellion. God knows what to do with those who have confirmed their wills in rebellion. But He is merciful to those of His children who fall frequently while learning to walk.

Recognize That Jesus' Authority Is Ours

A further prerequisite to authority is to accept the fact that it is ours. Jesus gives us the authority to imitate Him, to be as close to God the Father as He was, to do what He did and even more (John 14:12). These are our rights as Jesus' followers and friends.

Many Christians think, as I have said, that they have no right to make this kind of assertion. They fail to recognize the extent of Jesus' self-imposed limitations and what that means for us. If we ignore the fact that Jesus never used His deity while on earth, choosing to work entirely under the power of God's Spirit, we will have no confidence in our ability to function in the authority He has given us. Many without such confidence hold back, fearing they might overstep their bounds as Christians. What a tragedy, and what a victory for Satan!

Scripture allows a much greater possibility of imitating Jesus than evangelicalism has ordinarily allowed. As we obey Jesus' command to imitate Him by being filled with the Holy Spirit (Luke 24:49; Acts 1:4–5, 8), we receive Jesus' authority to move into a ministry like His and actually do what He did (John 14:12).

Garner Prayer Support

It is important for anyone engaging in spiritual warfare to be supported by as much prayer as possible, especially intercession by those who know how to pray with authority. We are not expected to fight all by ourselves. We are to enlist others, especially those with the gift of intercession, to keep our ministry constantly before the Lord and the enemy. We are parts of a Body, and those of us who assert our gifting in ministry need the support of those whose gifting gives them special authority in praying.

The equation is simple: The more prayer support, the more authority; the less prayer support, the less authority. The kingdom of darkness knows and believes in the power of prayer, and Satan and his helpers fear most those who have the most solid prayer backing. The clear message is that we should get as much prayer support as possible, from as many as possible who have the gift of intercession.

A good place to start understanding the importance of prayer for those who operate in Jesus' authority, and the way to go about building prayer support, is C. Peter Wagner's book *Prayer Shield* (1992). In this book he discusses three kinds of intercessors needed by those in ministry:

> *I–1 Intercessors.* These are one or more persons with whom we have a close relationship, who possess the gift of intercession and who commit to praying continuously for us, agreeing to be available to us and to the Lord for whatever the Lord wants to say or do in relation to prayer (and often prophetic) support. Wagner suggests we need at least one but no more than three such persons.

> *I–2 Intercessors.* These have a casual relationship with us but covenant to pray daily for us. Some will have gifts of intercession; some will simply be faithful pray-ers. For those in public ministry, it is good to have up to a hundred or more at this level. For others the number may be smaller. But it is good in any case for us to know who they are and to keep them informed concerning what is going on in our lives.

> *I–3 Intercessors.* These have a more remote relationship with us, and we will not necessarily even know who they are. They may pray for us sporadically or regularly. Those in public ministry should have a large number at this level. For others the emphasis should be on building up the I–2 level, even if there are few I–3s.

How much prayer support do we need? I have no idea, but I try to get on as many prayer lists as possible. The way God frequently works, especially on ministry trips, makes it obvious that the people back home are supporting us in our part of the battle.

Find a Spiritual Mentor and Accountability Partner

It is good, especially when we are first starting to work in Jesus' authority, to have a spiritual mentor to assist and encourage us in our learning and to hold us accountable. This can be one person or more than one whose job is to teach us and keep us on track. Even after we have been at it for a while, it is important for us to have someone to share with and to be accountable to.

As we begin to learn about our authority and to assert it, we often assume naïvely that we can go it alone. On the contrary, it is especially important for those of us who assert Jesus' authority over the enemy to have one or more mentors, since we are the ones most likely to be attacked by Satan. Many of the Christian leaders who have fallen from high positions might still be effective for Christ if they had been accountable to another human being.

In addition to mentoring and holding us accountable, such persons should minister to us. Even though we are in active ministry ourselves, we often carry wounds that need to be attended to. At best we are "wounded healers," and it is good for us to work constantly toward greater health for ourselves. We also need the kind of encouragement and blessing from mentors that we seek to give others.

✦ The Responsible Thing to Do

Actually getting out and doing some of the things we are suggesting may seem scary. We may assume that the rest Jesus promised us in Matthew 11:29—"You will find rest"—involves freedom from having to be concerned with Satan and his kingdom. Some actually believe Jesus got rid of all the demons while He was on earth, or that He has worked things so that they cannot affect Christians. Sorry! Neither of these things is true.

Some try to pretend the enemy kingdom does not affect us, or that while others may possess the gift of spiritual authority, they do not. Some will try rationalizing, ignoring, theologizing or explaining away the warfare terminology in Scripture. They will do almost anything to avoid having to recognize that we are at war.

Unfortunately, none of these approaches changes the facts. Satan is still on the loose (though I do not pretend to understand why God allows it), and we are at war, whether we like it or not.

This being true, *we had better prepare to fight!* We have been given the authority and power to fight. Why do we not accept the responsibility God has given us? Here are three priorities that will, I hope, open us more to working in and with the authority we have been given.

The first priority on our agenda must be to *shed our ignorance.* My own ignorance was profound! So I began taking steps to learn what spiritual warfare is all about. I read everything I could get my hands on and looked for those who would disciple me, or at least let me watch while they worked in God's authority to do His works. Since I am a teacher, I sought opportunities to teach on physical healing, inner healing and deliverance and, as part of each of these areas, the authority God gives us to do His works. I felt the responsible thing to do was, on the one hand, get prepared, and on the other, start taking steps in ministry. These steps led me through what I consider to be my paradigm shift and my practice shift (see Kraft 1989 for a discussion of these terms).

Second on our agenda is to *shed our fear.* Once people begin to move into spiritual warfare, they often experience fear. The enemy does all he can to impress us with his power in order to chase us off. We hear stories of battles that have been fought with demonized persons, and we get scared. Television and movies, when they deal with demonization and deliverance, focus on the sensational aspects of the subject. Satan loves to have these stories repeated; they make him look so good! But as Paul said to Timothy, "The Spirit that God has given us does not make us timid [or fearful]; instead, his Spirit fills us with power, love, and self-control" (2 Timothy 1:7).

In this power, love and self-control, we need to accept the responsibility given by our Master and engage ourselves in the war He has called us to. As we are commanded in Ephesians 6, we are to put on the whole armor of God, to stand when our Master asks us to stand, to attack when He asks us to attack. We need to ask for and accept the filling of the Holy Spirit (Luke 11:13) and move out in the authority our Leader has given us: first to protect ourselves, our families and our ministries, and then to communicate God's love through words, through healing, through deliverance and in whatever other ways our Master shows us. Once again, as Jesus did when He was on earth, we are to do what we see the Father doing (John 5:19), speak what the Father shows us (John 8:38) and do what the Father wants us to do (John 5:30).

The third priority on our agenda is to *work toward spiritual maturity.* Just as physical, intellectual and emotional maturity enable us to handle the everyday problems of life, spiritual maturity enables us to handle problems that are spiritual in nature. It is sad that many Christians would rather not even think about spiritual warfare. I asked one pastor, "If there are demons, would you rather know or not know?" He replied, "I'd rather not know!" What if someone asked us if we would like to know that we are in danger from fire or poison? Would we take the same position? Would we contend that young people do not need to know of the problems that can arise if they are careless in driving, or with sexual intercourse?

A choice for spiritual ignorance is a sign of spiritual immaturity. We need to grow out of an immature approach to understanding and dealing with the enemy forces all around us, forces to which the Bible refers frequently. Often when those of us engaged regularly in spiritual warfare mention demons and their activities, we are accused of looking for a demon under every rock and behind every bush. Our attempts to bring scriptural balance to our lives and ministries by recognizing the prominence of spiritual conflict and demonic activity in the Bible are greeted with accusations that we are off-balance. They say that we give the enemy too much recognition. I wonder if they would argue the same way against studying our enemy in a physical war?

Spiritual maturity involves a Scripture-based recognition of the forces that fight against us, plus the scriptural good news of our authority over those forces. It also includes nurturing what the Church has traditionally recognized: love and the other fruits of the Spirit, much prayer, worship, witnessing and other spiritually edifying activities. But we cannot speak of spiritual maturity without including the subject of spiritual warfare and our authority under our Master in that conflict.

A choice for spiritual ignorance is a sign of spiritual immaturity.

With this discussion of our responsibility behind us, we will consider some of the rules that govern the relationships between the human world and the spirit world.

8

Rules for Authority in the Spirit Realm

✨ "You Do Not Have the Authority"

"You can't get this family free. You do not have the authority."

It was difficult for Josh, one of my ministry team members, to hear these words from a man with prophetic gifts. If it was a word from the Lord, it meant he will not succeed in his ultimate goal—to bring that family into freedom from demonic oppression.

We still do not know the full implications of this prophecy. In fact, we are not sure we know exactly how to interpret the prophecy. Nor are we sure if we need to rectify the lack of authority by turning the ministry opportunity over to someone with greater authority, or whether others need to be present to add their authority to Josh's. Or maybe it was simply satanic bluff.

What this situation brings to light, however, is that there are rules in the universe that must be obeyed concerning the exercise of authority. If they are not obeyed, the results we seek will not happen.

I receive telephone calls regularly from a woman I will call Virginia. She lives at some distance from me and is engaged in spiritual warfare constantly. Though Virginia is in her forties, she has adopted me as her father, giving me legal rights in the spirit realm to protect and free her from demonic harassment. It surprises me that when her husband uses his authority to attempt to free her, it often does not work. The demons respond quickly, however, when I assert the authority Jesus has given me.

In another case, I was working one day to free a young woman I will call Cathy (who has also adopted me as her father) from a demon. The demon had an especially strong grip on Cathy since her mother, who was into witchcraft, had dedicated Cathy to this spirit before or soon after she was born. We were unable to break the demon's power until I said something to the demon: "She calls me Daddy. So I assert my authority as her father to take away all your rights given by her mother." This broke the demon's power, and we were soon able to banish him.

> *There are rules in the universe that must be obeyed concerning the exercise of authority.*

My relationship with Cathy has changed, however, so that recently, in struggling to rid her of another demon, I claimed the same authority and it did not work. We were eventually able to get rid of the demon, but the fact that the father-daughter relationship we once had has now been "reduced" a bit had authority implications in dealing with the demon.

In another kind of case, we struggled for two and a half hours to release a man I will call Joe from a demon. Although we had the authority to cast out demons and knew it, nothing seemed to work. Then Joe confessed a sin he had committed (adultery). As soon as he confessed his sin and received God's forgiveness, the power of the demon was broken and we had no trouble getting rid of him. It was Joe's confession that, according to a rule of the spiritual universe, allowed our (and his) authority to be effective in dealing with the demon.

I do not claim to understand all that is going on in cases like these. But I know there are rules concerning authority that must be obeyed—rules as firmly fixed in the universe as the law of gravity. And as we learn what these rules are, we can be more effective in dealing with spiritual reality.

Our God is a God of order; He has created an orderly universe. Whether we are looking at the way the material universe is put together or the intricacy of the human mind, everything works according to rules. The same is true of the spiritual world. There are rules and principles by which the spirit world operates. Among the most important of these are the rules that govern authority relationships.

It is clear from Scripture that the beings in the universe are arranged hierarchically. God is at the top, of course, with humans made in His image immediately under Him (according to Psalm 8:5). The separation between God and humans is distinct. But ever since the resurrection of Jesus, a Man—the God-Man—has assumed the highest position in the universe (Philippians 2:9–11).

In the human world, status carries its own authority (more on human status and authority below). Under humans there are angels (including demons) and animals. Angels also seem to have various rankings (see below); perhaps animals do, too.

In the cases I just described, it seems clear that no one has the authority to banish a demon so long as a person hangs on to sin, unforgiveness or other spiritually disabling conditions such as anger, shame, rejection or similar attitudes. The rules allow the enemy specific rights in these situations. With respect to cases in which I claim my authority as a father (even a father by adoption), the rules appear to give me great authority in a "daughter's" life—an authority I no longer have if our relationship lessens. With respect to Josh's situation, sometimes the rules appear to require the authority of several people or permit certain people, but not others, the necessary authority.

As we minister, we often discover techniques that work. Often (as I have said) this is the result of experimenting. When ministry colleagues and I experiment, we try to share with one another any successes, as well as any failures, we pick up along the way. Then we can try new approaches in our own ministries and report on them at our meetings. In this way we are building up a body of insight to add to what we learn from Scripture, Christian books, lectures and sources outside our group.

What follows is an attempt to codify some of what we think we have learned so far about the way spiritual authority operates in the universe.

The Spirit World and the Human World

Scripture is clear that there is a close connection between the spirit world and the human world. In spite of our habit of regarding spiritual things and human things as separate, in Scripture these realms are not compartmentalized. They are tightly interrelated, with events in the spirit realm having repercussions in the human realm and vice versa. Furthermore, the same rules seem to govern the interactions between humans and God and humans and Satan. The authority of God to do what He wants, for example, seems enhanced when His devotees obey Him, acknowledge His authority, pray to Him or worship Him. Likewise, the authority of Satan to do what he wants is enhanced when his devotees respond in such ways to him.

An apparent major principle is this: *The way authority is exercised in the human sphere affects what goes on in the spiritual realm and vice versa.* We spoke in chapter 3 that binding or loosing on earth has effects in heaven. And when human beings commit themselves to God, we are told that there is a reaction in heaven: rejoicing (Luke 15:7). I suspect there is a similar reaction on the part of the satanic kingdom when someone commits himself or herself to their side.

The close relationship between the heavenly and earthly realms is seen when Satan challenges God to allow him to attack Job (Job 1). The resulting agreement had tremendous repercussions on the lives of Job and his family. Then in Daniel 10:13 we see a spirit being, called the prince of Persia, preventing the answer to Daniel's prayer from being implemented. Apparently such activities in the spirit realm can have great impact among humans without our knowing it.

All such interactions and repercussions stem from the ways in which authority relationships are used. There is, first of all, *inherent authority*. This is the authority that is automatically part of the position and power of the various beings in the universe, whether spirit beings or human beings. Much of this book is about inherent authority and the rules that pertain to that authority.

The way authority is exercised in the human sphere affects what goes on in the spiritual realm and vice versa.

In addition to the authority inherent in a being's position is what we may call *specially granted authority*. This authority is granted at specific times to given beings, whether spirit or human, for particular purposes. In addition to the authority inherent in Satan's position in the universe, he was granted special authority over Job and his family. He was also given special authority to afflict the apostle Paul with what Paul called his "thorn in the flesh" (KJV) and "Satan's messenger" (2 Corinthians 12:7). There have probably been numerous times in history when Satan has appealed to God for similar special authority and been granted it.

Many human positions carry with them inherent authority, including various statuses and giftings. We will deal with these throughout these pages. But humans, like angelic beings, may be granted special authority at particular times as well. A frequent instance of this is when God chooses to use us to minister in ways for which we have not been gifted. When He uses a person to heal who does not have a gift of healing, for example, it is by means of specially granted authority. Likewise when one who does not have gifts of hospitality or administration is called on to serve these functions and is temporarily given by God the authority and gifting to do a good job of it.

The Importance of Obedience

One rule we may miss in Job's story (and in many other biblical stories) is that God had great opportunity to work in Job's life because of Job's allegiance and obedience to Him. In fact, it was Job's obedience that lay beneath his righteousness and that engendered Satan's animosity toward him.

When people are obedient to their masters, the ability of their masters to work in and through them is increased. Both God and Satan gain new rights and authority when humans choose to obey them. Furthermore, when people, especially people of status, obey one or the other, the one obeyed seems to gain more authority to work in the human context than was otherwise true. This leads to this principle: *Through human allegiance and obedience to one or the other, God or Satan gains greater authority to work in human affairs.*

A corollary of this principle is that there seem to be limitations to what God and Satan can do in the human realm, based on the cooperation received from humans. It seems that God has made for Himself (and for Satan) a rule that He will not work in the human arena without a human partner.

Thus, if certain people, especially those with status, stand for God and against Satan, Satan will have a difficult time carrying out his will within those people's spheres of influence. Likewise, if certain people stand for Satan and against God, God will have difficulty doing what He wants to do within their spheres.

To put it another way: On God's side, obedience to His rules—including committing ourselves to Christ, praying, worshiping, doing righteousness, loving others, confessing sin and (in Old Testament times) sacrificing—enables God to carry out His will both in and through us. On the enemy's side, disobedience to God's rules—by sinning, not forgiving, hating, committing oneself to Satan, seeking help from him, worshiping him and doing unrighteousness—gives Satan authority to work in and through us.

As long as Adam was obedient, partnering with God, God could work His will in Adam's life without hindrance. When Adam disobeyed God by partnering with Satan, however, the enemy gained the right to infect Adam and all that he had authority over, including his descendants and the physical world. The obedience of Noah gave God the authority to reach down into the human world and rescue a remnant at the time of the Flood. The obedience of Abraham enabled the Lord to raise up a people who would, He hoped, be faithful to Him. When Abraham's descendants obeyed, God was able to do mighty things through them. When they disobeyed (meaning they obeyed Satan), God's plans were thwarted, at least for a time.

The Need for Human Cooperation and Partnership

The ramifications of obedience affect the strategies of both God and Satan. The exercise of their authority in any given situation can be thwarted by a lack of human cooperation—the lack of a human partner. God's plan for His people to enter the

Promised Land had to be revised when they refused at Kadesh to obey Him (Numbers 13–14). On the enemy's side, it took some time for Satan to get a Pharaoh to partner with him to harass Israel. Finally, however, a Pharaoh came to the throne who partnered with Satan in refusing to honor the agreement made with Joseph (Exodus 1:8), and Satan was able to get that king to carry out his plan. Then, on God's side, through an Israeli mother who partnered with God, plus an Egyptian princess who disobeyed both Pharaoh and the gods of Egypt and unconsciously partnered with God, God was able to save Moses. He then, after a false start, could appoint and train Moses to partner with Him to rescue His people.

A similar circumstance occurred shortly after Jesus' birth, when Satan was able to get Herod to partner with him to kill the baby boys in hopes of killing Jesus (Matthew 2:16). Joseph and Mary, however, in submission to the authority of God, were able to partner with Him to save Jesus (Matthew 2:13–15).

When a person is tempted but refuses to give in and partner with Satan, what the enemy tried to accomplish does not happen. If, for example, a person is tempted by a demon to commit suicide but does not carry out the act, the death cannot happen. A spirit cannot bring about suicide without the person's agreement (partnership). Likewise, when God seeks to enter a person's life, it will not happen unless the person gives Him the authority to enter. When believers do not obey God—do not join God in partnership—by praying and witnessing, people are lost, in spite of the fact that it is not God's will for "anyone to be destroyed" (2 Peter 3:9). When God's people obey by praying, repenting and turning away from evil, however, God has promised to forgive and bring revival (2 Chronicles 7:14).

When a person disobeys his or her master, whether God or Satan, the relationship is weakened (though not broken), unless the person pledges a new allegiance. If a Christian sins but continues to be committed to Christ, the relationship is damaged but not forfeited. And if he or she repents quickly in obedience, the relationship with God is restored to what it was before.

When those committed to Satan in occult movements such as New Age or Freemasonry assert their wills to change their allegiance and begin following Christ, a new relationship is begun that replaces the old. And although demons left over from the previous commitment to Satan remain in the person, they can function only as hindrances to the person now owned by a different Master. They cannot have the same control as they had when Satan was in charge. (Unfortunately, those who come into a relationship with Christ while carrying demons do not attain complete freedom in Christ until the demons are ejected.)

On the positive side, the more the followers of God partner and practice obedience to God, the closer their relationship to their Master grows. As Jesus said, "If you love me, you will obey my commandments" (John 14:15), and, "If you obey my commands, you will remain in my love" (John 15:10). Obedience brings and maintains closeness (John 8:31).

Satan's working is frequently frustrated by God's. But even God does not get His way all the time. He does not, for example, want anyone to go to hell (2 Peter 3:9), but apparently many will. God wants great things to be done in the areas of evangelism, healing, deliverance and church planting, but much of it does not happen because God's people do not cooperate adequately. God is still looking for partners to join Him in these activities (Isaiah 6:8). Jesus prayed that we, His people, would be one, as He and the Father are one (John 17:21). But this has not happened yet. Apparently Satan, through the obedience of humans to his designs, has been able to frustrate many of God's plans.

But God frequently frustrates the enemy's plans as well. Down through the ages He has been able to gain the allegiance, obedience and partnership of millions of people who have converted to Christ and served Him faithfully in ministry. I have encountered many frustrated demons whose major problem was that they could not get the persons in whom they lived to do their will, because these persons were busy obeying God. "I can't get him to look," said a frustrated demon of lust to me once. "Every time I bring a pretty girl across his path, he turns his head." Although this man's obedience to God did not succeed in getting rid of the demons, it did hinder them greatly in carrying out their plans.

The Power of God through Rituals

Rituals such as sacrifice (in the Old Testament), worship and prayer seem to especially enable God or Satan. When God is honored through such rituals, enemy forces have to stand back and cannot carry out their purposes. When Satan is honored in these same ways, the forces of God are pushed back. Again, obedience seems to be the key. When we obey God by praying, worshiping, fasting and living faithfully by His commands, we grant Him authority to do what He wants in and through us. The same seems to be true on the other side.

A hierarchy of rituals, with accompanying increases of authority, seems to make things happen by spiritual power. Blood sacrifices are the most powerful kinds of sacrifices. Among pagan peoples, as well as with the Old Testament sacrificial system, we see this spiritual rule exemplified. The sacrifice of animals was at the low end on the scale of blood sacrifices. Much higher on the scale was human sacrifice, and near the top, the sacrifice of the heir to a king's throne. The clearest scriptural example of the enemy's use of this principle is recorded in 2 Kings 3:21–27, in which the king of Moab sacrificed his oldest son to the Moabite god Chemosh on the city wall.

The sacrifice of Jesus, another Heir to a throne, was the most powerful sacrifice in all of history. It unleashed an incredible amount of God's power and has had cosmic consequences. But there were also immediate, lesser consequences; among these were an earthquake, the rending of the Temple curtain and the emergence of many dead people from their tombs (Matthew 27:51–53). Another result, I believe, was the spiritual cleansing of Jerusalem so that such spectacular events as the coming of the Holy Spirit and the conversion of thousands could take place (Acts 2).

Below blood sacrifices, several other kinds of sacrifice involving food and drink can be used to enable either God or Satan. There are also various kinds of nonsacrifice rituals, including prayer, worship, fasting, Bible reading, meditating on Jesus, practicing intimacy with other Christians, giving, witnessing, sharing with those in need and many more. All these enable God to do more of what He wants to do, because they are done in obedience to His will.

Obedience in areas such as these is crucial to authority. The reason such obedience is so effective and important is that there is a rule in the spiritual realm that empowers it. When we pray, worship or fast, we tap into God's rules for the interaction between the spirit world and the human world to bring about the ends our Master seeks (see Kraft and DeBord 2000). Unfortunately, the same rule applies on the satanic side. Those who pray, worship, fast, meditate or share on the basis of an allegiance to Satan enhance his authority and help accomplish his ends.

An Angelic Authority Structure

Under God there seems to be a hierarchical structure of spirits that we call angels, archangels, cherubim and seraphim. The function of these beings is to serve God, and they play important roles in the operation of the universe. From various statements made in Scripture, we can infer that angels at different levels have differing levels of authority.

The discussion in Daniel 10, for example, leads us to infer that the angel assigned to take God's answer to Daniel was outranked by the demon called "the angel prince of the kingdom of Persia" (verse 13). The original angel, however, was able to get help from the archangel Michael, who outranked the prince of Persia. At the highest level under God that we know of, then, we have the archangels. Two

We can infer that angels at different levels have differing levels of authority.

beings at this level are mentioned by name: Michael, who is called "one of the chief angels" (an archangel) in Daniel 10:13 and "the chief angel" in Jude 9, and Gabriel, who introduced himself to Zechariah as one who "stand[s] in the presence of God" (Luke 1:19). It was Gabriel's assignment to announce the conceptions of John the Baptist and Jesus. An archangel is also mentioned in 1 Thessalonians 4:16.

It is likely that Satan was one of the highest, perhaps *the* highest, archangel before his rebellion (Isaiah 14:12–15). God would have delegated to him a large amount of power and authority. It is clear that Satan still possesses great power and authority—perhaps the same amount he had before he rebelled. But he, like any other angel, has no power or authority apart from God's permission.

We have no names for the remaining ranks of God's angels. We are told in Ephesians 6:12, however, that under Satan there are demonic angels with names like (depending on the translation) *rulers* or *principalities, authorities* or *powers* and *cosmic powers of this dark age* or *mighty powers of darkness.* Though there is some debate over whether these names represent a hierarchy, it seems probable to me that a hierarchy with at least three levels exists before we get down to the ground-level demons—the foot soldiers of the satanic kingdom. These foot soldiers may be divided into family demons, occult demons and "ordinary" demons, with the former wielding more power. If there is such a hierarchy, we can assume that the demons higher on the ladder have more authority than those lower down.

We know that at least some angels have specific responsibilities that apparently involve greater or lesser authority. The cherubim and seraphim seem to have important assignments relating to the presence of God (for seraphim, see Isaiah 6:2, 6; for cherubim, see Ezekiel 10:5) and protection, lest humans come near the Tree of Life (Genesis 3:24). Then there are the nameless angels, sometimes referred to as *the angel of the Lord*, that appeared to Abraham (Genesis 18:1–15), to Gideon (Judges 6:11–21) and in the fiery furnace with the three Hebrew men (Daniel 3:25). These were given authority to carry out specific important assignments and were therefore probably of high rank.

Some angels have assignments, and consequent authority, relating to children (Matthew 18:10). There are, I suspect, several levels of authority among God's angels, and many angels down through the ages have been assigned by God to such specific tasks with accompanying authority.

In addition to these assignments, we find when we are dealing with demons that God apparently assigns certain of His angels to assist us, giving them whatever authority they need to handle the situation. As I work to free people of demons, I sometimes hear the demons comment on the activities of angels. They report that we are protected by angels as we minister, that they (the demons) are surrounded by angels and that the angels punish them when they lie or disobey us.

A picture of the two angelic hierarchies, based on the names we have in Scripture, might look like this:

God	
Humans	
Archangels	**Archangel**
(Michael, Gabriel)	(Satan)
Cherubim, seraphim?	?
Angels	Rulers/principalities
Angels	Authorities/powers
Angels	Cosmic powers/mighty powers of darkness
Angels	Occult spirits/demons
Angels	Ordinary demons

Our enemy is allowed by God (as I pointed out in chapter 1) a certain degree of self-determination, as well as the authority and power that go along with the position granted him, even though he uses these to oppose God. He has thus set up his own kingdom within which he dispenses authority and power. There are certain restrictions, however, under which he works. These are important for us to know for our understanding of both Satan's authority and our own:

1. *In spite of the amount and extent of Satan's power and authority, they are much less than God's.* Though we talk of two kingdoms headed by two kings and may be impressed with Satan's power, the kingdom of Satan is infinitely smaller and weaker than the Kingdom of God.

2. *Although the two kingdoms are at war with each other, there is absolutely no chance that the satanic kingdom will emerge victorious.* Satan was defeated miserably at Jesus' cross and empty tomb. Beyond that, Satan and his followers have been "made a public spectacle" and led "as captives in [Jesus'] victory procession" (Colossians 2:15). Thus Satan's authority is restricted by both his limitations and his defeat.

3. *Satan's power and authority continue only at the level God allows and only as long as God allows.* God, working according to the rules He has built into the universe, limits Satan's activities and will sooner or later call a halt to Satan's ability to function (see the book of Revelation).

4. *Satan gained authority over creation from Adam (Luke 4:6).* Just as in that event, whatever authority Satan presently holds or gains is that permitted by humans.

5. *The satanic kingdom is literalistic in the way its members follow the rules that have been laid down for them.* When working to get rid of demons, we find that they obey the letter of the law with regard to authority structures and every other area. So must we.

As with the rest of human life, with authority we live in a structured universe, governed by spiritual rules. Now we turn to the relationships that flow from these spiritual rules.

9

Authority Relationships

✣ A Certain Degree of Autonomy and Authority

Though there is a bit of repetition in what follows, I believe it is important to review the human authority situation. Flowing from the fact that humans have been created second in the universe (Psalm 8:5) with a good bit of freedom and authority are facts and principles like the following:

1. Since we are created in the image and likeness of God (Genesis 1:26–27), we are higher in both position and authority, by nature of our creation, than even Satan and his angels. We are God's masterpiece, created high above every other creature, including the angels.

2. At Creation God gave Adam authority over the created world (Genesis 1:26, 28). It was apparently God's intent that humans live in obedience to Him as stewards over His creation.

3. God also built into the universe certain authority rules for humans. Among these are the following relative positions of authority:

- Husbands over wives (Ephesians 5:23; 1 Timothy 2:11–14)

- Parents over children (Ephesians 6:1–3; Colossians 3:20)

- Pastors and other leaders over the people in their churches (Ephesians 4:11–12; 1 Timothy 3)
- Rulers over their people (1 Timothy 2:2; Romans 13:1–2)
- Masters over slaves (Ephesians 6:5)
- Leaders over followers (1 Peter 2:13–14)
- Jesus over the Church (Ephesians 5:23)
- And, I believe, older people over younger

Although the authority in each case (including that of Jesus over the Church) is exercised by humans in the human world, it is a spiritual authority. However, *the one with greater authority does not have greater value than the one with lesser authority.* Indeed, I would argue that what we call authority in this regard is not so much a matter of those with so-called "higher" authority possessing the power to take advantage of those under their authority as it is being assigned the task of protecting those who are more vulnerable. Indeed, the principle by which those with greater authority are to be governed is the principle of service (Mark 10:42–45). These authority rules, then, are a matter of *organization*, not *value*. And there seems to be at least one counter-rule: that of the believing wife (1 Corinthians 7:14), who has authority both in relation to her unbelieving husband and to her children.

In dealing with demons we have found that they take all these authority relationships, including this counter-rule, very seriously. They regard the authority of husband over wife, parents over children, leaders over followers as well-nigh absolute. We must, therefore, take such rules seriously in dealing with demons, regardless of whether, as contemporary Westerners with our own views of authority, we like such rules. We will discuss these matters again later.

4. Adam *squandered the authority he was given* through his disobedience (Genesis 3). This gave Satan the authority he bragged about in Luke 4:6.

5. Through the work of Christ appropriated by faith, however, *humans can regain their lost relationship with God.* Those who receive Jesus through faith in Him are given "the right [i.e., authority] to become God's children" (John 1:12). On this basis, then, we who are committed to Jesus in faith have the authority to do what Jesus did and "even greater things" (John 14:12).

6. A proper relationship with God means *the restoration of the authority we were intended to have* over creation and even over evil spirits. As we learn from the sons of Sceva (Acts 19:13–16), those without a relationship with God do not have the authority to cast out demons. Jesus and His followers, on the other hand, demonstrated that such authority is available to those with this relationship.

Spirit World–Human World Interaction

Satan is, as I said, a literalist—or, rather, he is required by God to strictly obey the rules of the universe. Both God's Kingdom and Satan's are bound by whatever authority relationships God has set down. Among the principles governing these relationships:

1. There are conditions under which humans can give authority in their lives to either God or Satan. Human obedience, as we have seen, whether to God or to Satan, gives the master specific rights in a person's life. God's purpose for Adam was that he live a life of obedience to Him. But not until Jesus, the second Adam, do we see what human life was intended to be. Disobedience to God (sin), which is automatically obedience to Satan, gives the satanic kingdom rights over the person. And when a person wallows in sin, Satan has the right to send a demon to live in him or her.

2. Dedicating a person to God or Satan, whether self-dedication or dedication by someone in authority over that person, gives the master authority over him or her. When people commit themselves or their children to God, a kind of spiritual label is

put on that person that says, "This one belongs to God." Likewise with any dedication to a satanic being. Many people in non-Christian religions or occult organizations dedicate themselves to false gods or spirits, thus putting themselves under the authority of a demon, cult leader or false religion. Others who belong to organizations such as Freemasonry or Scientology commit themselves unconsciously to the enemy. When a parent dedicates a child to Satan, the parent gives the enemy authority to work in and through that child's life.

3. As I have indicated, the spirit world honors human authority patterns, both natural and delegated. We have spoken of "natural" patterns—those relating to the authority of husband over wife, parents over children and the like. But delegated authority is also honored by the spirit world. I have frequently been authorized by people to take authority over demons in themselves or in their houses. When I do so, I work with their permission and under their authority. Once I ministered to a man in his thirties who had carried a demon since he was five, authorized to be there by a nanny! When his parents had turned him as a child over to the nanny, which they did daily, they had given her their authority, which she used to invite one or more demons in.

> *The spirit world honors human authority patterns, both natural and delegated.*

As husbands, we can delegate to our wives our total authority over home and children when we go on a trip. Likewise, the leader of an organization can delegate his or her authority for certain purposes. When we do so, the spirit world has to listen to the one to whom authority is delegated, as if that person were the top authority figure. Before I learned this, when I would go on a trip it was predictable that something would go wrong at home. But when I took a bit of time and told the spirit world that my wife had my complete authority while I was away, such problems stopped.

4. What leaders do with their authority affects those under them. Those in authority over others need to be careful not to take their authority lightly. We see in Scripture that disobedience on the part of those in spiritual or civic authority over others (for example, Israel's kings) affects the whole group over which they have authority. In the case of Achan (Joshua 7), the sin of one, apparently not even a leader, affected the relationship of the whole nation to the Lord. Many evangelical churches in our day are hindered spiritually by the fact that some of their leaders are under satanic authority through immorality or occult involvement.

Practices such as horoscope reading, fortune-telling, eastern mysticism, New Age and Freemasonry give Satan permission to operate right within our churches (and homes). Many older churches have been dedicated to Satan by virtue of the fact that Freemasons laid the cornerstone when the church building was constructed. Churches can also fall under the influence of Satan if some of their leaders are living in sin.

5. Any commitment, dedication, curse or blessing entered into by a person in one generation may give authority to either master—God or Satan—over that person's descendants. Commitment to God in one generation blesses its descendants, especially if they do not turn their backs on God. But satanic power may enter the family line through conscious or unconscious commitments, such as those mentioned above or through cursing. If such commitments are not canceled, the interference gets passed on to the following generation. Because of this rule, many children come into the world already demonized because of agreements their ancestors made with the enemy.

Exodus 20:5, describing the second of the Ten Commandments, may mean that such satanic interference is limited to four generations. I sincerely hope so. I have frequently found demons, however, that claim to have been in a family for many generations, stemming from such commitments or curses. One way or the other, we observe from Scripture a mystical relationship between members of the same family, which means that children participate in commitments made by their parents.

God kept His commitments to Abraham for many generations, even after Israel ceased to be faithful to Him. We also see the blessing of God on David extending to Solomon and to one after another of his descendants (1 Kings 11:34–36), in spite of the fact that first Solomon and then many of his descendants were unfaithful to the Lord. In 2 Kings 8:19 we learn that "the Lord was not willing to destroy Judah, because he had promised his servant David that his descendants would always continue to rule." This they did until the fall of Jerusalem (2 Kings 25). When God curses, as He did in the Garden of Eden, those effects, too, go on from generation to generation.

6. On the basis of relationship and obedience to either master—God or Satan—these spirit powers delegate authority to humans. Spiritual empowerment in the human world can be granted by either God or Satan. On God's side, we note again that Jesus gave His disciples authority and power over all demons and diseases (Luke 9:1) while He was on earth. After His ascension, He sent the Holy Spirit to empower His followers (Acts 1:4–8) to do the works He did, and even more. With the Holy Spirit inside us, Christians carry the authority and power of God Himself.

Satan, too, can give people authority to work in his power to do miraculous things. The amount of authority and power available to individuals on Satan's side depends on the rank of the inhabiting demons. Higher-ranking demons can give a person power to do signs and wonders, as with Elymas (Acts 13:8–11) or the demonized girl in Philippi (Acts 16:16), even to move around out of the body as in astral projection.

✄ Authority through Cultural Forms

Cultural forms such as words, material objects, places and buildings can be instruments of authority and power. Blessings and curses, talismans and shrines, rituals and music all fit under this principle. The empowerment of words is basic to most of the ways in which spiritual authority is wielded. Words usually serve as the vehicles through which other items are empowered.

1. Words used on the authority of God or Satan are empowered. Blessings and curses spoken on the authority of the one to whom the speaker is committed are ordinarily empowered, with one exception (noted below). As Christians we have the authority to bless individuals with specific endowments like peace and joy. We can also use our authority to bless objects or places such as cars, homes, computers or offices with protection from enemy interference.

Although blessing in the name of God or Jesus gives rights to our side, there is also a satanic "blessing" that can be practiced consciously or unconsciously by his devotees. And there is cursing, by which enemy authority can be introduced into a person's life. I am not sure I know all the conditions under which a curse can be effective, but we are told in Proverbs 26:2 that a curse cannot land without a reason. By implication, then, a curse *can* land when there is a reason, such as sin in a person's life.

The exception to the source of empowerment I mentioned above is when a servant of God speaks words that serve Satan's purposes rather than God's. Negative words spoken against God's people, even on the part of Christians, can be empowered by Satan since they are in obedience to his temptations and are invested, therefore, with his authority. This means we have to be careful how we use our words.

Power was passed the opposite way when the prophet Balaam attempted to curse Israel but was prevented by God (Numbers

22–24). Apparently, God would not let Balaam prophesy against his calling as a prophet, committed to prophesying for God, even though he was hired to curse Israel.

I find that many people have cursed themselves or those close to them through negative statements. Self-cursing, often when a person simply says nasty things to himself or herself, gives the satanic kingdom rights to affect, influence, even live inside that person. Vows and oaths not made in God's will, or vows made and broken, also give the satanic kingdom rights. Satan is quick to empower and take advantage of vows and oaths designed to harm people or to win power or prestige in the human or spirit worlds.

> *The disciples' words and the power that flowed through them lay under their own authority.*

Words blessed on the authority of God (or of Satan) may be used to affect life for good if empowered by God or evil if empowered by Satan. On our side, it is an enormous privilege given us by God to bless in Jesus' name.

2. Blessings and curses are the property of those who utter them. We have seen that when Jesus gave His disciples authority and sent them out to witness, He commanded them to bless a home as they entered it, then to retract the blessing if they were not welcomed there (Luke 9:4–5; 10:5–6). The very fact that the disciples had given the blessings meant they could also retract them. Their words and the power that flowed through them lay under their own authority.

If we have cursed ourselves, then, we retain authority over those words and can renounce them and be freed from the power we have unleashed. We can usually break such curses fairly easily by saying something like, "In the name of Jesus, I renounce all curses I have put on myself/my body/my . . ."

3. The dedication of objects to spirit beings enables spiritual power to flow through those objects. Substances like anointing oil, water, salt and food, when dedicated to God, convey God's blessing to the user. In Scripture the Ark of the Covenant (1 Samuel 4–7; 2 Samuel 6:11), Jesus' cloak (Matthew 9:20; 14:36) and Paul's handkerchiefs and aprons (Acts 19:11–12) are examples of objects that conveyed blessing. Jesus' and Paul's items, moreover, conveyed God's power for healing and deliverance.

In ministry we often (but not always) find blessed oil to be effective in healing (James 5:14) or lessening the power of demons. Some people find it effective to bless with healing power such objects as water, salt, a cross, a Bible or the Communion elements. Lest we take a magical attitude toward such items, though, we must recognize that the power is not *contained* in the object itself, as animism would contend. Rather, the power comes from God and is merely *conveyed* through the blessed item.

The power of Satan is invested through dedication in such things as idols, the cups and tables of demons (1 Corinthians 10:21), even doctrines (1 Timothy 4:1). In many societies it is customary for those who make implements used for worship, work, decoration or other functions to use their authority to dedicate those items to their gods or spirits. Many groups of Christians use the authority we have from Jesus to dedicate articles used in worship, including sanctuary furnishings, anointing oil, the Communion elements and holy water. Once dedicated, physical objects are enabled to convey the power of the God or god to whom they are dedicated.

4. As with the Ark (1 Samuel 5) and cursed items retained by the Israelites in Joshua's day (Joshua 7), empowered items in the hands of the other side can cause great disruption. Apparently, dedication and cursing are able to carry the authority of God or the gods into the territory of the other being. Often when missionaries or Christian travelers bring back objects from other

societies and keep them in their homes, there is disruption by demons until the objects are either cleansed spiritually or gotten rid of. My colleague C. Peter Wagner had such a disruption in his home several years ago until he got rid of a group of items he and his wife had brought back with them from Bolivia. Unknown to them, these items had been dedicated to evil spirits.

5. We can use our authority to empower nonmaterial cultural forms as well. Music is frequently empowered through dedication to either God or Satan. So are rituals, dances and other worship activities. The blessing we feel in Christian worship is likely due to a combination of the pleasantness felt at the human level and the blessing of God flowing from the spiritual level.

Certain musical groups active in America and Europe serve Satan openly and use their authority to dedicate their music to him. There are probably other groups that do so unconsciously. Such music conveys satanic power to its devotees. Dr. Ed Murphy has recounted how his committed Christian teenage daughter unknowingly became demonized through association with certain rock music groups and their followers (see Murphy's article listed in the bibliography).

As Christians we have the authority to empower worship music to convey God's power to those who sing and listen to it. Blessed music played in our homes and cars is effective in suppressing enemy activity and protecting against satanic attacks in those places.

Authority over Places and Organizations

Authority rules govern the relationship between God or Satan on the one hand and places or organizations on the other:

1. Spiritual authority can be used to invest buildings, land or other places with spiritual power. Christians and non-Christians alike dedicate buildings to their divinities. Such dedications or blessings in the name of God or Satan give that spirit being

specific rights over the building. The Old Testament Tabernacle, the Temple and contemporary churches are dedicated places where God manifests His presence in special ways. The homes, land and other possessions (for example, cars, furniture, clothing and computers) of Christians can be dedicated as well, giving God specific authority over them.

Places like churches, buildings, shrines, homes and land can be made spiritually clean by being dedicated to God. They can also be dedicated to Satan, giving him authority over them. Or they can become empowered satanically through regular use for evil purposes like prostitution, gambling, pornography, homosexual activity, financial swindling, abortions and occult meetings. I have found that certain places can be dangerous for Christians to enter without claiming God's protection. Among such places are Masonic lodges, pagan shrines, temples, occult bookstores, abortion clinics, offices of occult and sin-enhancing organizations and some establishments doing commerce in health food, environmental concerns or martial arts.

When Adam sinned, he gave away his right to the land and its productivity (Genesis 3:17–19). So it was that Satan could claim ownership of the whole world (Luke 4:6). The enemy gains more specific rights, however, when people consciously dedicate property to him. Pagan temples, the meeting places of false religions and cults, shrines, occult bookstores and even the homes of those committed to Satan often show tangible evidence of his property rights. Those sensitive to spiritual things can feel the enemy's presence in such places.

On occasion I have been asked to clean out, spiritually speaking, homes and rooms that have been dedicated to Satan or that have come under his power due to people's sin and rebellion against God. A demon I once found in a woman claimed the right to inhabit her because she lived in a house in which a previous occupant had committed adultery. Only when we claimed the woman's authority as the new owner of the property, in order to break the power granted the demon by the previous owner, were we able to cast him out. I have dealt with other demons who seemed to have rights to homes through occult activity or a death that occurred in the home. On one occasion a demon claimed a church through adultery that the pastor's son had committed in the building.

A pastor once called me to ask my advice concerning a place where his church would meet. In searching for a place he had found an auditorium that met their needs very well at the right price. The problem was that the building was a Masonic temple. My advice to him was that if they chose to meet in that building, they were walking right into a territory strongly dedicated to Satan. They might be able to spiritually clean the place out each Sunday, but what if some Sunday they missed part of the building? And what if a part they missed was the nursery? I felt that it was just too dangerous to use a building that regularly got rededicated to Satan between Sundays. If the church were to buy the building and cleanse it, as has happened with a Christian school that I know of, the situation would be different. The Christians could use their authority to banish the enemy spirits and not allow them back in.

> *When Adam sinned, he gave away his right to the land and its productivity.*

I was asked about a different situation by a mission leader who had a colleague who regularly became disruptive during mission meetings. I asked the leader if he cleansed the meeting place (his office) spiritually before each meeting. He did not but started to do so after our conversation. The disruptive person's behavior changed dramatically when he was in that meeting place. Several teachers have told me they have found their students' behavior changed for the better after they started blessing their classrooms.

2. Cosmic or higher-level spirits wield authority over territory. In Daniel 10:13, 20–21, we are introduced to this concept overtly by the angel who has to deal with the ruling spirits called "princes" (NIV) of Persia and Greece. Territoriality of high-level spirits is implicit in much of the Old Testament, however, especially in the historical books, in which we see that the Canaanite people (and probably many in Israel) assumed Yahweh was a mountain God, while the Baal gods ruled the plains. In 1 Kings 20:23 this belief is stated explicitly, and Yahweh, whose authority over the plains is questioned, demonstrates that He is more powerful than the pagan gods even in "their" territory.

3. The territory over which spirit beings wield their authority seems to be defined by humans. It is humans who work out the boundaries over which they will have authority. These human boundaries seem to be honored in the spirit world. The fact that the territories of Persia and Greece (Daniel 10:13, 20), over which satanic principalities held sway, are labeled by human territorial names points in that direction. So does the impression gained by those who study and deal with territorial spirits that there are national spirits, regional spirits, spirits over cities and spirits over sections of cities.

C. Peter Wagner's book *Engaging the Enemy* (1991) recounts the story of a missionary distributing tracts in a small border town along a street that divided Brazil from Uruguay. He found that people accepted the tracts on the Brazil side but refused them on the Uruguay side. Furthermore, some who had refused them on the Uruguay side received them gladly after they had crossed over into Brazil. The missionary's interpretation was that the prayer of Christians in Brazil was what made the difference. There were gradations in the enemy's ability to control the responses of the people on either side of the human political border, calibrated to the authority exercised by Christians to break through the enemy's defenses.

4. There seem to be cosmic-level spirits with authority over organizations, institutions and activities. I believe there are cosmic-level spirits whose job it is to promote pornography, abortion, homosexuality, prostitution and occult organizations. These spirits probably aid, empower and encourage organizations devoted to such sins. In Evanston, Illinois (according to Wagner in *Engaging the Enemy*), Pastor Steve Nicholson was fasting and praying in an attempt to discover why his church was not growing. As he did, he was approached by a high-level demon who identified himself as a spirit of witchcraft and claimed to own the area in which the church was located. Steve felt led to claim a certain amount of territory for his church and was able to break the spirit's power over it. From that point on, his church began to grow, largely through a steady flow of converts from witchcraft.

In the Kingdom of God we know of angels assigned to children (Matthew 18:10) and to churches (Revelation 1–3). I assume there are also angels assigned to Christian activities like missionary and other parachurch organizations. Institutions such as churches, seminaries and Bible schools probably all have high-level angelic spirits and also high-level enemy spirits assigned to them. Possibly social institutions such as marriages, governments and educational institutions do, too.

5. In order for spirit beings to have authority over territories and organizations, they must have legal rights. Such rights are given them either overtly or below the level of consciousness, through the allegiances, dedications and behavior of humans who now use and have used in the past the territories and organizations. Land and organizations can be dedicated consciously to the Kingdom of God or the kingdom of Satan. They also seem to be consecrated by the purposes for which they are used, whether to God or Satan. Such dedications appear to continue from generation to generation until broken by the

current authority figures. The dedication of a place or organization can be weakened, sometimes broken, by subsequent opposite usage.

In Papua New Guinea, I learned that a whole mission compound was built on territory formerly used for tribal warfare. This use gave the enemy legal rights to the area. In an American community I was told that a church and high school were built on an ancient Indian burial ground. Since spirits do not all leave the places where their hosts die, it is likely that the strange things that happened both at the church and the high school were caused by enemy spirits who had legal rights to the area. In neither case does it appear that the power has been broken simply by opposite usage. Until those with authority to operate in the power of God break the legal rights given to the enemy over those territories by evil activities, Satan will continue to have great ability to interfere with God's activities in those places.

In Sierra Leone, on the other hand, a mission compound that was built on "spirit hill" was recaptured through missionaries taking authority and canceling the enemy's rights. When the first missionaries arrived there over a hundred years ago, they looked for a place to build their homes on and were directed to this place, known to the locals as "spirit hill." They built several homes on that hill. For over a hundred years missionary after missionary who lived in those homes had to leave involuntarily with sickness, emotional problems, or marriage and family difficulties. This problem was not solved until a recent missionary who understood spiritual warfare led the group to take their authority over the hill and cancel the enemy's legal rights.

Authority to Counteract Authority

When one with authority confronts another with authority, the one with the greater backing has the better possibility of winning.

Through bluff, mice are able to defeat elephants. The same is true with satanic spirits, if those of us working in God's power do not know what we are doing. One reason for this book is to reveal that we have greater authority than do the enemy's servants and to teach how to exercise that authority to defeat them.

1. By working in the authority and power of God, we can free people who are in satanic bondage. Under God we have the authority to cast out demons and minister in other ways that cancel enemy rights at ground level. We will deal with this more specifically in chapter 14, "Authority in Ministering to Others."

2. The rules for breaking the authority given by people through the dedication of territories, buildings and organizations are parallel to those for breaking such authority over individuals. In working to free an individual from demons, we deal first with the "garbage," then tackle the demons. In the same way, when we break satanic rights we go for the garbage first, the spirit rights second. In this case, the words spoken to dedicate territories, buildings and organizations constitute the garbage that needs to be dealt with. We claim the authority God has given us to cancel the dedications, then command the demons to leave.

At least sometimes, the garbage of usage can be broken by opposite usage. The dedication to Satan of places or institutions can be weakened, sometimes broken, through either the opposite dedication or through usage for the opposite purpose. With individuals committed to Satan, we need to look for and clean out the garbage that gives satanic spirits rights in the individual. For territories, buildings and organizations, it is crucial to find and break the power of commitments, dedications, curses and sins that have been made on the land, as well as agreements forged consciously or unconsciously by those in authority over the land that gave legal rights to the enemy.

Examples of this are cities, buildings and organizations dedicated by occult groups such as Freemasons (such as Masonic lodges, cities like Washington, D.C., and several Argentine cities dedicated by Freemasons), places where blood has been shed unjustly (for example, Wounded Knee, South Dakota, and buildings where murder took place) and buildings, sections of cities and organizations given to violence, prostitution and homosexuality. Just as for individuals, an important step in breaking the enemy's power is for the people of an infested place to confess sin, repent and turn from their wicked ways (2 Chronicles 7:14).

The power of the enemy over areas infected by sinful usage can be broken through repentance on the part of those now in authority over them. We call this *identificational repentance.* It consists of contemporary representatives of groups that sinned against other groups taking responsibility for the sins of their ancestors and repenting (preferably in public) to contemporary representatives of the groups wronged. Both Nehemiah (Nehemiah 1:5–11) and Daniel (Daniel 9:4–19) model identificational repentance. Such ground-level human activity prepares the way for more aggressive offensives against evil powers.

3. There are rules for exercising authority when we attack the spirits assigned to territories and organizations. For servants of God attacking evil spiritual beings, the most important weapon of attack is prayer, especially intercession. Prayer is an act of war. Servants of God, as individuals and groups, attack regularly through prayer, worship and fasting; they need to add repentance, both individual and corporate. Those praying need to rid themselves of as much internal garbage as possible so that the enemy can find nothing in them on which to get a grip (John 14:30).

In prayer we need to break all historical and contemporary commitments, curses and dedications holding a territory or organization in Satan's grip. We must repent of any sins committed in that territory. Next, in authoritative prayer, we speak the power of God over "the spiritual powers in space" (Ephesians 2:2), laying claim to the territory or organization in the name of Jesus.

✒ Learning the Rules

I have tried in this chapter to articulate the rules I have learned that relate to spiritual authority. As in all of God's creation, the spirit world is organized according to the principles and rules God has laid down. These rules are, I believe, as firm as any of the laws of physics or mathematics, and when discovered and recorded, they will constitute a science in the spiritual sphere.

But little attention has been focused on the study of these rules (unlike the study of the rules governing the physical universe), especially those governing the relationship between the spirit world and the human world. So we understand little. But in dealing with spiritual authority, and the relationships between that authority and what goes on in the worlds above and below, we do well to find out what these rules are and how to operate by them. I and David DeBord have written a little book on this subject called *The Rules of Engagement* (2000).

> *The principles and rules God has laid down are, I believe, as firm as any of the laws of physics or mathematics.*

Now it is time to begin discussing specific applications of these principles.

10

Authority in Our Personal Lives

✦ Knowing Our Authority

"Just who are you?" the demon said with a strong, arrogant voice.

"That doesn't matter," I replied. "I don't come in my own name. I come in Jesus' name. Do you recognize that name?"

"Oh yes," he replied. "I know Jesus."

"And do you recognize that I have the authority of that name?"

"Oh yes," he answered again.

"What does that mean?" I asked.

"It means I have to obey you."

"In that name, then, I command you to obey," I said.

And he did.

I have had this kind of interaction with many demons. Although some question whether we should let demons speak, I have found that a short conversation like this can pay off in at least three ways: (1) It can be very helpful to the client as a clear demonstration of who is in charge; (2) Pressured by the Holy Spirit, demons often reveal valuable information; and (3) Being forced to go against their nature by telling the truth, demons get weakened. For further discussion of talking to demons, see the section on this topic in chapter 15.

In such confrontations with the enemy, I never cease to be thrilled over the privilege Jesus has given us to use His name and His authority to free others. Unfortunately, most Christians do not seem to know the authority they have in Christ, so demons harass us at will, interfering with all aspects of our lives and crippling many. How gratifying it was for me to have a demon say to me, "You really know what you're doing, don't you!"

The apostle Paul said that his hearers knew the enemy's schemes (2 Corinthians 2:11). But those who are alive today are much less likely to know what the enemy is doing. The people of Paul's day understood the spirit world. We, due to the blinding effects of our worldview, do not. And because we do not know our enemy in a time of war, we fight (or hide or run) at a severe disadvantage.

I believe (as I have said) that Satan attacks us primarily in the area of self-image. He is desperately afraid we will discover who we are and make life difficult for him. Like a mouse bluffing an elephant into fearing a creature with much less power, the devil bluffs us and often wins because we do not know who we are. As Dean Sherman points out in *Spiritual Warfare for Every Christian* (1990), Satan does his best to keep us from "confidently believing in the authority God gives us." He wants us "out of the race, sidelined by our doubts, fears, and weaknesses." It is up to us to accept the truth of who we are and to operate in it. God's Spirit does live within us, no matter how we feel, so we do not lack the power to defeat the enemy.

> *The people of Paul's day understood the spirit world.*

It is absolutely true that "the Spirit who is in [us] is more powerful than the spirit in those who belong to the world"

(1 John 4:4). "But if we don't embrace that truth," writes Sherman, "then it might as well not be true." Instead we will submit to our feelings and circumstances as they are manipulated by the enemy. But God's truth is God's truth. We need to believe it in the depths of our being. As Sherman says, our authority stems from a legal right given to us by God Himself. This is a right much like marriage, granting us rights and privileges. We need to speak it out to let the enemy know that we know who we are, and then we need to act on it.

To quote again from Sherman's helpful treatment:

> When I ask people if they are married, I never hear, "Well, I'm not sure. Sometimes I feel married, and sometimes I just don't know." They always say, "Yes" or "No." If we are married, we are totally convinced of it at all times, and have a legal document to prove it. Feelings, thoughts, and personalities do not change the reality of that legal arrangement.
>
> Our spiritual authority is just as real and legal as marriage. It is not just a concept; it's an actual thing.
>
> p. 110

This legal authority God gave us at creation was so important to Satan that he stole it from our ancestor Adam. And stealing it from us is still at the top of his agenda (John 10:10).

✎ Filling Jesus' Shoes

The position and authority we have been given is to "fill Jesus' shoes." He said, "As the Father sent me, so I send you" (John 20:21), and He meant just that. As members of God's family, then, we are commissioned by Jesus to continue what He started while we are in the world. When He sent His followers to do His works throughout Palestine, He assigned to them two tasks (Luke 9:2; 10:9): to communicate that the Kingdom had arrived and to heal (including casting out demons). Furthermore He said to them, "I have given you authority, so that you can walk on snakes and scorpions and overcome all the power of the Enemy, and nothing will hurt you" (Luke 10:19). There are four ways we do this.

First, we must start, once again, where Jesus started: *with the filling of the Holy Spirit* (Luke 3:21–22). That is, to fill Jesus' shoes, we must first be filled with His Spirit (Acts 1:4–5).

Once empowered by the Spirit, we then need, like Jesus, to be *present and engaged*. We are not filling Jesus' shoes by receiving His empowerment and then simply sitting still. Jesus was representing the Father in the world with a mandate to establish His Kingdom here in enemy territory. He did not shun His responsibility, even though He knew He would not be treated gently in a world ruled by the enemy. He did not run away or hide from engagement. He was a man with a mission, which required that He be present and engaged. Being present, He provided a major threat to the enemy's reign on earth.

We, too, are to be present and engaged with the hostile world. As Jesus' representatives, we are to threaten the enemy kingdom. Too many Christians accept Christ and then lead basically secular lives. They seem to think they have been issued a rocking chair in which they can simply rock until the Rapture, as if all Jesus expects us to do is to wait for Him to return. But that is not the picture of the Christian life that the New Testament paints for us. We are told to put on our uniforms and go to war "against the wicked spiritual forces in the heavenly world, the rulers, authorities, and cosmic powers of this dark age" (Ephesians 6:12).

Third, we need to consider the *matter of protection*. In order to do what Jesus was commissioned to do, He needed a certain level of protection. The enemy came around frequently, whether as himself (Luke 4:1–13) or through Pharisees, government officials or other humans. In Nazareth, his home town, the people tried to push Jesus over a cliff, but the Father protected Him (Luke 4:28–30). Likewise, when the storm arose while He traveled by boat across Lake Galilee, the Father protected Him (Luke 8:22–25). Doubtless there were other situations in which the Father ordered angels to protect the Lord Jesus because "his hour had not yet come" (John 7:30; see also John 2:4; 7:6; 8:20).

God grants us, just as He did Jesus, an incredible amount of protection as we battle the enemy. Just as God granted His protection to Job, David and scores of others mentioned in Scripture, I believe all of us are protected by God in ways beyond number. I wonder how many accidents would have happened to us that did not because God kept them from happening.

But there is another level of protection we need to be concerned about. We need a high level of protection any time we challenge the enemy and enter territory specifically dedicated to satanic use. At this level we cannot be passive but must claim greater protection than normal. I have mentioned the need to claim such protection in health food stores, occult bookshops, pagan temples and when driving on highways or staying in motels.

God grants us, just as He did Jesus, an incredible amount of protection as we battle the enemy.

I believe Jesus claimed such protection for Himself regularly as He fought the enemy. He also claimed it for His followers. Before His crucifixion, as the intensity of opposition grew, Jesus said to Peter, "Satan has received permission to test all of you. . . . But I have prayed for you, Simon, that your faith will not fail" (Luke 22:31–32). Even so, as we know, Peter failed, though later he came back.

Living and carrying out warfare in Jesus' shoes, then, means that we need protection at both levels, normal and beyond. And although we need not fear the enemy because the normal level of protection is great, we do need to be conscious of our need to claim extra protection. Often God Himself tips us off to the need to claim more.

Dick Margeson, a ministry colleague of mine, was used in a special way recently to minister to students in a class I was teaching. After he left to return home, one of the members of the class felt nudged by the Holy Spirit to ask if we could take a moment to claim God's special protection for Dick. We did, and we found out later that as he was driving along the freeway, a large sign slid off a truck in front of him. It was headed for the windshield of his car, sure to smash it and hit him in the face, when it lifted and flew over his car, merely scratching the roof as it zoomed by. We know God protected Dick, although we do not know whether this was God's normal protection or a special protection granted because of our prayer. I think it was the latter.

A fourth indication that we are filling Jesus' shoes is that *all we do in His authority is done in love.* As I pointed out in chapter 5, only if God's power is wrapped in love is it truly used in God's way.

With God's love, the infilling of His Holy Spirit, our own presence and engagement and God's protection, we are prepared to use the authority credit card in ways Jesus demonstrated for us—doing the things He did in the ways He did them. He passed on to us the authority to heal, cast out demons, bless and forgive. We will discuss these one by one. But first we will return to the important issue of authority asserted in love and power.

✤ Relationship of Gifting to Authority

We are told that when Jesus ascended into heaven, He "gave gifts to people" (Ephesians 4:8, 11) and that "each one of us has received a special gift in proportion to what Christ has

168

given" (Ephesians 4:7). Some of these gifts are listed in Romans 12:6–8; 1 Corinthians 12:1–11, 28–31; and Ephesians 4:11. I believe these gifts are given at conception. This is why the enemy works so hard to gain control of those with the most spectacular gifting.

On occasion, as I have engaged in inner healing and deliverance, I have asked demons why they work so hard to keep a particular person in bondage. The demonic response is something like "We don't want him [or her] free to live for Jesus," or "We're afraid of what she [or he] might do for Jesus." Demons seem to understand that *certain individuals have greater potential than others to serve Jesus Christ and, therefore, to hurt the demons' kingdom.* Over and over I have found people with gifts such as words of knowledge, discernment, prophecy or healing who have been tormented by the enemy from childhood. People with the greatest gifting seem to be more often attacked by the enemy.

One dimension of gifting is that God has given different gifts to different people. And different giftings designate a different range over which one has the right to exercise authority (in the same way that one does not have authority over another's bank account or credit card).

There are at least three kinds of gifting, which I will call *roles, ministries* and *offices.* At any time God can enable one of His people to bring about healing. If this does not happen to a person very often, we say the person assumes the *role* of healing or whatever other gift was appropriate at that time. If, however, a person is regularly used to operate in a given gifting but is not paid for it, we call that a *ministry.* If a person is appointed to a position in which he or she regularly functions in a given gifting, we can call that an *office.*

The most obvious kind of gifting is ministry gifting. When a person has a gift of healing, intercession, teaching, etc., and exercises it regularly, we can say he or she has a ministry of whatever that gift is. Personally, I have been gifted by God to help people get free in emotional and spiritual areas. By exercising this gift, I have a ministry of inner healing and deliverance. I also have a gift of teaching. If I exercised this gift as a layperson, it would classify as a ministry gift. But because I was employed (and am now retired) as a teacher, I was in the office of teacher and was using this gift as an office gift.

The distinction between ministry gifting and office gifting is thus simply a matter of whether or not one is appointed (and usually paid) by an organization to function in one's gifting. I know people who are appointed as official intercessors and one who is ordained to a deliverance ministry (office), though without pay.

What I call *role gifting* is when a person is put on the spot, needing to function in an area in which he or she is not normally gifted, but God supplies the gift needed for the occasion. As nearly as I can tell, I have little or no gifting in the hospitality area. But when my wife (who does have the gift of hospitality) is not at home and I need to fill in, the Lord is gracious and gifts me for the occasion. Nor do I think I have the gift of physical healing, since most of the people for whom I pray for physical problems do not get healed. But God often uses me to bring physical healing as part of inner-healing sessions (within my gifting) and infrequently to bring purely physical healing (as role gifting).

> *God supplies the gift needed for the occasion.*

Given what we think we know about gifting, then, it appears that we have greater authority in areas of our gifting than in other areas. Even when the gifting is a matter of role, the authority can be great, if only for that single occasion. There may be times in role situations, however, when God does not give a person enough authority to do the job.

The level of authority in ministry or office gifting (unlike role gifting) is constantly high. Not that the success rate is 100 percent, but those who know their gifts and practice them regularly develop a high degree of confidence about what the results will be. They are, therefore, ready to tackle any problem within the area of their gifting, knowing they carry authority into every situation commensurate with the problem. They know who they are—both in general and in terms of their specific gifts and calling.

Those who do not take seriously their responsibility to use and develop their gifts, however, may find after a while that they are no longer able to use them. Or they may retain the gifts in much diminished measure, at least until such time as they begin to use them again regularly, since, according to Romans 11:29, "God's gifts and his call are irrevocable" (NIV).

What Authority Comes with Our Status?

The human and spirit worlds are, as we have noted, tightly connected. One of the implications of this fact is that the level of one's status in the world affects one's spiritual authority. Leaders in human affairs, for example, carry great authority in the spiritual realm. As we can see from the history of the kings of Israel, the spiritual fortunes of God's people were tied to the faithfulness or unfaithfulness of their leaders.

God does not take lightly the responsibility over precious people given to those who lead politically, corporately, in education or in any other context, large or small. For "no authority exists without God's permission, and the existing authorities have been put there by God" (Romans 13:1). Those in authority, therefore, are directly accountable to God for what they do with that authority. I tremble to think of the punishment awaiting leaders who stand for the murder of preborn infants and who cater to the unreasonable demands of certain homosexual groups. By the same token, as with ancient Israel, God is a rewarder of leaders who stand for righteousness.

Since spiritual authority and status are thus linked, we need to be especially careful how we exercise whatever human authority comes with our status. Those of us who are parents need to recognize that the decisions we make regarding our children have spiritual implications as well as human ones. We husbands need to recognize the same with regard to the way we treat our wives. Teachers are accountable for the way we treat students and co-workers. We who are older should use the status of age carefully and responsibly. Heads of organizations need to take seriously their responsibility before God for the ways in which they treat His people. When we use our authority to oppress, we are offending God as well as those we encumber. When we bless people and treat them lovingly, we are using our status the way God intended.

I have already recounted stories of problems that stopped when teachers took up the authority of their status over their classrooms. One fourth-grade teacher whom I will call Martha was having an awful year. Her kids were unruly, apparently undisciplined, and not learning much. Then a couple on my ministry team suggested that Martha begin first to pray for specific children, then start getting to class a little early each morning and going around to each desk, anointing it with oil and blessing it. They further urged Martha to take authority over her classroom and kick out any demonic intruders, taking the same authority silently whenever the children showed signs of becoming unruly, as if a demon were causing it. Martha followed these instructions, and God transformed her year as well as several of her students.

I have mentioned a friend who served as an interim pastor and told me about a badly divided church he was asked to serve. Discouraged and desperate, he went into the sanctuary several

Saturdays in a row, exercising his authority as pastor over each seat and its occupant as he visualized the person who regularly sat there, in order to break any bondage that person might be under. My friend also consecrated pulpit, choir loft, musical instruments, Communion table and everything else, and he prayed fervently for unity. Unity soon came, as the exercise of his authority as pastor banished the enemy spirits that were disrupting the congregation.

11

Past, Present and Future

❧ Claiming Authority over the Past

One area of our authority that is not obvious to many is our right to cancel any claims the enemy may make due to events and agreements of the past. Our personal aim for the past (as for the present) is to be as "clean" as Jesus was so that Satan would have no claim on us stemming from things we do in the present. In John 14:30 Jesus, while referring to Satan as "the ruler of this world," stated that he "has no power over me," or, as other versions translate it, "He has no hold over me" (NIV), "He has nothing in Me" (NKJV) or "He has no rights over me" (NEB).

Some of the rights the enemy has over people come through inheritance. Believers have the authority, however, to cancel those rights. The place to start is with the recognition that God has planned and chosen each of us from before the creation of the world (Ephesians 1:4). We can then assume that He has superintended the coupling of each pair of our ancestors and the transmission of both genetic and spiritual influences down through the generations. Then, according to Psalm 139:13, He formed and framed us in our mothers' wombs so we would come out just right.

Nevertheless, the enemy may have had ample opportunity through this process to influence and often intrude on us through our ancestors. Demons may have entered, taking advantage of physical and spiritual issues. The job of these agents is to find and exploit any defects in a person's physical and spiritual DNA. Through choices our ancestors have made, doors are often opened into our bloodlines, permitting the enemy to produce damage and insert his agents that will be inherited from generation to generation.

Some of the rights the enemy has over people come through inheritance.

To help free people from such bondages, I find it important to take authority over five major areas—vows, curses, dedications, sin and trauma—to cancel all rights the enemy may have gained through them. It is important for us, whether by ourselves or with the help of another, to take authority over these issues in our heritage so as to cancel the rights the enemy may have gained in our lives through inheritance from people and events of the past.

Our authority over the past extends to land, buildings, cars, curios and other items that come into our possession. We need to assert our authority to break any agreements that have given the devil rights over such property before we acquired it. (see chapter 13 for more on taking authority over homes and land.)

And we can mention again that objects we bring back from foreign places may have been dedicated to enemy gods and spirits. Usually these can be prayed over and the power in them broken quite easily. I pray routinely over whatever I buy overseas, from Native American sources or from places that may have New Age connections. I am told (though I have not experienced it) that some objects contain so much enemy power that it is better to destroy them than to fight continually with the spirits in them. Perhaps, as a rule of thumb, we can say that if the object has no purpose other than a religious one, it ought to be destroyed. But I do not believe in simply destroying everything that looks suspicious; we should be *capturing* things from the enemy rather than giving in to him.

Vows

Merriam-Webster's Collegiate Dictionary (2008) defines a vow as "a solemn promise or assertion . . . by which a person is bound to an act, service, or condition." People vow regularly to do things or not do things. Vows that fall in line with Satan's purposes get empowered by him. One such vow that is commonly made and looks fairly innocent is "I will not be like my mother [or father]." Somehow the enemy is able to use such a vow to establish a stronghold in a person. Other damaging vows that come up fairly often are these: "I never want children" (from someone who had a difficult upbringing or who gets disturbed by children's behavior); "I will never allow myself to enjoy sex" (from abuse victims); "I will never let another man [or woman] get close to me again" (after a broken relationship); "I refuse to grow old"; "I'll never amount to anything" and "I'll never be able to get it right."

I once ministered to a man who had vowed at age five never to cry again. Many men and a few women have made similar vows. A colleague of mine dealt with the descendant of a woman who had made a more openly evil vow. She had actually written a letter to Satan, vowing to give him her firstborn son and every firstborn son of her descendants if he would make her rich and famous. She became rich and famous, and, sure enough, her firstborn son and her firstborn grandson paid a high price for her wealth and fame.

Two kinds of negative vows need to be broken: ancestral vows and those made by the person himself or herself. To break the power Satan is able to wield in our lives through ancestral vows, we simply claim authority in the name of Jesus to break their power. Doing this in a general way usually takes care of things.

But sometimes the power of Satan through a given vow is so great that we must discover what the vow was and break it quite specifically. God can reveal what we have to know in order to break the vow, either through a word of knowledge or by forcing a demon to tell us.

Usually I deal with ancestral vows—as well as curses, dedications and sins—in each ancestral line (father's and mother's) separately. I usually say something like this: "In the name of Jesus, I take authority over all vows in the father's [or mother's] line to cancel any power given to the enemy, and to break his power through vows that may have been made by any of [name of person]'s ancestors in his [or her] father's [or mother's] line."

In addition to ancestral vows, any vows made by the person on him- or herself also need to be broken. This can be done in the same way. It is good to be as specific as possible. One may say something like "I cancel any vows I've put on myself," or "I cancel the vow that I would not be like my mother/father."

Cursing

The second kind of past event to be canceled is cursing. It is likely that both we and our ancestors have been the target of curses, whether leveled at us formally (for example, through a set ritual) or informally. This is especially likely if we or our ancestors have served in non-Western societies where curses are commonplace. Missionaries and others attempting to witness for Christ are frequent targets of such cursing.

Unfortunately, many of the curses that need to be broken have come from parents or other close relatives. An unwanted baby may be cursed while in the womb by mother or father or both. Those whose parents did not want them, especially those who have been adopted, can usually count on having been cursed. (I will share more on this in chapter 13.) Saying "I cancel the curse of unwantedness" is how I usually deal with it.

A common form of cursing is *self-cursing*. I have ministered to many who grew up with strong negative feelings toward themselves or some part of themselves. Many people curse their bodies during their teenage years. Victims of abuse often curse their sex organs. Many women tell me they have cursed such things as their hair, faces, breasts, hips, minds and personalities. A man often curses such things as his emotions, his sex drive (for example, in relation to masturbation), his sex organ and his ability to perform tasks such as a job

Cursing, whether from others or from oneself, often gives Satan a right to a person.

or athletics. Again, our authority enables us to say something like "I cancel all curses that I have put on myself" (or "my sex organs," "my hips," etc.).

Another kind of curse that needs to be broken is the one recorded in Matthew 27:25, when, at Jesus' crucifixion, the Jewish leaders said, "Let the responsibility for his death fall on us and on our children!" A friend of mine with Jewish ancestry experienced a radical change in his life when the one ministering to him broke the effects of this curse on him. When we have spoken against this curse in others of Jewish ancestry, we have often seen major changes. The testimony of demons (for whatever it is worth) is that all Jews are affected by this curse and that the demons' power is significantly lessened when the curse is broken. In one of my recent ministry sessions, a Jewish believer experienced major physical as well as emotional and spiritual changes when this curse was broken and the demons attached to it were expelled.

Cursing, whether from others or from oneself, often gives Satan a right to a person. But we have the authority to take away all rights the enemy has obtained over ancestors or over the person himself (or herself). My practice is first to claim God's power to cancel any rights obtained through cursing that affect the person I am working with. Then I have that person renounce any self-curses, and finally I break the power of any curses leveled at the person from conception up to the present.

Members of secret societies such as the Freemasons are often directed to pronounce curses on themselves, which can be powerful. There are published helps for people who wish to break such curses (a useful one for Freemasons is made available by Selwyn Stevens of New Zealand). For a child or grandchild of one who has belonged to a secret society, the curses can usually be cancelled more easily. In one case I was working to free a lady from a spirit of Freemasonry. The demon ridiculed me and claimed that I could not expel him since I did not know the curses she was under. I simply said, "I cover all the curses with the blood of Jesus." The demon looked at me and said, "I have no more power!" So we kicked him out.

Formal curses require greater attention. Often such curses involve the cursing and burial of some article, such as clothing, that has been close to the person cursed. To break them, then, may require finding where the items are buried. When discovered, the curses on the items can be canceled and the items burned.

Dedications

The third category of past events that need to be canceled is dedications. Individuals who come from (or whose ancestors came from) Asia, Africa or Latin America, or those with American Indian ancestry, can count on having been (or their ancestors having been) dedicated to false gods and spirits that are really demons. People who have belonged to false religions such as Buddhism, Hinduism, Islam, Shintoism (Japan) or shamanism (Korea), or to cults such as Freemasonry, Mormonism, Scientology, New Age, Christian Science and the like—or if their ancestors have belonged to these false religions—need to have the effects of dedications broken.

My practice is to cancel any power the enemy is able to wield through ancestral dedications, whether I suspect they are there or not. I speak against inherited spirits especially with non-Westerners, but I also do so with Westerners, just in case. Better to be safe than sorry. I treat specific dedications that I know about, whether ancestral or in the person's life. To do this, I simply assert the authority of Jesus Christ to cancel any enemy rights and to break all power gained through dedications (to the specific god or spirit, if known). Then I cover any rituals used in these dedications with the blood of Jesus Christ.

Sin

The fourth aspect of past influence that needs to be dealt with is sin. Often Satan has gained rights in our lives through sinful behavior on the parts of various ancestors. Many of us know of alcoholism, aberrant sexual behavior or even criminal activity in our family trees. Such behavior allows the enemy rights, on the basis of which he can often make claims on us. Any wallowing in sin on our part can, of course, give the same rights.

With the authority we have in Christ, we can claim freedom from satanic interference in our lives coming through this channel as well. We simply assert the power of God to break any power Satan has gained in our fathers' or mothers' lines through sinful behavior.

It is a good idea to precede such taking of authority with identificational repentance, claiming the authority that is ours as the current representative of our family line and *repenting for the sins of our ancestors.* Like Nehemiah (Nehemiah 1:6–7) and Daniel (Daniel 9:5–11), we identify with our ancestors in their sinfulness, taking responsibility for their sins as if they were our own and confessing our participation with them. We then assert our authority to repent on their behalf to remove family guilt from ourselves.

We do not have the right to grant our ancestors forgiveness, but we can free ourselves from any guilt that attaches itself to us and any rights their sin gives the enemy over us. To do this, we may say something like "As the current representative of my father's [or mother's] family, I assume responsibility for the sins of my ancestors and humbly repent for their disobedience in the name of Jesus Christ, who paid for their sins as well as mine." This act of identificational repentance breaks the power of inherited demons.

Trauma

The final area to cover when breaking enemy rights through inheritance is *trauma*. We often find, in dealing with present demonization, that the enemy is able to enter when a person experiences trauma or abuse. Given that such experiences may have happened to our ancestors, it is good to cancel any rights the enemy has gained in our family lines through trauma. This is done in the same way as recommended above for any of the other four areas.

Another dimension of the authority God gives us over the past is highlighted in chapter 15 in the section on deep-level healing. Most of us have experienced emotional wounds in the past that have the power to affect our present life negatively. In prayer most people are able to take themselves back to those events, first experiencing the pain again and then picturing the truth that Jesus was there when the event happened. Jesus does not change what actually happened, but He enables us to experience the fact that He was there, keeping His promise never to abandon us (Hebrews 13:5). This usually brings tremendous healing, whether for ourselves or for those we minister to. The authority that enables people to see and experience Jesus in a past event is the key to great freedom from the crippling effects of bad memories.

✎ Claiming Authority in the Present

As we have mentioned, we can assert God-given authority in the present over a home, classroom, office or church building. In addition, it is important that we assert the authority of Jesus over our workplaces. Those of us who work in offices should cleanse them by claiming the presence and power of Christ to banish any enemy spirits. We may or may not use anointing oil in the process. As I cleanse an office, I like to make the sign of the cross with blessed oil over the doors and windows. Then I speak a blessing of Jesus' presence on the office and all that goes on in it.

What is the "shelf life" of such cleansing prayers? The cleansing lasts until demons are given another right to enter. When a room is utilized by others before you use it again, it is a good idea to cleanse it whenever you are again in charge of it. As for workplaces like classrooms, workstations and offices that others (including cleaning personnel and night watchmen) enter after hours, I suggest taking authority over them daily to clean them as often as they are likely to get re-infected.

We do not need to discuss protection again except to note that this is a present authority we have been given. God's promise to "put his angels in charge of you to protect you wherever you go" (Psalm 91:11) is important to claim. We should also claim special protection for our children (Matthew 18:10; I will discuss authority within the family in chapter 12, including the authority coupled to our responsibility as parents to protect them).

It appears that, at least on certain occasions, we can use our authority to disable or disrupt the enemy's communication system to keep demons from hearing what we say. I do not know whether there are restrictions as to when we can do this, but I have been experimenting. When leaving on a trip, for example, I take authority over the enemy's communication system, forbidding it to be used to inform burglars or others who might do mischief or damage.

One Wednesday a woman called me from a city about twenty miles away to ask for prayer. As we talked it became obvious that she was probably demonized, and I decided to go to her home to minister to her. But before I made the appointment, I spoke to the spirit world, saying, "In the name of Jesus Christ, I forbid any spirits to hear what I'm about to say." Then we made an appointment for that coming Saturday. Three days later, I asked one of her demons if he had known I was coming. He replied, "No. She knew but wouldn't tell us." Then I asked if he had consulted the demons in the Pasadena area, where I live, to find out about my coming. "I couldn't," he answered. "You built a hedge around me so I couldn't get to them."

In dealing with demonized persons, I have frequently found it helpful to explain to the person what my strategy is and why I am doing something. But before doing so, I forbid the demons to hear what I will say. It seems to work, for when I have tested to see if they know what I talked about during the "blackout" period, they do not seem to. When we do this, however, we should remember to release demons from their inability to hear when we are finished dealing with the confidential matters; otherwise they will not respond to our direct commands, since they cannot hear us.

If you're not fighting, you're losing every time.

Guidance is another present need that we have authority to claim. When Jesus said He did only what He saw the Father doing (John 5:19) and said only what He heard the Father saying (John 8:28), He was speaking of guidance. He lived by that guidance—a blessing He could claim on the basis of His relationship with the Father rather than something He had to ask for. In claiming His right to guidance, though, He had to keep His eyes and ears open to the Father so as not to miss Him. This was Jesus' right. It is ours also.

✦ The Nature of Personal Attack

I already mentioned that I am often asked, "If I get into spiritual warfare, am I or my family in danger?" My answer is usually "Yes, but you're already on Satan's hit list by virtue of being a Christian. And if you're not fighting, you're losing every time. Wouldn't you like to learn how to win when you're attacked?"

Personally I can reflect with a good bit of regret on nearly four decades of such failure after my conversion. My ignorance of the authority God has given me enabled the enemy to keep me from either offensive or defensive interference with his activity. I have sometimes complained to God about the fact that He allowed me to be so ignorant for so long. He never answers such complaints, of course, but He did bring home an important truth while I was on a plane returning from an overseas trip.

The night before my flight, I had fought unsuccessfully for more than five hours to free a woman from a demon. In any war there are battles lost as well as battles won, and we had lost this one. Now, as I sat on the plane, I began to complain to the Lord about the fact that He had not enabled us to win this battle. Sometime during the discussion came the inaudible but distinct reply: *Well, at least this time you were fighting!* It was true. This time I had not been avoiding the battle out of ignorance, nor had I run or hid. And the Lord, without explaining why we had lost, expressed His pride in me that for once I had done the right thing.

There must have been many battles the Lord wanted me to wage during the first 38 years of my Christian life. But I lost them because I did not even know I was in a war. My commitment now is never to go down knowingly without a fight. And most of the time we get to win.

185

The enemy does not like it that we are here and connected with God. Frequently he attacks spiritually. Sometimes the attack is emotional in nature. It may even be physical. During one of my seminars a woman told me she had been accosted by a man with a gun. Having learned the authority she has in Christ, and assuming an evil spirit was motivating the man, she spoke to the spirit and forbade it to attack her. Looking straight at the man, she said, "This body belongs to Jesus Christ, and I forbid you, foul spirit, to hurt it." At that, the hand holding the gun fell to the man's side, he turned around sheepishly and he walked away!

Another woman told me of an incident with a dog. As she was out for her daily walk, she noticed a large, fierce-looking Doberman coming at her. Suspecting there might be a demon, she spoke to it authoritatively, much as the woman had addressed the spirit in the man with the gun, and the dog turned and slunk away without touching her.

The enemy likes to attack us when our resistance is down. When we sleep, we relinquish conscious control over our senses, making it easier for either God or Satan to get through to us. If the enemy has rights either to us as persons or to the building we are occupying, we can be attacked. Such attacks usually seem to happen, for some reason, between midnight and three o'clock in the morning. To prevent them, it is a good idea to claim the Lord's protection before going to sleep.

Often when a spirit attacks at night, people feel pressure on their bodies or on some part of their bodies. They may even experience a kind of paralysis. A friend of a colleague was asleep one night when she was attacked. She could not move and woke up in a panic, thinking she was dead. Although she was unable to talk, she could pray in her mind, and pretty soon she could say the name of Jesus. As her tongue was loosened, she began to rebuke the demon and it left her. Shaken, she called a friend, and they spent the rest of the night praying together. Later, in a deliverance and inner-healing session, the woman was delivered from a spirit of death that was generational. It seemed to be trying to scare her in her sleep.

Another friend woke up on several occasions feeling that claws were digging into his face; on one of these occasions, the pain in his eyes and mouth was so great that it prevented him from speaking. Each time this happened, he began calling on the name of Jesus in his mind, and before long he could speak Jesus' name aloud. Once he could do this, he was able to rebuke the demon and go back to sleep. It turned out that the owners of the house in which he was living kept a large collection of Indian and tribal art, and many of the objects were infested with demonic power.

Not infrequently the enemy attacks in dreams. Some people have reported to me that when they were attacked this way, instead of simply calling on Jesus and ending the dream, they attempted to stay in the dream long enough to invite Jesus to come and fight the enemy. It took some practice to stay partly asleep, but when they did, they were able to call on Jesus to take over, and He did, in some cases casting demons out of them during the dream.

Whether by night or day, attacks can often be stopped by using the authority we have to pray in tongues (if we have that gift). One friend tells me that whenever he begins to move into a mode of stress and fear in his work situation, he spends a few minutes at his desk quietly speaking in tongues. Invariably the tension lifts and God's perspective for his work returns. Whether through prayer or tongues, though, the result is merely to suppress the demonic activity, not to stop it permanently. To make the demons quit for good, their rights have to be taken away. This entails discovering what gives them their rights and then taking those away from them forever by the power of the Holy Spirit (see chapter 15).

✒ What to Do When Attacked

When we are attacked or suspect we are in danger, we need to assert our authority to protect ourselves. With that authority we can tell the enemy to back off because we belong to Jesus Christ.

There are several ways to assert our authority. My favorite way is to say, "If this is the enemy, stop it!" Sometimes simply calling out the name of Jesus is effective. At other times, reminding the enemy that we are members of God's family and under the blood of Jesus is appropriate, as is speaking in tongues or referring to or quoting Scripture. In any case, it is important to address the enemy directly in the authority of Jesus Christ.

Spiritual and Natural Weapons

When we are attacked, we must resist with both spiritual and natural weapons. If we are too tired and worn out to resist, we must sleep. If we have not eaten, a good meal may give us the strength to resist. We may need to exercise. We may need to cut some things out of our schedules so we have more time for God. We cannot count on Him to protect us if we are disobedient to natural rules.

A weapon that is both natural and spiritual is the support of the Body of Christ. Incredible strength can be imparted to us by those with like faith when we are under attack. We can join their authority to ours and be helped and uplifted by their gifting. When members of the Body of Christ find themselves under the weight of spiritual attack, therefore, calling on other believers for such things as prayer, advice and encouragement can enable them to overcome and defeat the enemy. The ones successful in spiritual warfare are those who have learned to surround themselves with other believers who share the struggles with them.

A man I will call Jared discovered the importance of the Body one Sunday when he came forward in church for ministry. Through tears he explained that the day before, he had been driving on the freeway when an intense fear overtook him in the driver's seat. He saw pictures in his mind from every angle of people around him trying to kill him by ramming their vehicles into his. The enemy was whispering in his ear, *I'm going to kill you. All these people want to ram you. You're going to die right here in traffic.* His drive turned into a nightmare of fear that almost paralyzed him in his seat. He was barely able to make it home,

When we are attacked, we must resist with both spiritual and natural weapons.

and he remained gripped by fear even after he got there. All that night the enemy came to him with threats, until by the time he came forward for prayer, he was a jumbled mess of frantic nerves.

As the team members prayed with Jared, they asked the Holy Spirit to enable them to break the power of this irrational fear. They asked God to show him that the threats he was hearing were lies, and they commanded the enemy to "stop it in the name of Jesus!" They claimed protection for Jared by the power of the Holy Spirit and felt impressed to speak strongly and decisively against fear, proclaiming to him the truth that God's protection rested on him as a believer and as one who walks with Jesus. They asserted the truth that, as a Christian, Jared was under the authority of Jesus, whose power is far greater than the power of the enemy. He was to respect the enemy's power and be wise to his schemes but to reject any fear of him, especially irrational fear.

As the ministry team spoke to and prayed with Jared, his countenance began to change. The truth, more powerful than the lies, permeated his heart and mind. He began to breathe more easily and comfortably, resting in God's peace and rejecting the lies of the evil one. His tears dried up, while hope and courage were visibly restored to him. Jesus had broken into the jumbled mess of his emotions, reorienting them in the truth of His sovereign protection.

Jared then needed to experience a complete inner-healing ministry to rid himself once and for all of the enemy spirits and what they were attached to. But for the time being, the enemy was called off and the harassment stopped. Such is often the case when people are invited forward in church. The presenting problem is addressed then and there, but longer ministry is needed to get the person completely free.

Using Scripture

One of the great privileges of the Christian life is the authority we are given to use Scripture when we are attacked. This is an especially good defense when the attack is sustained over a period of time.

We learn from the example of Jesus to use Scripture when confronted by the enemy. As Jesus submitted His life to God, the Holy Spirit led Him into the wilderness for forty days of fasting and prayer. There the devil tempted Him powerfully (Luke 4:1–13). Because Jesus was getting ready to begin His public ministry, the devil sought to divert Him from the Father's plan and get Jesus (like Adam earlier) to give up His authority. But Jesus countered each temptation from the enemy with Scripture.

Satan's suggestion that Jesus use His authority to turn stones into bread was met with Deuteronomy 8:3, which says that "you must not depend on bread alone to sustain you, but on everything that the Lord says." The temptation for Jesus to use His authority by throwing Himself down from the Temple, in order to stage a rescue and be caught by angels, was met with a quotation from Deuteronomy 6:16: "Do not put the Lord your God to the test." Finally Jesus countered Satan's offer of a quick way to authority over the world by quoting Deuteronomy 6:13: "Honor the Lord your God, worship only him."

In dealing with the enemy's temptations, Jesus was modeling the way for us to use Scripture when we are attacked by the enemy. We can and should hide God's Word in our hearts, as we are advised in Psalm 119:11: "I have hidden your word in my heart that I might not sin against you" (NIV). And we should speak it forth with our mouths to defeat the enemy in spiritual conflict—either quoting Scripture or reading it aloud.

The enemy does not like to hear Scripture! It is there that we learn we have the authority to "resist the Devil" and see him run away from us (James 4:7). The verse the enemy hates the most is the reminder in Colossians 2:15 of his defeat and humiliation. I have had demons cry out for me to stop reading that verse to them:

> On that cross Christ freed himself from the power of the spiritual rulers and authorities; he made a public spectacle of them by leading them as captives in his victory procession.

An especially rich source of scriptural ammunition to bring encouragement to those under attack is the Psalms. Many of these, called laments, were written by a person actually under enemy attack. Knowing that roughly 40 percent of the Psalms are of this nature helps me to know I am not alone in experiencing enemy attack. Some of the most useful passages I have found are Psalm 3:4; 6:8–10; 72:12–14; and 82:1–7.

David and many other Bible figures really went through it! Reminding ourselves of what God has done in the lives of His people in the past can take us from a place of confusion to a place of clarity with Jesus. This can be a source of great strength when we are under attack.

✽ Suggestions for Engagement

We can help people better handle the pain and suffering they will face when they move into spiritual warfare. The first thing is that we want to help free them from any internal garbage the enemy is using to attack them. After this, however, we need to remember Jesus' prediction that since the world hated Him, it will hate us also and will persecute us as it persecuted Him (John 15:18–20). Thus, when people come to me who are obviously under enemy attack, my first words to them are usually words of congratulation. They must be doing something right to attract the enemy's attention!

My friend and ministry colleague Mark White has developed the following list of ten suggestions to enable us to combat satanic activity:

1. *Always be alert.* Without becoming paranoid or mentioning spiritual warfare to any but those who understand, keep your spiritual eyes open to enemy activity. He likes to focus our attention on lies about ourselves and others and to disrupt relationships with others and with ourselves. Talk a lot to God about these things, claim His protection regularly and use your authority to plunder the enemy kingdom.

2. *Respond in love if Satan uses someone to attack you.* The enemy is the enemy, not the people he sucks into his operations.

3. *Respond in prayer.* Do not panic. Invite the Holy Spirit immediately into every volatile or potentially volatile situation. Use tongues if you have that gift.

4. *Do not fear.* Remember, there is nothing that can separate you from His love. You can trust this. Respond to the situation remembering this as a foundation.

5. *Be submissive to God.* The power for fighting lies in the place of reverent obedience to the Father.

6. *Rebuke the enemy with confidence and boldness.* Remember, the infinite power of God is on our side, and Satan's primary weapon is not power but bluff. Call his bluff and bring the love and power of Christ to bear on the situation.

7. *Ask the Holy Spirit to reveal spiritual strongholds in you that need to be broken and activity or attitude in your life that*

may be inviting the spiritual attack. Repent of any known sin and respond in forgiveness toward any person the Holy Spirit brings to your mind. When you find anything within yourself that you cannot take care of alone, seek others who know how to minister in God's power and work with them to get free.

8. *Read Scripture aloud.*

9. *Worship.* Play worship music. The enemy does not like to hear Jesus glorified.

10. *If physical and emotional stress is involved, as it often is, do the natural things to reduce the problem.* Take a nap. Rest. Eat a good meal. Take a hot bath. Bless yourself. Bless your head, your mind, your heart, whatever part of your body is tired or in pain.

Since we are to assert our authority not only as individuals but in the context of our families, we now turn to family matters.

12

Authority in Families

‎ಀ Family Devotions

Robert is a committed Christian who, like many fathers, has had great difficulty getting his children interested in family devotions. For years Robert tried everything he could think of, from enticement to coercion, to motivate his children to spend a bit of time each day with him and his wife reading the Bible and praying. But their cooperation was always grudging at best.

Then, in one of my seminar sessions at a church, Robert heard me suggest that fathers should let the evil spirit world know they are in charge of their families by making a statement such as "If you want my wife or any of my children, you have to go through me. And I'm not going to allow that." Robert went home and spoke those words. Apparently the enemy kingdom heard them, for something changed.

A couple of days later, in a follow-up meeting to the seminar, I asked if any of the participants would like to share anything. Robert stood and, with tears in his eyes, said, "Many of you know how fervently I've been praying that my children would willingly participate in family devotions, and how resistant they've been. So the other day, when Dr. Kraft taught us to take authority over our families by forbidding the enemy to go around, over or under us to get to our children, I tried it. And this morning my oldest son came to me asking if we couldn't get together for family devotions. It's a miracle!"

✠ The Husband/Father: Spiritual Gatekeeper

There is an ordering in the human world (as we have pointed out) that has spiritual significance. God is a God of order. And just as He has structured the universe in an orderly manner, He has structured the family so that each member has his or her place with its own privileges and responsibilities.

The purpose of differences within the family, as with the functioning of gifts in the Church (1 Corinthians 12:12–30), is so that the members will work complementarily for the good of the unit. And, as with the body called the *Church* (1 Corinthians 12:28), so with the body called the *family* do different members have different authority.

We have to be careful, though, not to attach more value to greater authority or visibility. Difference in function or status in no way makes one person worth more than another. In God's sight all humans are of equal value, whatever their position on the human scene. To God the poorest, least significant person (humanly speaking) is just as valuable as the president of a country or head of a bank. Likewise, in a family, the youngest child with the least authority is just as valuable to God as the father to whom, according to Ephesians 5:23, God has given authority over that family.

Differences in authority have important implications, however, for what God expects of a person. Those with great authority carry great responsibility, as well as risk of harsh judgment if they misuse their authority. In God's eyes, one in authority is a steward of that over which he or she has responsibility, and "the one thing required of such servants is that they be faithful to their master" (1 Corinthians 4:2). Jesus underlined this point with the parables of the talents (Luke 19:11–27), the faithful and unfaithful servants (Luke 12:42–48) and several others.

Faithfulness in heading a family is an awesome responsibility and challenge, especially since husbands are expected to use the authority we have been assigned as Jesus did—to love, serve and give ourselves to and for our families, even to death (Ephesians 5:25). "How did your family turn out?" is a question we husbands and fathers can expect God to ask us at judgment time.

Differences of authority are important not only to God; they are respected in the evil spirit world as well. It makes a difference, when we work to release a wife from demons, whether or not her husband is in favor. Often a husband's negativity toward our efforts makes it necessary for us to override his authority, as well as to break the demon's power, in order to get the wife freed.

One of my abiding memories from a recent seminar is the look of desperation on the face of a young wife who, though tormented by demons, could not get her husband's permission to receive ministry. With his agreement we could easily have freed her. Without his permission we could probably have freed her with difficulty. But he, probably following the orders of his own demons, watched her like a hawk and would not allow us to help her.

The apostle Paul was pointing to a rule of the universe when he stated that the husband has authority over the wife (Ephesians 5:23), extending even to authority over her body (1 Corinthians 7:4), just as the wife has authority over her husband's body. But although this rule confers privilege on husbands, there are corresponding rules for how this authority is to be exercised. Whatever privilege is thus allowed to husbands is to be tempered by their responsibility to exercise it according to God's guidelines.

Even though we are told that "a husband has authority over his wife just as Christ has authority over the church" (Ephesians 5:23), the rule is that such authority is to be exercised lovingly and with a giving, serving attitude, with Jesus Himself as our model (Ephesians 5:25; Colossians 3:19; 1 Peter 3:7). The command to love their wives was a shocker for first-century Greeks, since the ideal for a wife in Greek society was to never be noticed, either for bad or for good. By such a command, then, Paul was not only articulating God's rule but challenging Greek custom.

Ours is an authority to relate to our wives as Christ relates to His Church.

As husbands we are given authority under God over our wives. This is a law of the universe that, if broken, interferes with a husband's prayer life (1 Peter 3:7). Let's dissect what this authority involves.

It is authority first to love, then to care for, to respect, to sacrifice for and to protect our wives as more vulnerable (even "weaker," according to 1 Peter 3:7) than we are. Ours is an authority to relate to our wives as Christ relates to His Church. Indeed, we are commanded to treat them as Christ treats the Church, giving our lives for them as Jesus gave His life for His Church. This is an incredible mandate. It is authority involving far more responsibility than privilege—an authority that challenges our tendency to see authority as more a matter of rights than of duties.

One important responsibility of a husband is to protect his wife and family. Gary Runkle-Edens, a former student who has an inner-healing ministry with his wife, writes about how he learned to take this responsibility:

One day in a course I was taking from Dr. Kraft, I heard him mention that he believed we husbands have the responsibility to declare to all spiritual forces that they are forbidden to bother our wives. He advised us to speak out to the enemy powers in the universe, saying, "If you want my wife and family, you must go through me."

Honestly, I didn't take this advice very seriously, feeling it was a novel idea but impractical. I figured demons would bother whomever they were going to bother. But a few weeks later I noticed that Betsy seemed not to be sleeping well. In talking with her, I noticed how stressed and bothered she was from all she had experienced recently—leaving the church she was pastoring, moving across the country, looking for a new church, etc.

So one night I decided to do what I had been challenged to do. I declared to all cosmic powers, principalities and demons that I was God's appointed head to Betsy and our home. I ordered them to quit harassing Betsy and told them they had to go through me from now on if they wanted to get to her.

To my surprise Betsy's personal joy and zest for life seemed to return that week. She started sleeping better and being more carefree about life. I also noticed, however, that I seemed to be more spiritually attacked on all sides. A few days later it dawned on me that some sort of *enemy attack had been transferred to me!* So I started dealing with the enemy that was now harassing me.

This area is so important that I will give another testimony, this one from Natalie Stangl, a Swiss lady who has attended several of our seminars in Switzerland:

I was used to fighting by myself against the attacks of the enemy. My husband would pray for me every day. But he did not know the authority and responsibility he had as the head of our family.

I suffered for more than two years from one throat infection after another. There was not a month when I did not have throat pain and get hoarse to the point that I could not even speak. Since I am on the worship team at our church, this was a real problem. I began to get very discouraged.

Many people prayed for me, but the problem continued. I went twice to a throat specialist because I feared there might be some kind of growth on my vocal cords. But after looking at my throat and vocal cords, the doctor couldn't find anything wrong except an infection. He simply advised me to use my voice very carefully and to wait it out. I took some treatments from a vocal therapist. These helped. But as soon as the therapy was over, the problem came back.

Then, at a seminar led by Dr. Kraft, I learned that husbands can use their authority to protect their wives. So I went home and asked my husband, Andy, if he would start taking authority in the way Dr. Kraft suggested. He agreed, saying something like "I, Andy, as Natalie's husband, take authority in Jesus' name to forbid that any evil spirits attack my wife. I take all such attacks on myself." He spoke this way every day.

The results: From that day six months ago, I have been free from any attacks. Though recently I caught a cold, it had no effect on my throat. Andy, however, began to have the same kind of terrible throat pain and hoarseness that I had had! This went on for two weeks, then stopped.

(I suspect that since Andy had the authority to protect his wife, he could probably have spared himself the throat pain, too, by refusing to allow the enemy to attack him. See Dick Margeson's account in the next chapter.)

With regard to the spirit world, our authority is great when we obey the rules but is interfered with if we do not use what is granted us as God intends us to use it. As Nee observes in *Spiritual Authority* (1972), "If husbands wish to represent God's authority, they must love their own wives." Disobedience to God automatically means obedience to the enemy. If we men use wrongly the authority we have been assigned with respect to our wives and children, we cannot expect to be as resistant to satanic activity in our lives as we are meant to be. We will not be able to say, as Jesus could, that the ruler of this world "has nothing in Me" (John 14:30, NKJV).

Since parents have authority over children (as we will discuss in a moment), the husband and father's authority extends to the children as well. But again, there are rules. We need to treat our children well if we are to use in the spirit world the authority God has granted us (Ephesians 6:4; Colossians 3:21).

↫ Authority of the Wife/Mother

Wives are to submit to the loving authority of their husbands as the Church submits to the authority of Christ (Ephesians 5:24; Colossians 3:18; 1 Peter 3:1). They are to submit gladly, lovingly, respectfully (Ephesians 5:33) and sacrificially. Such submission makes wives beautiful, according to 1 Peter 3:5.

These commands and the ways they are to be worked out are the ideals we are to strive for. Other passages see to less-than-ideal situations, such as when the husband is an unbeliever (e.g., 1 Corinthians 7:14). But even then Peter advises wives to submit so that if their husbands "do not believe God's word, [their] conduct will win them over to believe" without their speaking a word (1 Peter 3:1). And in 1 Corinthians 7:14 we are taught that an unbelieving spouse and his or her children are "made acceptable to God" through union with the believing spouse.

We do not get as much help from Scripture as we could wish to deal with cases in which husbands abuse their authority. When love and patience do not win over the husband but only allow abuse to continue, steps need to be taken to protect the wife and even get her out of the abusive situation. Here, I believe, our concern should be more for the need to protect a person God loves from the attacks of the enemy than for seeing to it that she fulfills the ideal of wifely submission.

The wife's authority in the family is second to that of her husband but is by no means small. I once experimented with the use of 1 Corinthians 7:14 in dealing with a "family demon" (one who resides in more than one member of a family) who lived in a woman I will call Grace. This verse says,

> For the unbelieving husband is made acceptable to God by being united to his wife, and the unbelieving wife is made acceptable to God by being united to her Christian husband. If this were not so, their children would be like pagan children; but as it is, they are acceptable to God.
>
> 1 Corinthians 7:14

Both Grace and her husband, Jim, are deeply committed Christians, and though Jim was not present, we believed he would be willing to be freed if we could use his wife's authority to bring it about. So I said something like "On the basis of 1 Corinthians 7:14, and on the authority of this believing wife, Grace, I command all demons who are under this demon's authority and living in her husband, Jim, to come here and be joined to this demon." At that, the demon exclaimed to Grace, "How did he know about that authority? Nobody knows about that!"

On the basis of the authority of the believing wife, then, we were able to banish her demons and at least some of his—those under the authority of the demon with whom I was dealing in Grace.

On another occasion I was working to get a demon out of a woman whose husband was a Hindu. As I was getting information from the demon concerning what gave him his right to be there, I asked him if he had any authority over demons in her husband. He said, "Of course." So, using the authority of the believing wife, I commanded all the demons in her husband over which this demon had authority—for we had no rights over any of his demons who were not under the authority of this one—to join the demon and to leave with him. The demon said they had to do this, and I believe they left the husband when the wife's demons left her. If so, it was a combination of the power of Jesus and the wife's authority over her husband that canceled the demons' assignments and enabled me to send them away.

A wife joins her husband in parental authority over their children. And since she is more likely than he to have primary responsibility for raising them, she may have more opportunity than he to exercise authority. She also has authority over her husband's body (1 Corinthians 7:4). And, in the case of a believing wife with an unbelieving husband, she may have even greater authority than he in the spirit world, according to 1 Corinthians 7:14 (quoted above).

This verse applies specifically to children but, I believe, has broader application to the spiritual authority of believing wives. Many women whose husbands are unbelievers have used this authority, though perhaps unconsciously, to protect their children from the vulnerability to satanic attack that would ordinarily be their lot. That is, *since the head of the house belongs to Satan, the enemy would ordinarily have permission to do whatever he could get away with in that household.*

A wife joins her husband in parental authority over their children.

The presence of a believing wife and mother, however, automatically puts severe restrictions on what the enemy can do in that family. If this woman becomes aware of her right to exercise even more authority, both over her children and over her husband, the enemy is restricted further and defeated at many points in his attempts to influence the family.

Probably we all can point to families that have been led spiritually by a believing mother because the father is either an unbeliever or merely nominal in his faith. Often the children in such families are well protected from spiritual attack as they grow up and become strong in the Lord, in spite of their father's lack of relationship with God.

A mother's prayers will often reveal that she has been making requests of God for her children from before they were born. This is a right and important kind of activity. But a mother should also recognize and employ her authority in relation to the spirit world, challenging the enemy's right to do what he wants with her children. Just as a mother, whether human or animal, is known for her ferocity in protecting her offspring physically, so she should be known for her refusal to allow satanic interference in the lives of her children. She should exercise her authority regularly to restrict enemy activity in her children's lives, to protect them from the enemy and, if necessary, to attack the enemy if he bothers or threatens them.

In addition to a wife's authority over family members, she can claim at least delegated authority over such things as parts of a house (for example, a kitchen or workroom), a car or other personal possessions. She can and should spiritually cleanse the objects and spaces that are hers, either by ownership or because she is the primary user. The section "Single-Parent Families" in chapter 13 discusses a woman's authority in less-than-ideal situations (1 Peter 3:1–6).

Learning from Rules Concerning Vows

In Numbers 30 we learn some important principles concerning how God regards male and female authority relationships, so long as we believe (as I do) that the whole Bible is inspired and to be taken seriously. Some dispute passages like this one on the basis of current sensitivities concerning male-female status. But since there is no New Testament contradiction of the teaching in this passage, and since the demonic world takes such father-daughter and husband-wife authority relationships seriously, I think we need to listen, whether we like the way God has set things up or not.

The principles emerge from God's rules concerning vows, especially those made by women. At the beginning of Numbers 30, the author shows the direct authority relationship between God and males:

> When a man makes a vow to give something to the Lord or takes an oath to abstain from something, he must not break his promise, but must do everything that he said he would.

Numbers 30:2

The rule for a widow or divorced woman is similar; the vow is directly between her and God with no intervening authority, and she "must keep every vow she makes and every promise to abstain from something" (verse 9).

The rule for an engaged or married woman, however, is that any vow she makes can be broken by the man in authority over her, so long as it is canceled by the day after he hears about it. A young woman still living at home must keep any vow she makes unless her father uses his authority to cancel it (verses 3–5). If she gets married and her husband does not agree to her vow, he can use his authority to cancel it (verses 6–8). The vow of a woman already married, then, can be annulled by her husband if he does not like it, as long as he does it within the one-day time period (verses 10–14).

This passage gives us insight into several ways the authority of males operates in the spiritual realm. First we see the authority of a father over his unmarried daughter. Then we see the change that takes place when that daughter gets married and begins to function under her husband's authority. In both cases, although the women who made the vows are accountable directly to God for them, the men in authority over them are responsible to God to either approve or annul the vows. (Males, widows and divorced women are each responsible directly to God without the possibility of someone in authority over them annulling their vows.)

Horizontal and Vertical Authority

A mystical, spiritual unity exists between members of the same family. It has both horizontal and vertical dimensions. Horizontally we are connected tightly to siblings. Vertically we are connected tightly to parents and ancestors on the one hand and to descendants on the other. We may diagram these relationships as follows:

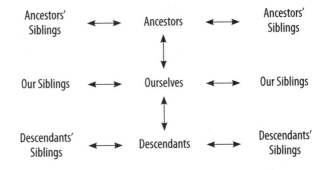

Such relationships involve authority. Since spiritual authority seems to be calibrated to human status, the normal horizontal authority hierarchy for most societies would have older siblings in authority over younger ones (although in some societies the youngest son has a special position). In all patriarchal societies and most matrilineal societies, brothers exercise authority over sisters. In Jewish and Greek societies, like most patriarchal societies, the first son has priority over the rest of the children in the family and enjoys a status about equal to that of the father. Again, brothers are over sisters.

Given these differences in status (not value), those with greater authority should exercise it to protect and bless those with less. On several occasions I have recommended to older sisters or brothers that they make use of their authority to break the enemy's power in what looks like an attack on a younger sibling. In some cases it seems to have worked. In other cases, either there was no report or else things did not seem to change.

A woman came to me recently as the youngest sibling in her family, and the only Christian, to express great concern for the salvation of her parents and other siblings, especially an older sister. My suggestion was for her to assert the authority of a believing younger sister (whatever that might be) and claim the breaking of the blinding spoken of in 2 Corinthians 4:4 in the lives of her loved ones. I have not heard whether there are any results. I would recommend, however, that my readers experiment with taking such authority in similar situations.

Those with greater authority should exercise it to protect and bless those with less.

Generational Ramifications

As for our vertical relationships, we have already pointed out that what we do with our authority has ramifications for our descendants. We see several examples of inherited blessing in the Old Testament. God was generous to Israel for several generations, in spite of their disobedience, because of the faithfulness of Joseph (Exodus 1:7), Moses, Joshua (Joshua 24:31) and, of course, David (1 Kings 11:34–36; 2 Kings 8:19), among others. The faithfulness of these men of God resulted in blessing and protection for a certain number of their descendants.

But God's patience is not without limits. He says in the Ten Commandments, "I bring punishment on those who hate me and on their descendants" (Exodus 20:5). We find references throughout Scripture to the accountability of succeeding generations for the sins of their ancestors. As Lamentations 5:7 states, "Our ancestors sinned, but now they are gone, and we are suffering for their sins." People like Daniel, Shadrach, Meshach and Abednego, who found themselves in captivity in Babylon (Daniel 1; 3), were not being punished for their own sins but for those of their predecessors. And Jeremiah 15:4 states that, several generations later, "all the people of the world" would be "horrified" at Israel's plight as a result of God's judgment on King Manasseh.

Among the most vivid examples of God visiting judgment on later generations is what He did to the descendants of Eli. God wiped out Eli's house because he did not rein in his sons, Hophni and Phinehas (1 Samuel 2:27–34; 4:11). The punishment was not simply because of his sons' disobedience but because of Eli's negligence (1 Samuel 2:29). God expected Eli to assert his authority to keep his sons on track even after they were grown. But Eli's sons had become "scoundrels" (verse 12), and although he attempted to bring them back into line, "they would not listen to their father" (verse 25). God held Eli responsible, therefore, and cursed his family because of the behavior of his sons, "so that no man in your family [except one who will become blind] will live to be old. . . . And all your other descendants will die a violent death" (verses 31, 33).

There is a single passage, however, that seems to counter the general teaching and illustrations from Scripture concerning the accountability of descendants for the sins of their ancestors:

> The Lord spoke to me and said, "What is this proverb people keep repeating in the land of Israel? The parents ate the sour grapes, but the children got the sour taste. As surely as I am the living God, says the Sovereign Lord, you will not repeat this proverb in Israel any more. The life of every person belongs

to me, the life of the parent as well as that of the child. The person who sins is the one who will die. . . . It is the one who sins who will die. A son is not to suffer because of his father's sins, nor a father because of the sins of his son. Good people will be rewarded for doing good, and evil people will suffer for the evil they do."

Ezekiel 18:1–4, 20

Whether God has changed the rules, I cannot say. But we learn from this passage that each of us is responsible for our own behavior, regardless of whether our guilt gets passed down to following generations.

An important part of the vertical oneness of families is our need to repent for the sins of our ancestors. This is what I am calling *identificational repentance*. In Leviticus 26:40 the Lord predicts that, while in exile, "your descendants will confess their sins and the sins of their ancestors," leading to God's forgiveness and restoration. In Jeremiah 14:20 the people of Judah confess both their sins and those of their ancestors. Such accepting and repenting for the sins of ancestors were an important part of Nehemiah's reforms (Nehemiah 9:2). Daniel, too, was led to confess the sins of his people and ask forgiveness for his ancestors (Daniel 9:5–19).

The Father As Spiritual Gatekeeper

A major implication of the headship of the father/grandfather is the fact that he is the spiritual gatekeeper for the family. This means that whatever spiritual influences enter the family come as a result of the exercise of his authority to consciously or unconsciously give or withhold permission. The father is in the position either to allow negative or to invite positive spiritual influences into his family; he is thus responsible to protect his family from enemy intrusion. Unfortunately, many men (like Andy, whose wife kept getting throat infections) have no idea of their authority and responsibility in this regard, nor how to exercise it. Consequently the enemy specializes in going around, over or under the heads of family who neglect their responsibility as spiritual protectors.

I have ministered to many people whose lives are scarred by the influence of evil spirits invited by fathers or grandfathers who gave themselves and their families over to spirits of Freemasonry. Most of these people have not belonged to a Masonic organization or taken any Masonic oaths themselves. All the rights the spirits of Freemasonry had over them came from the authority granted by their fathers or grandfathers. These spiritual authority figures had not simply joined an organization; through the oaths they took and the allegiance they pledged to the god of that organization (Lucifer), they committed themselves *and their families*, often quite unconsciously, to Satan.

A father is in a position, by the same token, to provide protection and even rescue for his family. I have seen several instances of fathers who were able to free their children from problems by asserting their authority against the harassment of the enemy.

The husband/father's authority carries with it responsibility for whatever goes on in the home and family. He is to be the one who protects by providing the necessary prayer covering, who guides by listening to and following God's instructions, who rises up to defend when the family is attacked. "You can't have access to my wife or children" is his constant word to "the spiritual powers in space" (Ephesians 2:2). His shield of faith[fulness] is raised constantly on his and his family's behalf "to put out all the burning arrows shot by the Evil One" (Ephesians 6:16). His ears are to be open constantly to the voice of God.

Like the patriarchs of old, the husband/father is the family priest with responsibility and authority both under God and toward the family. This authority and responsibility relate to the spirit world, too, both to demons and to God's angels. And the authority of the husband/father over the family has a cosmic dimension, which seems to be the reason that Adam, not Eve, is blamed for the entrance of death (Genesis 3; 1 Corinthians 15:21–22). It was in Adam, not Eve, that we all sinned and forfeited our relationship with God and our sovereignty over the created world.

Authority of Parents

Ephesians 6:1–4 and Colossians 3:20 speak of the duty of children to obey and honor parents. This commandment, Paul says, is the first one with a promise attached: "So that all may go well with you, and you may live a long time in the land" (Ephesians 6:3). The authority of parents, although not stated explicitly, is assumed, and respect for that authority required.

But again, there are rules for the exercise of parental authority. As parents we are not to "treat [our] children in such a way as to make them angry. Instead, raise them with Christian discipline and instruction" (Ephesians 6:4). We are not to "irritate [our] children, or they will become discouraged" (Colossians 3:21).

I am not sure how long parental authority remains in effect over one's children, or how this relates to their own choices. Do I still have the authority to protect my grown children after they marry and establish their own families? I think I do. And I would point to the patriarchal structuring of Old Testament families, like those of Abraham, Isaac and Jacob, as possible bases for such exercise of authority. The way in which authority

The authority of the husband/father over the family has a cosmic dimension.

and honor were structured in those families may be more than simply cultural. It may be a transcultural pattern that points us to God's ideals for families of every society.

So I take what I believe to be my responsibility by exercising my authority as the head of my home, claiming protection regularly for my children and their spouses (even though they are grown and on their own), their children and spouses (my grandchildren) and their children (my great-grandchildren). I let the spirit world know that access to any of my children and their spouses, my grandchildren and their spouses and my great-grandchildren has to come through me, and that is not going to happen because of the authority Jesus has granted me.

If my children, grandchildren or great-grandchildren choose to disobey God, however, I am not sure how much influence my claim of protection has in their lives. The tragic story of the prophet Eli and his wayward sons seems to relate to this topic as well. Eli probably claimed protection for Hophni and Phinehas but because of their choices could not keep them from ruin. On the other hand, their bad choices probably stemmed from a lack of proper early training. Eli and his wife seem not to have done a good job at this.

As in our relationship with God, a father's desires can be thwarted by a child's choices. Even so, fathers carry a major responsibility for their children's choices and actions.

13

More on Family

🌿 Dealing with Adoption

When children are adopted, there are special considerations to be made. The first thing to remember, once again, is that the spirit world works according to human authority rules. When the adoption is official on earth, it is official in heaven. And from the time it is official, the new parents have the right to assert their authority over the child.

But the fact that the child is under new authority does not automatically cancel whatever rights the enemy may have had over the child. And the circumstances that led the biological parents to give up their rights to the child often mean enemy spirits have rights over the youngster. A child conceived through rape, adultery or violence, for example, or carried in the womb in a situation of abuse, unwantedness, mixed emotions, contemplation of abortion or abandonment is sure to be demonized.

This means the adoptive parents need to take authority over both the ancestry and the circumstances of the child's conception, gestation and birth in order to break any enemy power the child may be carrying (more on this below). It can be done while the child is asleep, if he or she is small, or with his or her participation.

The key thing to accomplish is the cancellation of all rights the enemy may have gained through the birth parents' family line and any rights he has gained due to the circumstances of the conception, pregnancy, birth and giving up for adoption by the biological parent(s). Among these rights may be those that have come through cursing, abandonment by the father, contemplating or attempting an abortion or miscarriage, or any of the other circumstances mentioned above. Much of this information may be hidden from the adoptive parents during the negotiations leading to the adoption. Even so, it is good to take authority over such things, even if you are not sure they happened. Why? Because it is better to clean a house that is not dirty than to leave one that is dirty simply because one is not certain that it needs cleaning.

In one seminar I was approached by an eighteen-year-old I will call Joe, accompanied by his adoptive parents. He could not understand why he hated them since, by his own admission, they had treated him wonderfully all his life. Joe was asking for prayer ministry to break through this problem. In addition, he hated himself and had wanted to die for as far back as he could remember.

To start with, I led him in a discussion of the probable circumstances of his biological mother's decision to give him up. My aim was to help Joe understand what it must have been like for an unmarried young woman who had made a mistake by getting pregnant and whose boyfriend had run off, taking no responsibility and perhaps even pushing for an abortion. Knowing nothing about the actual circumstances, we assumed all this to be true, plus the dilemmas his biological mother must have faced over when and how to tell her parents, whether or not to abort her child and what to do with him once she chose to carry him to full term—all the while hoping for a miscarriage. Joe could understand how his biological mother had probably concluded that adoption would be the most loving thing to do, rather than the irresponsible decision to abandon him.

On the basis of these understandings, then, and with the help of the Holy Spirit, Joe was able to forgive his biological mother, as well as his natural father. After this forgiveness step, we took authority over his ancestry (as outlined in chapter 12) and, in the name of Jesus Christ, canceled any enemy rights to him through sin, vows, curses or dedications in the family lines of his biological father and mother.

Having done this, I challenged any demons that might be there and found four main spirits (fear, anger, hatred and self-rejection). These spirits were severely weakened because we had gone over Joe's ancestry and he had extended forgiveness. So all we had to do was cancel the rights they had been given by his natural parents during his gestation and birth, and any rights Joe had given them during his life to this point. They went quietly, leaving Joe incredibly free and, for the first time in his life, expressing genuine love and gratitude as he hugged his adoptive parents.

To break enemy authority over adopted youngsters, we may use words such as the following:

> In the name of Jesus Christ, we take authority over all the circumstances of this person's conception, gestation and birth. He forgives his biological parents for their mistakes and attitudes and thanks God for allowing him to be adopted. On the basis of the authority given us by Jesus Christ and by his adoptive parents, we cancel all rights the enemy has been given, consciously or unconsciously, by his biological parents, grandparents or any others.

At this point I usually challenge any demons that might be there and seek to find out what, if any, additional ground they may have been given by those in authority over the person, or by the person himself or herself. Then I take that ground away and send the demons to Jesus.

I received a telephone call from a distraught mother I will call Adele. She could not figure out how to stop what was going on with her eleven-year-old daughter, adopted at age three from a war-torn country in southeast Asia. Apparently the daughter had spells of rebellion characterized by temper tantrums that disrupted the family greatly. Worse, she had a very low self-image, according to Adele, and spoke of suicide a lot. In fact, she had already made several small attempts to end her life, and the family feared she would accomplish her goal. Adele and her husband had taken her to a series of counselors, but the problem persisted.

Since this call came from a distance, I needed to advise Adele how to work with the Holy Spirit to bring freedom to her daughter. So I made several suggestions, all with the aim of helping her "do it herself," since she has the same Empowerer I have. Thankfully the family is Christian, so I could assume the power of the Holy Spirit at their end.

These suggestions can serve as a sort of outline for what to do if you find yourself, as Adele did, far from an expert in spiritual warfare:

1. *Assert authority over the family.* The first thing is for the father to assert his authority over his family. As we have seen from several illustrations, it is important for him to do this before the evil spirit world in order to cancel whatever other authority there might be, and to break whatever power the enemy has been able to gain. Adele's husband needed to make obvious both to himself and to the spirit world that he had legal authority over the child (since we have seen that the previous authority over the child continues until it is overtly canceled by the present legal authority).

I advised Adele to ask her husband to state to the spirit world something like this: "I am the head of this home, the protector of my wife and children. If anyone out there wants to get at them, they have to go through me. And I refuse to allow this."

2. *Take authority over the child's ancestry.* It is important to take authority over *any* child's ancestry, but it is especially important for adoptees and crucial for those coming from societies in which it is routine to dedicate children to spirits. I advised Adele to join her husband in canceling all rights the enemy may have gained over their child through agreements made by the child's biological parents and ancestors, in both the father's and mother's lines.

We have already noted that this involves the breaking of all vows, curses (both from the outside and from self-curses), dedications (in this case, generations of dedications to Buddhist and shamanistic spirits), rights given through sin and rights taken by the enemy in times of trauma and distress (as was likely in the warfare situation in which the child's parents lived).

3. *Cancel any direct dedications.* A third area to cover is the possibility (in this case, almost certain) that the child may have been dedicated to spirits or taken to spirits for healing or blessing. Given the girl's cultural background, it is likely that her parents dedicated her to their family spirits. It is also probable that she was taken to spirit healers at various times any time she became ill in the three years before Adele and her husband adopted her. It is important, therefore, to cancel all rights the enemy may have gained through dedication to or healing by evil spirits.

4. *Do housecleaning.* Next I advised Adele to do some housecleaning. I suggested that she and her husband take complete authority over their home and the land on which it sits. They needed to cancel any rights of the enemy to their property, gained through agreements or through sin that occurred under past owners or users, by asserting their rights as the present owners to break any power the enemy still had. Then I suggested they go through the house room by room, taking authority over every space—especially their daughter's room—for Jesus.

At that point Adele told me she had already had a disturbing demonic visitation one night in their bedroom. This suggested to me that the enemy probably had some rights in their home, stemming either from past agreements or rights related to their daughter.

5. *Assert your authority verbally.* A fifth suggestion I made is that Adele and her husband make use of the command "If this is the enemy, stop it!" It is likely that the assertion of such authority will help when the daughter acts up, when there is an argument or when there is indication that the daughter is struggling with thoughts of self-destruction or other problems.

6. *Get deep-level healing.* A sixth important area to deal with is the deep-level healing the daughter needed. For their little girl, working on self-image and early-life trauma was probably very important. She needed to experience the fact that Jesus was present and protecting her during what may have been very traumatic experiences before she was born and in her first three years. She also needed to know deep inside herself that she was planned "before the foundation of the world" (Ephesians 1:4, NKJV) and that she is now a princess in the Kingdom of the most high God. When she assimilates these truths, they will transform her self-image and set her on a new course of freedom in her life.

In such situations it is also a good idea to do inner healing with the parents and any siblings to cover the whole family tree.

Authority of Children

What authority, if any, does a child have? All the previous rules apply to them. Children have rights over whatever they own or whatever they are granted authority over. In the former category fall toys, bicycles, athletic equipment and other possessions. In the latter, a youngster who is assigned a bedroom, for example, has authority over that room.

At a seminar where I had been teaching on authority in the home, I was approached by a young Asian woman concerned about the ability of the enemy spirits in her home to influence her. She asked, "What rights do I have in my parents' home where I live? I'm a Christian, but they are devout Buddhists with a very large and obvious ancestral shelf in the living room, and countless Buddhist artifacts everywhere except in my room."

I recommended that she focus on three goals: keeping herself clean spiritually so the enemy would not have rights to her, claiming protection for herself when she was in any part of the house other than her own room and asserting her God-given authority over her room and any other parts of the house she had rights over.

These three areas are important for anyone to tend to, especially if living in a place belonging to someone else.

✦ Authority to Bless Unborn Children

Although there is some controversy over what preborn children are aware of, my experience leads me to accept what Dr. Thomas Verny and John Kelly have written in *The Secret Life of the Unborn Child* (1981). The following perspective assumes, with Verny, that life begins at conception and that a preborn child begins gaining consciousness of what is going on in the outside world after about six to eight weeks of gestation. Every attitude and event that goes on in the mother's life from at least that

A preborn child begins gaining consciousness of what is going on in the outside world after about six to eight weeks of gestation.

time, perhaps even earlier, gets recorded in the baby's brain and can affect him or her subconsciously. Thus, experiencing rejection at this early age can become a major problem later in life.

For this reason it is important that each child have a good experience in the womb. Verny's studies and others seem to show that preborn children know quite a bit about what is going on in the lives of their parents and siblings. If there is fighting, violence or abuse, the preborn child senses an uncongenial environment. And if the parents prefer a child of the opposite sex, or do not want a child at all, the preborn child knows it and may even make the birth difficult.

A major problem is that the preborn child does not have a context for the feelings that come his or her way. The child does not know that grown-ups can make mistakes, so he or she blames any problems on him- or herself. I had this problem myself, since my parents were not married when I was conceived. So the first signals I received in the womb were of rejection. With no understanding of adult life, I interpreted this as rejection of myself, which it was not, rather than as rejection of a pregnancy, which it was. As a result I assumed there must be something wrong with me and hated myself.

To make sure the child has a good prebirth experience, prospective parents can use their authority to bless and communicate love and acceptance to their preborn child. The best guide I know for expectant parents is Francis and Judith MacNutt's book *Praying for Your Unborn Child* (1988). Taking the authority we are given to pray over unborn children, as they point out, makes a big difference in the children's lives.

One of the illustrations recorded in the book contrasts a pregnancy without prayer with one in which the parents and their three-year-old daughter, Jenny, daily "took time to talk and pray with our baby." They prayed,

> Dear Lord, we ask you to bless and protect our baby, to fill [him/her] with your love, your peace and your joy—to surround this little baby with the warmth of your love. We ask you to help [him/her] grow and develop into the beautiful child you want [him/her] to be. Thank you for this baby and for blessing us and entrusting us with this new life.

Although the mother had been sick during most of her first pregnancy (before they had learned to pray over a preborn child) and labor and delivery had been "long and hard," things were different with this one. The second pregnancy was "much better physically—and much more peaceful." The birth took place in a "relaxed atmosphere" in a birthing room, and Jenny was allowed to join her parents soon after the birth. The baby, Albert, "just looked around and was very peaceful and content." The mother continues,

> He seemed to recognize each one of our voices, especially Jenny's. As the weeks went by, we noticed how happy and peaceful he was, and, to our surprise, others also commented on Albert's joyful personality. Finally, we realized that our praying for Albert in the womb accounted for his peaceful, pleasant personality. Now he is a year and a half old; his personality is still joyful and peaceful.

Former members of my ministry team, Gary and Kathleen Hixson, who now minister in Spain, had a similar experience with their firstborn daughter. As soon as they found out they were expecting, they began to systematically bless and communicate with their little one. Never has a preborn child been the recipient of more love, care and the impartation of the love and blessing of God than this one! Though we cannot be sure, I regard it as highly likely that this prebirth activity has a lot to do with the fact that Sarah, now a teenager, was and is one of the happiest, most content and best-adjusted children I have ever seen. And she is a big help to her father in ministry.

Authority over Our Homes

The authority of the head of a household extends to the territory in which the family lives. The head of the family, and the other family members as well, have legal rights in the spirit world over the family's residence. This right of ownership is respected in the spirit world. So are the legal rights granted through a rental arrangement, the loan of a residence or a less formal arrangement.

Sometimes a family buys or rents a home that has been dedicated to the enemy or over which Satan has gained authority through sin. Sins such as adultery, violence, occult activity or wrongful death that occur in a house may give the enemy enough authority to make life very difficult for the next owner or occupant. Again, the rules for such authority apply regardless of whether we know, understand or agree with them.

> *This right of ownership is respected in the spirit world.*

If a house or apartment has been used for evil purposes before we bought or rented it, the enemy may have rights to do things there without our permission. Our legal right to own or rent that house or apartment also gives us the authority, however, to cancel any claims the enemy can make because of previous agreements, whether those agreements were made verbally or through behavior. Likewise with land and other property.

A woman I will call Sue experienced strange fears and other disagreeable feelings when she got up in the night to feed her baby. The feelings always seemed strongest in the hallway just outside her bedroom door. Then we learned that a previous occupant of the house had been practicing New Age rituals in that hallway; indeed, there were still traces of candle wax there. So with the encouragement of her husband, we claimed their authority as the present owners of the house, plus the power of Christ, to cancel all previous agreements, and we were able to get rid of whatever enemy spirits were operating there. There has been no such problem since then.

We said something like this:

In the name of Jesus, we assert the authority of the present owner of this house to cancel all agreements with previous owners and all rights given to the enemy by them. We thus break all satanic power over this house and the land on which it stands, and we bless them with the power of Jesus Christ.

Then we anointed the doors and windows of the whole house with anointing oil that had been blessed, making the sign of the cross in oil on each place. (It is not necessary for the anointing to be in the sign of the cross; that is just the way I choose to do it. Some simply rub the oil on.)

With houses and land, it is good to pray back over their history, asserting the present owner's authority back to the beginning of time to cancel any enemy rights. Although I cannot claim to know all that is going on, I have been involved in many situations in which taking authority to break satanic power, obtained through events that have occurred in homes, has made a big difference. I have prayed over land that served as the regular place of warfare, land that was once Indian burial ground, houses in which violence and even murder took place, a college dormitory in which a New Age devotee had lived and other places in which strange things were happening, although we did not know the specific reason. To my knowledge, there were major changes in each place after we prayed.

In one case a demon claimed to have influence over a woman herself, not just over her house, because of adultery that had occurred there prior to her purchase of it. When we asserted the power of Jesus to cancel all authority given through the previous owner's sin, the demon's power was greatly weakened, and we had no difficulty getting him out.

The way the enemy works and what to do about it is well described in the personal experience of Gary Runkle-Edens:

After Betsy and I got married, I moved into the beautiful house and half acre she had purchased when she moved to Ohio. Despite the fact that we were very compatible, excited and happy together, I became troubled. I found that when I was home, I had a lot of critical thoughts about Betsy. I was thinking about all the ways she needed to change and grow. This began to affect our relationship.

As I prayed about it, I felt God revealing to me that I was being attacked spiritually. So I proceeded to go through every single room in our house, anointing them with oil and taking authority over any demonic intruders. Within a few hours I noticed a tangible difference in the atmosphere (and my thought life) in the house. But I failed to notice that when I went outside to do yard work, these thoughts continued to bother me. Because we had a huge yard, I was outside a lot, especially during the summer months. I worked really hard and fast and tried to think about anything other than Betsy's faults.

Finally one day I got down on my knees and said, "Lord, haven't I prayed over the house? Why is this still happening?" I heard the Lord reply, *You forgot the yard.* Though surprised that I would have to take authority over the yard, too, I went right to it. I grabbed my anointing oil and proceeded to walk the perimeter of our half-acre lot, taking authority over it.

After that I had some of the most peaceful and wonderful yard work experiences ever! Not only did I not think critical thoughts about Betsy, but in the following months God used my outdoor work as a time to birth an incredible new vision for ministry. If I sensed enemy attack in the yard after that, I commanded it away, and away it would go!

But this was not the end of Gary and Betsy's problems. When they moved across the country to California about a year later, they found themselves at each other's throats in the new apartment. Thinking this was due to the stress of the move, Gary did nothing about it at first, even though the unease and temper flare-ups lasted a full six weeks. Then Gary records,

As I struggled one evening in prayer, I heard the Lord say, *Go through the apartment and anoint it with oil and take authority over it.* Well, I was too worn out to do it that night. And the next day, in my busyness, I simply forgot about it. But by that next day, our sour moods became unbearable. It was then that the Lord reminded me again. So not only did I go through and take authority and anoint our apartment, but I even did this to the entire apartment complex! It was as if something broke immediately. Within a few hours we were back to being happy and compatible. God revealed to us that the enemy had lain in wait to ambush us on our arrival in California.

But that was still not the end of the story. Gary and Betsy were living in their apartment without a written contract, and when a notice came for them to appear at the housing office to sign their contract, they did not get around to it right away. Gary writes,

Then we began to notice that our problem of short tempers and negative attitudes had returned. Despite my taking authority over the apartment almost daily, these persisted. As I cried out to God over the matter, I sensed the Holy Spirit saying, *The enemy has found out you don't have a contract!*

It didn't take me long to get down to the housing office and sign our contract. That night it was as if the enemy was upset, and we had a difficult night. The next morning I declared to the enemy that we were now fully legal contractual renters and they must leave. We have been back to normal since that moment.

❧ Delegating Authority

Authority can be delegated to someone else. This can be done any time we leave home, even to go to work.

I have mentioned that husbands going on a trip can delegate total authority over home and children to their wives. Whenever

I Give You Authority

a husband goes away, it is important for him to assert his authority to protect his family in his absence. My approach to this is simply to claim protection, regularly and pointedly, when I go away. If my wife stays home or if someone else is left in charge, I let the spirit world know that that person has my full authority while I am gone.

Before we learned to do this, my wife, Meg, and I found that when I went away on a trip, things often broke down, or the children had accidents or got sick, and almost invariably she and I would have one argument before I left and another when I returned. So I learned first to forbid the enemy to cause us to argue, and then to speak protection over our home and all the people and things that reside there. Finally I would state to the spirit world that my wife has my full authority while I am gone. Things have changed dramatically since I learned to do this. Now things rarely go wrong when I travel, and Meg and I rarely even have a difference of opinion.

Authority can be delegated to someone else.

This kind of protection is especially important when children are involved. One of my ministry team members, Dick Margeson, shares the following illustration from his life:

I have been privileged to go on several ministry team trips. Somewhere along the way, it began to dawn on me that whenever I went away, my oldest son, Zachary, age five, would misbehave. He would often begin to misbehave as soon as I drove out of the driveway, and his behavior affected the other children. Out of concern for this problem, I consulted several I could trust, including a psychotherapist who had considerable experience with children. All felt, as I did, that Zach's behavior was in reaction to my leaving for these trips. Their suggestion was that I leave him with something of value that belonged to me.

Before leaving for our next weekend trip, I let Zach keep my pocket watch. On the second day of the trip, I called home from Arizona to find out how things were. My wife reported that Zach was up to his usual misbehavior, but that at least he had slept well that first night. He continued to struggle that weekend until I returned.

On my return, it finally dawned on me that the problem we were having had spiritual roots. I knew that the enemy spirit world takes the father's authority seriously but that I hadn't taken the steps to assure the safety of my family while I was away. While the high priest of the family is away, evil spirits will search for any advantage they can get to attack those left behind, especially if the father/husband is in a ministry they don't like.

So I decided to take the necessary steps to assure that there would be no more of this kind of spiritual problem, whether I am away or at home. The first thing I did was declare to all the spirits that I am the high priest in my family and that if I am away, at any time and for any reason, my wife, Marcia, assumes my role. Second, I let the satanic world know that my children have been dedicated to the most high God and that evil spirits do not have my permission to disturb my family. Third, I declared that since I am the high priest of my family, any spirits who would like to destroy my children, and particularly Zach, must come through me first. And finally I told them that, in addition to refusing to allow evil spirits to attack my family, I as the husband and father, in the position of authority in my home—a child of God, saved by the blood of the Lamb—absolutely forbade any of them to attack me either.

Marcia and I also embarked on a program to teach our children Scripture that they could speak out whenever they felt they were under attack. We instructed them that attacks might come in the form of dreams, temptations or anything that did not seem right. Teaching our children Scripture has given them authority of their own to deal with the enemy.

My next trip was to Toronto, Canada. This trip would be longer than the last, and busier. Before I left, I took authority over each member of my family, stating specifically that my wife was in charge both physically and spiritually. I also reminded Satan's army that I am a warrior in the army of the most high God, and that while I am away, my wife is the high priest in my absence.

Because we were busy in Toronto, I didn't get to check in at home until the second day. To my relief, Marcia was feeling great, the kids were doing very well and problems in general appeared to be minimal. The fact that I had passed on my authority to my wife seems to have done the trick.

And this approach has continued to work well. When I am home, I continually remind the enemy that the Spirit of the living God is in charge of our family. And when I go away, I let them know Marcia has my full authority.

If a husband goes to work and his wife stays home, especially if she has young children to take care of, it is a good idea to make explicit to the spirit world that she has her husband's full authority. A major reason for this: Demons are very active in attempting to disrupt family relationships. They like to goad children into behaving badly when Dad is away, even if he is just at work. Men have reported to me that after they started speaking to the spirit world in this way each day as they left for work, it made a big difference in the behavior of their children. And when they spoke protection over the home, they experienced fewer mechanical breakdowns in appliances or cars.

> *Demons are very active in attempting to disrupt family relationships.*

When parents go away and leave their children with someone else, they delegate their full authority—over the children and usually over the home as well—to those they leave in charge. It is good to recognize this when selecting babysitters, or even when leaving the children with relatives. When we turn our homes and children over to someone else, we are granting that person our rights for whatever period of time we are away. It is wise, therefore, to speak out into the spirit world that this person is operating under our authority, not simply on her or his own. This can keep pesky spirits from taking advantage of the situation.

Unfortunately, I have had to deal with several missionaries who left their children with the wrong caretakers, who either innocently or by design got their children demonized. Some situations in missionary schools have recently come to light in which the authority granted to the houseparents was misused. Such situations are especially sad, since they affect numbers of innocent children.

In an earlier chapter I mentioned a man in his thirties who had carried a demon since he was five. When I asked the demon what right he had to be there, he told me a nanny had given Arthur to him when he was about five years old and living with his parents in a Latin American country. It may be that while Arthur was under the authority of the babysitter, he got sick and the babysitter did what she normally did: Intending no harm, she called on some spirits to heal him. Or she may have been under demonic assignment and passed on a demon knowingly. In any event, the babysitter used the authority she was given over Arthur to invite demons into him. And Arthur, with no knowledge that the demons were there, had been struggling against them all his life.

Single-Parent Families

It is good for parents to understand and take the authority God has given them. But what if either husband/father or wife/mother is missing? What about situations in which the mother or father is alone in raising the children because the spouse has abdicated responsibility or has died?

I believe the statements recorded in Numbers 30 concerning responsibility for vows point us to the right approach here. We noted in our earlier discussion that in verse 9, a widow or divorced woman has the same responsibility for her vows as does a man. I believe she has the same authority a man has as head of a home.

But some women are uncomfortable with this understanding of their authority. They prefer to find a man—sometimes a pastor, sometimes a relative—to be for them what is often called a "covering." This can be arranged simply by getting a man to agree to assume the spiritual authority that a husband or father would carry. This is an awesome responsibility, for it means (among other things) that any attempt to attack the woman might land on the man who has agreed to be her covering. If he is vulnerable in some way, he can encounter difficulty (as Andy, mentioned earlier, did when he started getting the throat pain his wife had had). If the man is spiritually clean, however, so that the enemy can find nothing in him (John 14:30), any woman who puts herself under his protection gains great status in the spirit world.

To take such authority, the man must agree to be the covering for the woman. He may assume this role as a pastor, as a surrogate father or grandfather, as a leader of some group (for example, a Bible study) that the woman belongs to or just as a friend to whom the woman chooses to give this authority. In assuming this role, the man simply speaks to the spirit world, stating that he is claiming the spiritual authority over her that the woman has requested. Such arrangements speak loudly to the spirit world and provide great spiritual benefits to the women who make them.

I believe the same kind of covering can be effective with men as well as with women. Several men who work with me as members of a ministry organization find that my authority to protect or bring healing to them is greater than that of others who pray for them. I believe this is because they have granted me a kind of spiritual covering for them.

✧ Relinquishing Authority

There are times and circumstances when we either relinquish or forfeit our authority. Less permanent forms of relinquishment occur when we give our authority to someone for a longer or shorter period of time. (We spoke about husbands giving their authority to their wives when they go on trips, and about parents turning over their authority to babysitters.)

At certain times we give over our authority gladly and voluntarily to someone else. I think of my daughter's wedding as an example: At one point in the ceremony, the pastor asked, "Who gives this woman to be married to this man?" My response was, "Her mother and I do." At that time two things happened in the spirit world: My daughter came under the authority of her husband, and they both came under my authority (and my father's) as the patriarch(s) of the family. I retain some authority over my daughter, but the major transaction was one in which I relinquished to her husband my role as her primary authority figure.

A more permanent form of relinquishment can happen at death. A friend of mine has told me that his last words to his terminally ill wife were, "It's all right to leave." And as he left the room, she acted on his permission and died. In saying those words, my friend relinquished his authority over her, giving her permission to die. Another friend, who pastored Chinese congregations for a number of years, recalls several times when he gathered the families of terminally ill loved ones and asked them if they agreed that their loved one could die. In each case it was only a short time after they relinquished their right to keep the loved one alive that he or she died.

We can point to several times in Jesus' life when He relinquished His authority to the Father. The first was when He came to earth, putting aside His rights as the second Person of the

Trinity (Philippians 2:5–8). Then, in John 5:19 and 8:28, Jesus stated that He had relinquished to the Father His authority to act and speak on His own behalf. It might even be said that He surrendered His authority to Pilate when He made it clear that the Roman governor had no authority over Him except that granted by God (John 19:11). In the agony of His final hours, then, having begged the Father to "take this cup of suffering away," Jesus relinquished His right to life itself, saying, "Not my will . . . but your will be done" (Luke 22:42).

Divorce is another kind of relinquishment. A divorced woman can, however, still be interfered with by her ex-husband unless she asserts her new position out from under his authority. My recommendation to such a woman is that when the divorce is legalized, she speak to the spirit world asserting her freedom from the authority of her former husband.

When a person is under the influence of an ungodly soul tie, he or she is affected by the authority of the one to whom he or she is tied (or bonded). Sexual relationships outside of marriage are the most common way in which a person comes under a soul tie. A soul tie can also be created when a person is bonded under another's authority, as when a very controlling pastor demands to be consulted on every major decision or when an older mother asserts control over her grown daughter. Such authority needs to be broken, and the control cancelled and taken away from the perpetrator.

Using Authority Wisely

One of the most important areas in which we are to assert our authority is within the family. Those of us who are heads of families especially need to carry out our responsibility by making good use of this privilege. Those who are in other positions in the family may have more spiritual authority than they realize.

It is my prayer that this discussion will help us all to recognize the authority God has given us and enable us to use it wisely. It is sad that we have not learned more about this area in most of our churches. May this discussion contribute important insight that enables us all to make use of our authority to enhance God's work in our families.

Now let's turn to the authority Jesus gives us to minister to others. He came to set captives free (Luke 4:18), and He sends us to continue granting freedom to those harassed by the enemy.

14

Authority in Ministering to Others

Discovering Her Authority

A woman I will call Teri has written me about discovering that she really does have spiritual authority. I was leading a seminar she attended at a California church. Teri and a friend had come along as apprentice ministry leaders, and they had just finished working with someone when they became aware of another ministry group that seemed to be having difficulty. This group had aroused a demon that was manifesting loudly and violently, and they were unsure what to do next. Although Teri was headed for her lunch break and had no experience dealing with demons, she felt led to help the group as she passed by. Then she remembered some of my teaching, and she rebuked the demon, forbidding it to be violent or to cause the person to throw up, thinking she would then go on to lunch.

The demon responded immediately, and the people in the group thought she was an expert! Teri suddenly realized she was now in charge of the ministry. Without a clue what to do next, she called on the Lord for help and immediately felt led to ask the demon who had more authority, him or Jesus. The demon admitted that Jesus did. Teri writes,

> Then I told the demon that I came in Jesus' authority and that it had to obey me. What happened next really startled me! The demon agreed with me that I had authority over it, and it tried to convince me that I should let it stay in this man. It took me a few moments to get over the initial shock of discovering that the authority Jesus gave us is real. After a brief pause, I continued with deliverance, commanding the demon to leave the man and go to the feet of Jesus. It disagreed three or four times, then gave up and left the man.

Teri testifies that this experience brought about a major change, both in her thinking and in her practice. What we had been saying in the seminar about working in the authority of Jesus became more than mere theory; the discussions suddenly made practical sense as Teri began doing something she knew she could not do alone. "My authority was no longer mere head knowledge and theology," she says. "It became reality! That was the start for me of learning to walk in His power and authority and to do the things Jesus did."

Authority to Invite the Holy Spirit

Jesus said that whoever believes in Him will do the works He did and "even greater things" (John 14:12). Then He said He would "do whatever you ask for in my name, so that the Father's glory will be shown through the Son. If you ask me for anything in my name, I will do it" (John 14:13–14). What incredible authority these statements give us!

A few verses later, Jesus let us know that the first item on our "want list" should be the Helper called the Holy Spirit (John 14:16). As we have mentioned several times, we are to start where Jesus started: with the empowerment of the Holy Spirit, whom (as Jesus said) God will give us if we ask for Him. As Luke 11:13 says, "You know how to give good things to your children. How much more, then, will the Father in heaven give the Holy Spirit to those who ask him!" What an inestimable privilege—having the authority to invite the Holy Spirit to come and take charge of our lives and ministries, and being sure He will do just that.

We see the pattern in Jesus' life: He came into the world, committed to living in total dependence on the Father, as Adam was intended to live. We have noted Jesus' dependence in John 5:19: "I tell you the truth: the Son can do nothing on his own; he does only what he sees his Father doing. What the Father does, the Son also does." We have also seen that Jesus' dependence on the Father was worked out in such a way that He did no mighty works before the Holy Spirit came on Him at His baptism (Luke 3:21–22). And we have seen that whatever authority the Father granted Jesus before that time did not impress the people of His hometown, Nazareth, for they marveled at His authority and power once He began His public ministry (Matthew 13:53–58). They also rejected Him.

We are to follow the same pattern Jesus did: receive the Holy Spirit, then move out in authority and power. We start as His disciples did by waiting (Acts 1:4–5) and, presumably, asking to receive the gift Jesus promised. We use our authority first to ask for the baptism in the Holy Spirit. Then we are to live as Jesus lived—in the fullness of the Spirit.

But we note an ebb and flow of the Spirit's activity in Jesus' ministry. Although Jesus was filled with the Holy Spirit, we see that He did not have the authority to override the lack of faith of the people of Nazareth, and so He "did not perform many miracles there" (Matthew 13:58). At other times the Holy Spirit came in a special way "to heal the sick" (Luke 5:17) and to fill

Jesus with joy (Luke 10:21). I take it, then, that although the Holy Spirit is always with and in us, once we have invited Him in, He comes with special power and gifting at certain times, either by His choice or because we ask Him to come.

There are two times, then, when it is appropriate to use our authority to ask for the Holy Spirit. The first is when we ask to receive Him in His fullness; the second is when we want Him to come for some special purpose, such as ministry.

The purpose of this chapter and the next is to discuss the various kinds of ministry for which the Holy Spirit empowers us. We will deal with these ministries under eight headings: blessing, breaking bondages, physical healing, deep-level healing, deliverance, forgiveness, death and higher-level spirits. As we look at Jesus' ministry, we see most of them in focus regularly. As He ministered in authority and power in these crucial areas, so should we.

Authority to Bless

First of all, we have been given the authority to *bless*. As usual, Jesus modeled this area of authority for us. In the Beatitudes He blessed people for specific behavior and attitudes (Matthew 5:3–12). When He sent His followers out to minister in Luke 9 and 10, He told them to bless those who cared for them (Luke 10:5). Blessing is especially noticeable after His resurrection (John 20:19, 21, 26). Then, when Jesus left the earth, He commanded His followers to teach their followers "to obey everything I have commanded you" (Matthew 28:20). And the command that His followers be taught to minister as Jesus did comes down to us. So, just as Jesus blessed, we are to bless.

The authority to bless (Matthew 5:44; Romans 12:14) is one of the most precious gifts God has given us. Genuine spiritual transactions take place when we speak blessing in Jesus' name.

The Bible is full of blessing. Not only did Jacob and other Old Testament fathers pronounce blessings on their sons (for example, Genesis 48–49), but Paul starts each of his letters with a blessing (see, for example, Romans 1:7; 1 Corinthians 1:3; 2 Corinthians 1:2; Galatians 1:3). Jesus was blessed before He was born (Luke 1:42) and afterward (Luke 2:34–35). Jesus blessed children (Mark 10:16), people who lived

> *The authority to bless is one of the most precious gifts God has given us.*

Kingdom values (Matthew 5:3–12), His disciples after His resurrection (John 20:19, 21, 26) and those present at His ascension (Luke 24:50–51). Further, He commands us to bless those who curse us (Luke 6:28).

We find about three hundred references to blessing in Scripture. There would undoubtedly have been more if it had not been so universally practiced by those with a Jewish worldview. The more familiar something is, the less it gets mentioned, and invoking God's blessing on those you favor was, for the Jews, almost as natural as breathing. The favorite Jewish blessing was *peace*; in each of Paul's letters, he spoke peace on his readers. And since he was working in the Greek world, he added a favorite Greek blessing, *grace*. Thus his usual opening blessing was *grace and peace*. In his letters to Timothy, he added *mercy*, another favorite Jewish blessing (1 Timothy 1:2; 2 Timothy 1:2). In each case, these are not to be taken as mere words of favor but *as the invoking of God's spiritual power for the benefit of those addressed*.

The authority to bless is a wonderful gift from God. We are to use it often to minister to people; in fact, blessing someone is a *form of ministry* in and of itself. I mentioned in chapter 3 that as I have blessed people with peace, many have experienced a noticeable peacefulness coming over them like a warm shower or mild electricity. I have blessed myself with peace many times when I have been upset and found that it usually works wonders. People blessed with joy often find their minds filled quickly with God's praises. Once I blessed a woman with joy, and a demon manifested itself! The demon could not stand the praise for God that welled up in the woman's heart. On one occasion I blessed a woman with "a deeper experience of the love of God than you have ever had before," and the Holy Spirit started a major work in her life.

I make it a practice in my seminary teaching and seminars to bless the students as we close class. I have frequently blessed them with things like peace, patience, freedom from tiredness and good rest (after they go home from an evening class), and many have remarked on the changes these blessings seem to have initiated in their lives.

Blessing in Ministry

Blessing is also an effective vehicle for initiating more extensive prayer ministry. It is my practice to bless the person I am ministering to at the beginning of each session. Often he or she needs the peace of God to combat fear and discomfort. The blessing usually changes such fear to peaceful anticipation of what God is about to do.

Recently Gary Runkle-Edens began to take a new approach to working with a man who had been coming to him for several months. The man's male identity had been damaged in childhood through sexual abuse, homosexuality and much more. Gary began to bless his client with a rebuilt self-identity as a male. After a few sessions of such blessing, the client reported having "strange new thoughts" and urges about "working on cars and trucks, doing furniture refinishing and going fishing!" He did not know how to handle these urges. So Gary explained to him that he thought God might be rebuilding the male part of him.

The client looked at Gary, amazed by what it felt like to have male urges and surprised by God's power to do this!

While working with a man I will call Ed, I was finding no success in ridding him of a demon of defiance. So, more out of frustration than anything else, I began blessing Ed with an infilling of God's love. At this the demon started shouting, "No, no, no!" And soon the demon was willing to leave because *he could not stand this influx of love through the blessing.*

Partly as a result of the ministry session with Ed, I have begun to experiment with a new use of the authority to bless. At the end of our time together, I bless my client with the *opposite* of whatever damage or demon we have dealt with. If we have been doing inner healing for a damaged self-image, I bless the person with new self-love and self-appreciation. If we have just kicked out a demon of anger, rage or violence, I bless that person with gentleness and self-control. If the problem or demon is fear, I bless the person with confidence or faith. Sometimes I just use a general blessing, saying, "I bless you with the opposite of each of the problems [or demons] we have dealt with."

Kinds of Blessings

A blessing may be either general or specific. "I bless you in Jesus' name" is general. When we bless one another with peace, mercy, grace, patience or joy, we are being more specific. It may be that in the Beatitudes, Jesus intended His statements to confer specific blessings, not simply to describe the blessings available to those with the qualities He mentioned. Perhaps He was saying, "I bless you who are spiritually poor by giving you the Kingdom of heaven," and "I bless you who mourn with the comfort of God" (Matthew 5:3–4).

Those who pronounce the blessings own the blessings they speak and can take them back if they choose to. Jesus commanded His disciples to do just that (as we saw in chapter 3) if they were rejected when they went out to proclaim the Kingdom (Luke 10:5–6). They were to go to a home and ask for hospitality; if the homeowner invited them in, they were to accept the invitation. If not, they were to leave and take their blessing with them.

"Peace be with you," or, better, "I wish you total well-being," was Jesus' favorite blessing, especially after His resurrection (Matthew 28:9; Luke 24:36; John 20:19, 21, 26). Jesus would have used the Aramaic word *shalom*, meaning far more than simply "peace"; it is more like "general, total well-being." This was probably the blessing He pronounced as He ascended to heaven after the resurrection (Luke 24:50–51).

I love to bless people! My favorite blessing (following the examples of Jesus and Paul) is peace. General blessings such as "I bless you in Jesus' name" are fun to use and minister God's blessing effectively to those who are receptive, although I prefer to use more specific blessings as often as possible. One formula I use often is, "In Jesus' name I bless you with [peace, forgiveness, confidence, release from worry/fear/guilt]."

Material objects such as food and the Communion elements may also be blessed. I believe it is the power of God conveyed through blessing that explains how Jesus' garment (Matthew 9:20; 14:36), Paul's handkerchiefs and aprons (Acts 19:12) and Peter's shadow (Acts 5:15, assuming it worked) could bring healing. Jesus blessed food regularly. The disciples who walked to Emmaus with Him recognized Jesus as He blessed and broke the bread (Luke 24:30–31). Before distributing the food to the five thousand, He blessed it as He thanked God for it (Luke 9:16). With regard to the Communion elements, Paul spoke of blessing the cup used in the Lord's Supper (1 Corinthians 10:16, KJV). I have seen God minister healing to people during Communion as they ate and drank the elements that had been blessed.

I have gotten into the pleasant habit of starting and concluding both private and public ministry sessions with one or more blessings. I also send a blessing with each email and letter. This is one of the most wonderful privileges we have as representatives of the supreme Blesser. And He Himself has given us this authority.

Authority to Break Bondages

A second important area of authority in ministry is the authority to break bondages. People can be in bondage to Satan due to such things as sin, soul ties, contemporary or generational curses, self-curses and authority relationships. A relationship in which one person is dominated by another, for example, can be empowered by Satan and affected through a soul tie. Likewise, participants in adultery become bonded by satanic power and affected through soul ties. Curses are obvious bondage creators. And there seem to be generational bondages, held in place by demons, in which particular sins or compulsions occur generation after generation. In each case we have the authority to renounce such bondages if they are in us and to cancel them in others.

Cursing by Others

The topic of cursing has come up frequently in these pages; this is because we have to deal with cursing so often as we minister to people. Many societies have those who practice what may be termed "formal" cursing. With New Age and Satanist groups emerging in the United States, formal cursing is becoming more prominent. In this kind of cursing some ritual is performed, sometimes involving a sacrifice. During the ritual, words are said and sometimes an image or statue of the person being cursed is used in order to invoke satanic power against that person. Sometimes something that has been close to the person will be cursed and buried.

More common is "informal" cursing. This may happen through careless or angry words. Such negative statements as "I wish you [or I] were dead," "I hate you [or myself]," "You'll never amount to anything" or "You're worthless," especially if uttered by someone in authority over the person cursed, can convey enemy power into anyone who accepts the statement or prediction (see below for dealing with self-curses).

I was told by one of our ministry team members recently that he had to break a curse on a young woman put on her by her pastor! The pastor happened to say something like "Spiritually you're just a midget." Somehow this statement, made by one in authority, dug its way into her to such an extent that the enemy could use it significantly in her life. In ministry, my colleague treated those words as a curse and asked a fellow team member to stand in for the pastor, asking forgiveness on his behalf and renouncing the curse. At that time its power was broken and she became free.

Sometimes we have to break the power of a doctor's prediction based on a diagnosis concerning a serious disease or accident. The enemy's ability to use such predictions against us seems to relate directly to whether or not, under the guidance of the Holy Spirit, we accept the prognosis as valid. If we do, the enemy seems able to use that belief to empower the words as a curse. If we reject the prediction, its power as a curse seems to be broken.

Another form of informal cursing is embodied in curse words or "swear words" such as "You bastard" or "You son of a bitch," or perhaps even "God damn you" or "F——— you." Matthew 5:22 adds "You good-for-nothing" and "worthless fool" to the list. These and other negative words invite enemy power into that person's life. This is especially true when the curses are uttered by someone in authority over a person and/or if there is internal garbage the enemy can latch onto.

The curse may go back to prebirth, if the pregnancy was not wanted or if the parents wanted a child of the other sex. During pregnancy either parent may put a curse of *unwantedness* on the child by saying or thinking things like "I wish I [we/you] weren't pregnant" or "I hope there will be a miscarriage." Many people curse preborn children by contemplating abortion. It is amazing how much power the enemy is able to wield throughout a person's life when such words or wishes are uttered.

> *Many people curse preborn children by contemplating abortion.*

Can Christians Be Cursed?

Does the enemy have the authority to empower curses directed at believers? Unfortunately the answer seems to be yes. I have heard of and ministered to many missionaries who have experienced evil of various sorts after being the target of curses. Indeed, missionaries working in other societies, as well as Christian workers in the United States, seem to be special targets of such cursing. These choice servants of God have experienced significant freedom when we used our authority to break curses over them.

A curse, according to Proverbs 26:2, must have someplace to land if it is to be effective. And internal garbage coming from various sources provides ample opportunity for the enemy to carry out at least part of his assignment in a person's life. Spiritual and emotional garbage can come by inheritance, by our own choices, by the choices of those in authority over us or by our reactions to difficulties and abuse. If any such conditions result in unresolved sins such as unforgiveness, bitterness, lust, anger, hate or self-rejection, even in Christians, these provide landing places for curses. The ideal, once again, is the condition Jesus could claim for Himself when He said, "The ruler of this world is coming, and he has nothing in Me" (John 14:30, NKJV).

A related question that comes to me from time to time: Does Satan have authority to afflict Christians who enter territory dedicated to him, such as temples, shrines, occult bookstores or Oriental martial arts studios? Again, I think he has that authority on the same basis as with curses: if there is something inside that he has a right to. I have toured several temples and only once, in a Buddhist temple in Taiwan, was I attacked, with a pain under my sternum.

I also believe, however, that demonic beings know if we are there as tourists or for warfare. I have learned to be cautious, especially after that visit to the Buddhist temple. Ceremonies were being conducted in honor of the dead—ceremonies that I believe provided more power than normal for the spirits inhabiting the temple. So now I ask for extra protecting angels when I visit such places.

Self-Cursing

Many curse themselves, usually without realizing it. I do not know when negative words uttered against ourselves constitute a curse, but I have ministered to numerous people whose problems were lessened when they took their authority in Christ to renounce any curses they had put on themselves. As with blessings, the person who makes the curse owns it. This means that he or she can break its power by renouncing it.

The most frequent target of such self-curses seems to be our bodies, often during adolescence. As our bodies develop, we may perceive ourselves to be the object of critical words or looks from peers, especially if the speed of our development differs from that of others. If so, we may say things to or about our bodies that constitute self-curses. I often minister to men who have cursed themselves, and whose struggle with shame is intense, due to the taunts of their peers in junior high locker rooms over the small size of their sex organs. Shame and insecurity over adolescent development is also a frequent problem in women. Either because of dissatisfaction with how they developed or because of abuse, I have found that many women have cursed themselves. Or they have cursed some part of themselves, such as their faces, breast size, hips, hair, minds, emotions or some other parts that they do not feel are adequate.

As I was teaching on self-cursing in one of my seminars, a lady raised her hand and said, "I think I've cursed my hair!" From the looks of her hair, I think she was right! And I think I've seen quite a few ladies with cursed hair.

The impression that we should not have been born, or that we should have been male rather than female (or vice versa), is often the source of self-cursing. I ministered to a woman who was the fourth daughter in a Chinese family. She was in her late thirties and came to me because she had cancer in several parts of her body. I asked her if she had ever wished she were a boy. "Every second of my life!" she replied. Then she admitted to having cursed her body thousands of times. I helped her renounce those curses, and later I received a letter from her reporting that she was well.

Abuse can be another reason for self-cursing. A woman came to me whose doctor had discovered lumps in her breasts. As I asked God what to pray for, the word *abuse* came into my mind. It turned out that she had been abused sexually and that the abuser had focused on her breasts. So she had cursed the fact that she had breasts. After she renounced the self-curses, her next examination showed no lumps.

A general rule regarding curses is that the person who has put the curse on has the authority to cancel it. Those who have cursed themselves, therefore, usually simply need to renounce the curses in the name of Jesus to break their power. They probably will then have to get rid of the demon who empowered the curse.

Breaking Curses

Whatever the source of the curses, we have been given the authority to break them. Our gracious God wants to free people from any power of the enemy that has come through cursing, and we get to assist. Since the power in which we work is infinitely greater than that of the enemy, most curses are fairly easy to cancel once they are discovered or suspected. I usually say something like this:

> In the name of Jesus Christ, we take authority over this curse [or these curses] and speak the canceling of the curse, and all its effects, and the breaking of all enemy power that affects or has affected this person's life.

We have authority in Christ to break *ancestral curses* as well. Often I find demons that have rights in people through curses leveled at their ancestors. Routinely, therefore, I speak the canceling in the name of Jesus of all curses that have given the enemy rights, either through the father's line or through the mother's, including curses coming from others and self-curses.

If we become aware that someone has cursed us, we are commanded to bless him or her (Matthew 5:44; Romans 12:14). I like to do what I learned from one of our ministry team members.

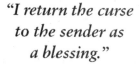

"I return the curse to the sender as a blessing."

If the source of the curse is a human being (as opposed to a demon), I say, "I return the curse to the sender as a blessing." Sometimes I make the blessing more specific: "I return the curse as a blessing aimed at bringing that person to salvation" or "I return the curse as a blessing of peace [or patience, or whatever]." If, as often happens in deliverance, the source of the curse is a demon, I return the curse to the demon as a curse. This usually stops him from cursing, since he is receiving what he is trying to send me and he does not like to receive his own curses.

Since we as Christians have the authority to speak empowered words, we need to be especially careful how we talk, especially when we are angry, lest we curse others or ourselves. But it is appropriate to curse germs, viruses and whole diseases when praying for healing. I have done this on several occasions, especially with "big ones" such as diabetes, arthritis and cancer.

Canceling Authority over Us

We spoke in chapter 11 about the need to break enemy power over our ancestors due to authority granted through vows, curses, dedications, sin and trauma. The authority to cancel such enemy rights may be referred to as the "authority to renounce satanic authority" that has been given us. This authority, while it has been implied in several places throughout this book, deserves a bit more focus.

We can renounce agreements (as we have seen) made by our ancestors. Since we are the contemporary representatives of our family line, we have authority over all such agreements. When anyone in our family line has made vows giving the enemy rights, it is our job to ferret these out and renounce them. Likewise with curses that our ancestors have put on themselves, dedications to occult involvement they have made and power they have granted Satan through sinful practices.

Often a general renunciation is sufficient to break the enemy's power through such ancestral involvement. The person seeking freedom can say, "I renounce all vows, dedications, curses and authority given through sin or reaction to trauma in the name of Jesus Christ." But sometimes the enemy's grip is so strong that we need to discover at least the generation if not the specific occasion on which the ancestor gave the enemy authority over that person and his or her family. The Holy Spirit usually provides the information necessary to discover the event, either directly through a word of knowledge or indirectly through the confession of a demon. The rights can then be renounced very specifically.

Rights granted through vows, dedications, curses, sins and reactions to trauma should also be renounced if any have occurred in the life of the one being ministered to. A fair number of persons who come to me for prayer ministry have participated in occult activities such as palm reading, Ouija boards, satanic computer games, and organizations like Scientology, Mormonism, Freemasonry, Christian Science, Buddhism and even Satanism. The rights given the enemy through such involvement must be renounced. Usually it is best to have the person renounce them specifically and to include the renunciation of all rights the enemy has thus gained over spouse, children and anyone else under that person's authority. Once the rights have been renounced, the demons attached to these rights need to be cast out.

Canceling Soul Ties

Other authority-granting connections should be renounced as well. An important area to explore in ministry is the possible presence of soul ties. These bondings empowered by Satan come about in a variety of ways that usually involve sex, close friendship or dominating relationships. Sexual relationships bond people spiritually. This is why Paul put sexual sin in a special category—something that, unlike other sins, works within and against the body, which is God's temple (1 Corinthians 6:18–20). People bonded by sex to persons other than their marriage partners carry a major source of satanic interference in their lives. Likewise with those who are soul-tied (bonded) to people who dominate them, or with whom they have an unnatural or super-intense friendship or dependency relationship.

The bonding we call a soul tie often happens in situations in which a pastor is very dominating and produces a church that is cultlike in its demands on people. Often there are strict rules and regulations, and members are required to ask the leader's permission before they do anything major in their lives. A dominating relationship with a parent can also produce a soul tie. I have ministered to several women who were so dominated and controlled by their mothers, emotionally and sometimes even physically, that they could hardly turn around without consulting them. Often such women have to call their mothers every day or even live at home to care for them as if their mothers were children. An unhealthy codependent or dominating friendship with someone of either sex (even in marriage) can likewise produce a soul tie.

The way out of immoral sexual bonding or soul ties is to use our authority to renounce the relationship and claim the freedom Jesus gives when we break such enemy power. Usually it is enough for the person to state something like "I renounce the sexual bonding [or soul tie] I have with [person] in Jesus' name, and I break the power Satan has gained over me through this relationship." Breaking the power is often easier, however, than breaking the habits that have enabled the relationship. Once the power is broken, the person needs to work hard at establishing new habits. Although the habits are easier to break with the new freedom from enemy interference, they still may be a problem. Often the person needs others to assist.

In the next chapter we will continue our discussion of the various ministries in which we function under the empowerment of the Holy Spirit. With His power often comes His healing, and it is to healing that we turn next.

15

Authority to Heal

Authority for Physical Healing

Physical healing is the third of our eight areas of authority in ministry. It is obvious that Jesus was active in this ministry. The Father gave Him incredible authority and power to heal the most difficult kinds of physical problems: leprosy, lameness, paralysis, hemorrhaging, blindness, deafness, dumbness. Contrary to the way we often describe it, however, Jesus never prayed for healing; He commanded it. He took authority over whatever the condition was—for example, when He "ordered the fever to leave her" (Luke 4:39), or when He said to the leper, "Be clean!" (Luke 5:13), or when He cast out demons. When Jesus sent out His followers to speak about and demonstrate the Kingdom of God, He gave them authority to heal as He had demonstrated it—by commanding it (Matthew 10:1, 8; Luke 9:1; 10:9).

The ministry of physical healing that Jesus taught the Twelve while He was with them continued after He left. The book of Acts contains many references to healing through the apostles and others (Acts 2:43; 5:12–16; 14:3; 19:11–12; 28:8–9). General references to the healings of Stephen (6:8) and Philip (8:6–7),

253

plus the specific reference to Ananias' healing of Saul's blindness (9:10–19), demonstrate that not just the apostles were involved. Peter and John healed a lame man (3:1–10); Peter healed Aeneas of paralysis (9:33–34) and raised Dorcas from the dead (9:36–41); Paul raised Eutychus from the dead (20:9–12) and healed Publius' father of fever and dysentery (28:8).

It is plain from history, and from the fact that many people today are being healed of physical maladies, that the authority to heal is still present. Marvelously gifted people like Benny Hinn, Pat Robertson and his associates on *The 700 Club*, my colleague C. Peter Wagner and many others are active in physical healing. Several years ago Yonggi Cho, pastor of the world's largest church in Seoul, Korea, sent a woman suffering from degenerating hip bones to Peter Wagner for prayer. He took authority over the physical problem and brought healing to the woman. She announced it by giving us her crutches, which she had needed badly when she came, and walking out of our office without a limp.

I have seen physical healing combined with inner healing in abundance.

Jesus did not distinguish between physical and deep-level healing (see the next section). When He extended forgiveness to the man let down through the roof (Luke 5:17–26), He healed him both physically and spiritually. Forgiveness is a major focus of inner healing and often results in physical healing as well.

Most of the purely physical healings I have been involved in have either been "small" or have been in conjunction with deep-level healing, since physical healing does not seem to be my gifting. But I have seen physical healing combined with inner healing in abundance. A woman has been free for several years now from what was diagnosed as terminal cancer since the time I helped her deal with fear. At least two women were healed immediately from major back problems when I helped them deal with certain emotional and spiritual issues. A pastor's wife had a severe back problem healed when we helped her turn over to God the problems of others that she was in the habit of carrying herself. We watched as the leg of a woman that had been fully one and a half inches short grow out in spurts after we had done deep-level healing with her. Many have been freed of stress- or unforgiveness-related stiff necks, headaches (sometimes migrainous) and stomach or back problems as we dealt with their inner issues in the authority and power Jesus gives.

The point is, Jesus gives us the credit card to assert His authority over physical problems. Those gifted in physical healing see more such healing in their ministries. Those of us with gifting in deep-level healing see many physical healings in the process of doing inner healing. Even those without these healing gifts may expect to be used in the role of physical healer from time to time, if they will be faithful and use the authority they have been given in this area whenever possible.

Should we assume God always wants to heal a person with a physical problem? We do not know, except to say that Jesus never told anyone to simply grin and bear it. Whenever He saw someone with a problem, the gospels show that He took authority and healed it. We also know, however, that He was getting His directions from the Father. And although Scripture frequently shows Him healing everyone who came to Him, He must have walked past several hundred needy people to heal the one bed-ridden man in John 5. The key, I believe, is listening to God on the one hand, and showing compassion by ministering to any who come to us on the other.

What about those who do not get healed? This is a tough one, especially when we feel deep compassion for someone who continues to live in both physical pain and the pain of knowing God has not chosen to heal him or her. Although I feel it keenly when I minister to someone who does not get healed (and I have had many like this), I have determined not to allow my disappointment to lead me to stop ministering to people. It is a matter of obedience to do as Jesus did by ministering to the hurting. And it is my responsibility to remain faithful to God by exercising my authority to help the hurting, no matter what the results may be. Those results are up to God.

✆ Authority for Deep-Level Healing

Deep-level or inner healing is another area of ministry for which the Lord gives us authority. Most of the people who come to me are suffering from wounds in the emotional or spiritual areas of life, even if they come with a physical problem. So when they come describing a physical need, I have learned to ask when the problem started and what else was going on in their lives at the time. Again and again a physical problem becomes the occasion for claiming God's power to heal something much deeper. Indeed, I am often thankful for the physical need, since we can usually gauge the progress of the deep-level healing taking place by the way in which the physical problem lessens and goes away.

Often the person is unaware of the underlying problem when he or she first comes for ministry. For others the problem is obvious, but they have not been able to get rid of it—often in spite of much prayer, counseling and consultation. Problems such as anger, worry, fear, bitterness, unforgiveness, lust, shame, guilt, pride, inadequacy, unworthiness, rejection and depression come up again and again. And in each case God gives us the authority and power to minister His love and grace to His hurting children.

In dealing with deep-level hurts, the Holy Spirit gives us authority to go back deep into people's pasts to bring healing. Usually through picturing led by the Holy Spirit, we can help people revisit the hurtful events and picture Jesus in it. It is true that Jesus was there at the time they were hurt, even though they were not aware of it. This experience of Jesus' presence in the event is usually very healing. As the person pictures the event, allowing him- or herself to feel the emotional pain, Jesus usually leads the person right through the pain, taking the problem and pain on Himself and bringing about a radical change of attitude.

Jesus died for our wounds as well as for our sins (Isaiah 53:4; 61:1). He thus releases the person from fear of the past and changes an emotional open wound into a painless and harmless scar. The memory of the event remains, since Jesus does not change history. But He does take away the fear of the past that Satan uses so effectively to cripple people, along with most, if not all, of the pain of the event. And the person goes free! The way Jesus treated Peter in John 21:15–19, as He reinstated him in ministry after his denials, is also classic inner healing.

Though most deep-level ministry sessions need take no more than two hours (see Kraft 2010b), sometimes God does not heal deep-level problems all at once. For some, ministry may requires several sessions. Often problems are reinforced by demonic beings that need to be banished. Such ministry provides great opportunity to demonstrate the caring and lovingkindness of Jesus. There is power in the authority we take and in the love we show. See my book *Deep Wounds, Deep Healing* (2010a) for more detail on inner healing.

Authority for Deliverance

Jesus' authority was most obvious in dealing with demons. Demons never questioned Jesus' authority over them; they responded immediately. He did not beg demons to leave, as we are told the Pharisees did. Nor did He pray to God the Father to release a person from them. He assumed they should not be there and He commanded them to go.

Some people deny that Christians can have demons living within them. Yet both Jesus' experience and ours contradict this assertion. Jesus healed and delivered people who came to Him. When they came, they came in faith. They were believers, people we would call "Christians." Our experience is that many believers are carrying demons; I personally have ministered to well over three thousand Christians who were carrying demons.

Jesus' example is the one we are to follow. The authority Jesus gave His followers in Luke 9 and 10 included "authority to drive out all demons" (Luke 9:1). It is an authority that amazed the disciples (Luke 10:17) and one that He intended to be ours as well (John 20:21). As with Jesus, the authority we have is most obvious in deliverance. Demons recognize it right away, even before we challenge them. With it we have the privilege of confronting and defeating them regularly. A demon once asked me, "Where did you get this power?" I replied, "Remember who we serve." He was convinced and obeyed me.

The satanic kingdom is active in this world, taking advantage of people as often as possible from inside. Apparently Satan has no access from the inside to those who are spiritually clean (John 14:30; Proverbs 26:2). But there are people (including many Christians) with enough garbage inside to make the enemy quite successful in his attempts to gain an inside position. I have found that many people, non-Christians and Christians alike, give demons opportunity to live within them by hanging on to emotions like bitterness, anger, unforgiveness, hate, fear, worry and lust. In addition, many inherit demons due to sins, vows, curses, dedications and trauma in their ancestral lines.

Demons are like rats, and rats go for garbage. With certain exceptions, then, it is the presence of spiritual and emotional garbage that allows demons to enter if they have not come by inheritance, or to stay if they have. Furthermore, their strength is calibrated to the amount and kind of garbage present in the person. Those with many problems of the kinds listed above will have strong demons; those with fewer will have weak demons. Though the presence of such problems may not in and of itself prove that there are demons present, if there *are* demons, it is because they have such problems to attach themselves to. Getting rid of garbage, then, weakens any demons that may be present.

One important implication of the rats-and-garbage situation is that demonic infestation always involves problems at two levels. There are, as it were, two causes of the malady, a primary one and a secondary one. *The human problem is primary and the demon problem secondary,* for demons piggyback on human problems (this is why demons often go by function names such as *fear, anger, lust* and the like). It is never *either* a demon or an emotional or spiritual problem; it is *both* a demon and an emotional or spiritual problem. If there are demons, we know there are emotional or spiritual problems that must be dealt with, either before or after the demons are cast out. Because I do not like strong demons, and because I want my clients to be healed (not just delivered), my preference is to deal with garbage first, then demons. This approach weakens the demons so that we almost never have any violence.

When we think of the strength of demons, it is important to remember that the term *demon possession* (as I pointed out in chapter 1) is unscriptural. The Greek words translated *demon possessed* in many of our English versions really only mean "have a demon." The translators have been irresponsible in using the word *possessed* and by so doing have given the impression that demons have more authority and power than they actually do. Demons have only the authority that a person (often ignorantly) allows them, and they never have complete control of a person all the time, as the term *possession* suggests. Even the Gerasene demoniac, who was more controlled by demons than any other scriptural example, came to meet Jesus of his own free will

(Mark 5:6–8). It is inaccurate, then, to call even him *possessed* in the sense of being under demonic control at all times. The only possible validity for the term *possession* is for cases in which a shaman calls on spirits to take over or possess him or her.

How to Proceed

To use our authority with demons, we usually have to challenge them. In most cases I try to do as much inner healing as possible before challenging demons so that if some turn up, they will be weak. Although the demons recognize our authority and see their strength diminishing as we do inner healing, they usually hide until challenged (though sometimes, when they feel threatened, they will make their presence known to try to stop us). Once they surface, they try their best to bluff us into leaving them there. One demon begged me to let him stay, saying, "If you'll let me stay, I promise I'll never hurt her!"

Most of what demons do in response to challenge is not power but bluff. They know we have much greater power; but they also realize that often we do not know how to use the power we have. So they use what tactics they can to keep us from getting them out. Seeing through their bluffing, and continuing to use the authority and power we have been given, is the name of the game.

When I suspect there might be a demon, I call for him to reveal himself by answering my questions. My usual "call" is, "I command the spirit of [fear, anger, etc.] to attention in the presence of Jesus Christ." I then ask if he has any legal right to stay in the person.

Whatever the problem is, I try to rouse the demon by calling him by the name of the problem. If fear is the problem, for example, I will call for a spirit of fear, usually after we have dealt through inner healing with the human roots of the problem on which the demon has been piggybacking. If the problem is worry, anger, self-hate, lust or pornography, I call that name. If the person has attempted suicide or had an abortion, I always find a spirit of death, suicide or abortion present. Often we have to call the demon's name several times before we get a response.

Sometimes, especially when working with a group, I may forbid any demons to speak in the first person when communicating with the person in whom they live. For years the person may have been hearing such statements as "I'm no good," "I ought to kill myself," "I don't believe demons can live in Christians" or "I can look at pornography [or drink alcohol or shoot drugs] without getting hooked." Since these statements start with *I*, the person has always assumed the thoughts were his or her own. But if these thoughts have been prompted by demons, as they often are, commanding them to refrain from using the first person results in new statements like "*You're* no good" or "*You* don't believe this stuff, do you?"

Recently I was teaching a class on inner healing and deliverance when a woman in the front row confessed that she had been hearing voices. Suspecting these were demons, I forbade them to use the first person and went on with my lecture. After a while the woman raised her hand to report that the voices, though saying many of the same things to her, were now using *you* rather than *I*. A man in the same class, sitting a row behind this lady, reported that he, too, began hearing *you* in similar contexts immediately after I gave my command to the demons in the woman.

In another class I spoke this command out to the whole class, just in case any of the members were carrying demons. One woman reported that as soon as I spoke out, she began to hear a whole series of *you* statements. She even saw that this change was made in her notes! This led her to suspect for the first time that she might be carrying demons, and it caused her to change her belief that demons cannot live in Christians. This event proved the first step in a glorious deliverance and radical change of life for her.

Though I will not go into detail here, it might be useful to note the steps we ordinarily follow in getting demons out:

1. The first step is always to pray, inviting the Holy Spirit to take over and to lead the session. I also ask for the right amount of authority and power to meet whatever challenge the enemy might bring. Next I usually bless the client with whatever the Lord brings to mind. He or she is usually at least in need of God's peace.

2. Claim authority over the place, time and people involved, and speak protection for all concerned from any revenge by the demons. Also, forbid any violence or any antics that might embarrass the client.

3. Do deep-level healing to get rid of the garbage and weaken the demons.

4. Challenge each demon by name (as suggested above). There will likely be several groups of demons, each with a head demon and helper demons in it. Commonly found groups will be *shame*, guilt and deception; *anger*, bitterness, resentment and rage; *fear*, worry, anxiety and panic; *rejection*, abandonment, neglect and self-rejection; *lust*, pornography, fantasy and adultery; *death*, suicide, death wish and infirmity.

5. Command the head demons to line up with their helpers behind them. Bind all helper demons to the head demons.

6. Force the demons to reveal if they have any further legal rights to be there. If they do, take away those rights through deep-level healing.

7. When they have no further rights, I like to ask Jesus or the angels to create a spiritual box to lock each group in. If any of the demons will not go into the boxes, this tells us they still have some right to stay. So we have to do more deep-level healing.

8. When they are all in their boxes, I send the boxes to the feet of Jesus and ask Him to separate the demons from the client as far as the east is from the west.

9. I then forbid any of the demons ever to come back or ever to send any others. Next I place Jesus' cross and His empty tomb between the demons and the person, to make sure they cannot get back.

10. We then bless the person with as many things as the Lord brings to our minds, especially things that are the opposite of the problems he or she was having.

God has blessed this approach enormously. Literally thousands of His beloved servants are free now because He has led us to use His authority in this way. They have discovered that, though they did not get entirely free when they accepted Christ, Jesus brought them the freedom they wanted through deep-level healing. This approach, however, is not a magic formula, and there are other approaches that God uses, too.

Talking to Demons

You have noted that my colleagues and I engage in the controversial practice of talking to demons. The reason we do this is that we have found it the easiest and quickest way to find out information we would not know otherwise—usually information that helps us to bring deep-level healing to the client. As we minister, the demons are under the complete control of the Holy Spirit, who over and over again forces them to reveal things that are against their own best interests. A typical question we ask demons is, "Does this person need to forgive anyone?" We find (because we can check up on it) that the demon's answer is almost always the truth. We then ask the person to forgive the one named. When the person deals with that important piece of garbage (the unforgiveness), the demon's strength is greatly reduced.

Do demons lie? Yes. But, interestingly enough, every scriptural account of demons speaking portrays them as telling the truth. And we find that under Holy Spirit pressure, they often reveal important information that we can use to defeat them. They are like hostile witnesses in court; you know they support the other side, so you weigh their answers and do not fully trust their testimony unless you can check up on it (which you frequently can). They are also weakened through being forced to tell the truth, which is against their nature. We do not engage them in long conversations, but by talking to demons just long enough to get key information from them, we can keep track of them, gauge their strength by the strength of their voices and be much more certain at the end of the ministry session that we have gotten them out.

We also depend on words of knowledge coming directly from God, but using the demons to give us information enables many to be successful in deliverance who do not receive much information via words of knowledge. The important thing to remember is that it is the Holy Spirit getting information to us, even though it is through coercing the demons.

Who Is Targeted

If you were the enemy, whom would you target first? Pastors and other Christian leaders, of course. I have had frequent opportunity to cast demons out of Christian leaders who, either by inheritance or by foolish experimentation with the wrong activities, ended up carrying demons. One pastor, in order to gain respectability, had joined a Masonic lodge, not knowing this is one of the most evil organizations in the world. As I was working to find out what grip the demon had on the man, I asked the demon when he got in. "When he cursed God!" he replied. This surprised the pastor so much that he asked the demon when that had happened. The demon told him that all the Masonic commitments the pastor had made were to Lucifer, the god of Freemasonry.

Many who have no experience with demonized Christians refuse to believe demons can live in Christians. I wish this were true. But I have been involved personally in several thousand ministry sessions in which we delivered from demons people unmistakably committed to Christ. Demons living in Christians is, unfortunately, a fact, not a theory. It can be demonstrated like any other social scientific fact.

What is theory is how we understand this fact. I assume that *demons cannot live in a Christian's spirit.* They can live only in mind, emotions, body and will. Interestingly, these are the places where sin can also live in a Christian. I believe that when a person comes to Christ, the Holy Spirit takes up residence in his or her spirit (the central place in us) and banishes any demons that might be present from that place, though they may still have residence in the other parts of the person.

Demons cannot live in a Christian's spirit.

When I ask demons if they live in the person's spirit, they always say no and state that they had to get out of that part of the person when he or she came to Christ.

Since my occupation is teaching missionaries and international church leaders, I frequently get to cast demons out of these dear people. Many have inherited demons; others have become demonized through cursing by the people they have worked among. At one mission station, I met at least four missionaries who had experimented with Satanism in their school days, and several who had been involved in communal experiments involving sexual promiscuity. Some were still struggling with pornography. What often happens to people with such backgrounds is that they get gloriously converted and give themselves for the Lord's work without getting cleaned up. The demons within them are smart enough to lie low until the people get involved in something really important to God's Kingdom, and then they sabotage them. I have met missionary after missionary who has had a crippling demonic experience at a crucial time in his or her ministry.

The fact that so many, including Christians, are demonized means there are many battles yet to be fought. The enemy is especially anxious to cripple believers to keep us from hurting him. But if we are to be engaged properly in spiritual warfare on behalf of our Master, we must equip and motivate ourselves and become active in using our authority in the cause of freedom.

God needs more of us using His authority in ministering deliverance. By doing so, we are imitating Jesus by freeing His creatures, especially those He has called to extend His Kingdom or feed His sheep. This is a loving thing to do, and God gives us the power and authority to do it. You can read more on this subject in my book *Defeating Dark Angels* (2011).

✣ Authority to Forgive

One of Jesus' surprising statements is recorded in John 20:21–23. After He told the disciples, "As the Father sent me, so I send you," He breathed on them, saying, "Receive the Holy Spirit," and added, "If you forgive people's sins, they are forgiven; if you do not forgive them, they are not forgiven." As Jesus forgave sins, so we are to forgive people's sins. This is an awesome responsibility and the sixth area of our authority in ministry.

Satan often cripples Christians through their guilt and failure to forgive themselves, even after they have ostensibly repented and given their sins to God. In ministry, therefore, God often leads us to pronounce as forgiven those who have already confessed their sins or who do so during the ministry session. I usually ask people if they have confessed all known sin before I pronounce them forgiven. The freedom such a pronouncement brings, then, may be dramatic.

Several years ago God led me to speak forgiveness to a woman who remarked, "I feel ten pounds lighter! Now I don't have to go on a diet!" She had been experiencing a heaviness in the chest that disappeared when I took the authority Jesus gives us and pronounced her forgiven. Often in such cases there are tears of joy, as a person who knows intellectually that God has forgiven him or her actually feels that forgiveness for the first time. Over the years I have seen several ministry sessions turn from so-so to spectacular after I, in response to a word of knowledge, pronounced the person forgiven.

Transactions take place in the spiritual realm when we assert the authority Jesus has given us to pronounce forgiveness.

But regardless of whether a person senses anything or not, transactions take place in the spiritual realm when we assert the authority Jesus has given us to pronounce forgiveness. I believe we must be very careful with this authority, however. We are not the forgivers, Jesus is. When we speak forgiveness, then, it is on the basis of the authority that Jesus has delegated to us. We are not the source of the forgiveness.

Authority to Raise from the Dead

The seventh area of authority is that over death. Jesus raised the widow's son from the dead (Luke 7:11–15), as well as Jairus' daughter (Luke 8:41–42, 49–56) and Lazarus (John 11:1–44). If we get to do whatever Jesus did, as He promised, raising people from the dead is included. Indeed, Jesus commanded His disciples to do so as He sent them out into ministry: "Heal the sick, bring the dead back to life, heal those who suffer from dreaded skin diseases, and drive out demons" (Matthew 10:8).

I have not had this privilege yet, but I know at least two people who have. The first is a Lutheran pastor who, while serving a church in Michigan, had the privilege of seeing two women come back to life while he was praying over them. One of them was in the hospital. The monitoring machines indicated that death had taken place, and the woman's skin had turned a brownish color. The nurses were calling the doctor to come and pronounce her dead. During the pastor's prayer, however, the woman's husband noticed her skin turning pink and healthy again. And as the pastor left the room, thinking his next job would be a funeral, the woman came back to life. I cannot forget his triumphal tone of voice when, concluding this account, he exclaimed, "There were three people in our church last Easter who had risen from death—Jesus and these two ladies!"

The second person I know who has been used by God to raise people from the dead is a missionary working in Irian Jaya. She has been the human instrument in raising to life two children who had drowned. (At the time of the first one, she did not even believe healing is for today!) A boy had fallen into the river and had been under water for about half an hour. When he was pulled out, he was quite dead, and the women began to wail over him. As this missionary reported the incident to me, she said something like, "I didn't know what to do, so I put a hand on the child and prayed that somehow God would help in the situation." And He did—the youngster came back to life!

About a year and a half later, this missionary had the opportunity to bring another drowning victim to life. Now both she and her husband are convinced God is still in the healing business. The people they work among are convinced they are the most powerful shamans around, and the true God has become their God!

In his book *Spiritual Gifts in the Local Church* (1985), David Pytches records more than a dozen contemporary examples, culled from various sources, of people who have been raised from the dead. One story, taken from Albert Hibbert's 1982 biography of Smith Wigglesworth (which reports "fourteen occasions when the dead were raised during Wigglesworth's ministry"), goes as follows:

> On one occasion he called at the home in which the family was mourning the loss of a five-year-old boy. Wigglesworth stood looking at the corpse in the coffin with tears running down his cheeks. Wigglesworth requested the father to leave him alone in the room. He locked the door behind the father, lifted the corpse from the coffin and stood it up in the corner. Wigglesworth rebuked death in the name of the Lord Jesus and commanded it to surrender its victim. An amazing miracle occurred when the child returned to life.
>
> On another occasion he was used to resuscitate a corpse. The man was raised, however, still suffering from the disease which killed him. Wigglesworth told the family that unless they repented and put matters right within their home, the man would die again. The family repented. Wigglesworth prayed for them and the Lord healed the man, who lived for thirty years more.

pp. 232–233

God is still raising people from the dead. Do not be surprised if He uses you to do it sometime.

Authority over Higher-Level Spirits

With regard to higher-level spirits, the eighth area, I am not sure we really know how much authority we have. Some interpret a verse like Jude 9 as indicating that we should not get involved in confronting higher-level spirits directly. Jude 8 (see also 2 Peter 2:10–11) refers to people who "despise God's authority and insult the glorious beings above," then goes on to say in verse 9, "Not even the chief angel Michael did this. . . . Michael did not dare condemn the Devil with insulting words, but said, The Lord rebuke you!"

But when Jesus was confronted with higher-level spirits, He did not back off. I believe there were two events in Jesus' ministry when He confronted territorial spirits. The first was at the temptations (Luke 4:1–13) when Satan himself tempts Jesus in the desert. The desert was considered to be Satan's territory. By winning that contest, I believe Jesus took away at least some of Satan's authority over Israel, opening the country up for Jesus to heal and deliver people and leaving Satan to scurry around gaining support to bring Jesus to trial.

The second event in which Jesus confronted territorial spirits was when He met the demons called "Legion" or "Mob" in the Gerasene demoniac (Mark 5:1–13). When Jesus encountered these demons, they begged Him not to send them out of the region (verse 10). I believe this request identified these spirits as territorial spirits who had chosen to live in the demoniac. Interestingly, the border of the region was where the water met the land; it was the pigs who carried the demons into the water and out of their region, thus opening up the region of the ten towns to the testimony of the former demoniac.

Few Christian leaders dispute the fact that there are cosmic-level spirits at work constantly, attempting to thwart God's plans and programs. They are mentioned in Ephesians 2:2, referred to as "the spiritual powers in space." There are ample indications in the Old Testament that Israel and its neighbors believed in territorial spirits (see 1 Kings 20:23 for one example). There is quite a bit of controversy, however, over what to do about these spirits.

Many contend that neither Jesus nor Paul nor any other biblical leader (for example, Daniel in Daniel 10:13, or Moses and Joshua moving through and into pagan territory) seems to have been led to confront such higher-level spirits directly. I would say, though, that the examples given above in Jesus' ministry show that He confronted territorial spirits at least twice. And Paul states that we are to battle "the wicked spiritual forces in the heavenly world, the rulers, authorities, and cosmic powers of this dark age" (Ephesians 6:12). Perhaps this verse means we are to oppose these higher-level beings directly.

Approaches to evangelism in Argentina and other places that involve direct attacks on higher-level spirits are producing impressive results. These results seem to be related to the power of territorial spirits being broken over the city or part of the city in which Christian meetings are held. One of the leaders encouraging this approach is Edgardo Silvoso. In his report on Argentina in C. Peter Wagner's *Engaging the Enemy* (1991), Silvoso states that, though up until recently churches in Argentina seldom had even a hundred members, lately they are burgeoning by a hundred or even a thousand times. One church in Buenos Aires grew to twenty thousand members in less than six months! At least a dozen evangelists and hundreds of zealous preachers are communicating Christ in all parts of the nation. As a result, *the Argentinean church has experienced more growth in the last four years than in the previous hundred* (Wagner 1991, 110).

The apparent reason for this incredible growth is warfare prayer undergirded by a tremendous surge of unity among church leaders. This unity includes a commitment to breaking the powers of darkness over the nation through authority praying (that is, asserting authority over the spirit world in prayer). When Argentineans pray, Silvoso writes, they focus on "God, to whom they address all honor and praise; and, Satan, whom they boldly and aggressively rebuke." They believe God requires their prayers, pointing to the biblical teaching that the initiative must come from the human side: We must ask, we must knock, "[w]e must bind and release for heaven to do the same. The action on earth not only precedes but to some extent determines the answer in heaven." When people pray like this, they expect God to take action: "They engage the enemy and they bind him. And then they move on and loot his camp."

This taking up of authority is exemplified in the ministries of the leading evangelists and pastors in Argentina:

Carlos Annacondia saturates all aspects of his crusade ministry—from the preparation to the platform to the prayer brigade *under* the platform—with authority prayer. Silvoso reports, "I have estimated that of the two hours that Annacondia spends on the platform ministering, over one hour is actually spent in prayer." Annacondia has won over a million people to Christ in less than four years.

Before beginning his campaigns, Omar Cabrera, whom some consider the leading power evangelist in Argentina, closets himself for five to seven days of authoritative prayer, during which he confronts the cosmic-level spirit commanding the darkness over the city or region. His prayer frees the area spiritually so that when he presents the Gospel message, the result is usually a stampede of people giving their hearts to Christ.

Floro Olivera, a Brethren pastor, with his elders in San Justo, a suburb of Buenos Aires, saw "massive conversions" in one area after declaring that they would take that section of town for Christ.

A Baptist pastor in Androgue named Eduardo Lorenzo and his staff have challenged spiritually the cosmic-level spirit in charge of the county in which their church sits, resulting in dramatic effects that have spread through the entire county.

When we read such impressive reports, resulting, as nearly as we can tell, from an authoritative approach to spiritual warfare against territorial spirits, it is hard to side with the skeptics.

It looks as though the enemy has specially infested certain places with both general and more specific kinds of power. (We often see certain sections of cities and countries, for example, characterized by specific sinful activities such as prostitution, gambling, abortion, homosexuality and deceit.) But if we Christians get together and assert our authority against Satan, things will change. As noted by the Argentineans, however, the activity that will result in such change has to start with us. We must knock, seek, bind and release before heaven acts—not because God is unwilling to take charge but because the rules He has laid down require such ministry to be a joint venture, with us as God's partners.

The strategy for tackling cosmic-level spirits is parallel to that for dealing with "ground-level" demons (those that live in people): It is rats and garbage again. When we deal with the garbage, we weaken the rats. With cosmic-level spirits, however, the garbage is things like sin, disunity of spiritual leaders, unrighteousness, unforgiveness, prayerlessness, failure to worship, failure to get people free from ground-level garbage and rats and the like. To set the stage to confront cosmic-level spirits, then, there needs to be repentance,

Authority in ministry is an exciting aspect of our relationship with God.

unity, forgiveness, righteousness, prayer (especially intercession), worship, getting people spiritually free and the like, followed by direct challenges to the cosmic-level spirits. A strategy will also include searching out the history of a place and dealing with past sin and commitments. An excellent guidebook for doing cosmic-level warfare is George Otis Jr.'s *Informed Intercession* (1999).

Authority in ministry is an exciting aspect of our relationship with God. It is my prayer that the set of considerations raised in this chapter will challenge those of us who are not already experiencing the excitement of participating with Him in authoritative ministry to begin doing so. Nothing is so spiritually enriching yet personally humbling as being involved with God in doing things we know we cannot do ourselves!

We will now turn to the use of God's authority in churches.

16

Authority in Churches

How Did Jesus Get outside His Church?

I was conducting a seminar on healing and deliverance for a group of Taiwanese pastors when God led me to put together two verses I had never seen as related. Just thinking about the implications of this connection had such an impact on me that I decided to attempt to communicate them to the pastors through faith picturing.

The first of these verses occurs in the first book of the New Testament, in Matthew 16:18, when Jesus states that He will build His Church on the foundation of Peter's confession, and it will not be overcome even by the power of death (called the "gates of hell" in many translations). Then, in the final book of the New Testament, in Revelation 3:20, we find Jesus communicating to the church of Laodicea that He now finds himself *outside* His own Church, knocking at the door, asking for permission to enter.

My question to these pastors was this: How did Jesus get to be outside His own Church? And if He is on the outside of *your* church, what are you going to do about it?

Because I wanted them to feel, not just think, their answers, I asked them to close their eyes and picture their church buildings with Jesus standing outside, knocking to get in. As they pictured that scene, I asked them to go to the door, open it and take Jesus by the hand, drawing Him inside. I asked them to lead Him up to the pulpit and give it to Him, returning the authority over the pulpit and all that comes from it to its rightful owner. Then they were to lead Him to the musical instruments, piano, organ, guitars, drums, whatever they used in their worship times, and give Him authority over the instruments and those who play them; then to the place where the music director stands, giving him or her to Jesus; and to the choir seats, picturing each choir member who sits there and giving every one to Him. And then down into the congregation, giving each seat and its occupant to Jesus.

Then I asked these pastors to go to their offices, or wherever they prayed or prepared for their opportunities to minister, and give everything here, too—all the people, books, computers, typewriters, telephones and office supplies—to Jesus. And to their homes, giving each of their family members to Jesus. And themselves, so that Jesus could have complete authority over His Church, as well as His servants and His servants' families.

There were tears and even some wailing as we allowed the Holy Spirit to show us areas we had held back from our Master, and as we made the transactions that would put these areas in the right hands.

❧ The Pastor As Spiritual Gatekeeper

Scripture is clear that people in authority, such as pastors and teachers, are responsible to God for what they do with that authority. The standard is very high: We are told that church leaders "must be without fault" (1 Timothy 3:2), that "teachers will be judged with greater strictness than others" (James 3:1) and that "they must give to God an account of their service" (Hebrews 13:17). Not only are pastors and teachers responsible for the way they handle the Word of God, they are accountable to God for the example they set for those under their supervision. The lives of church leaders are to be exemplary in every way, modeling the behavior of the Lord they claim to serve.

Pastors (called *elders* in 1 Timothy 5:17 and Titus 1:5) are responsible for asserting authority within and through the church, with primary responsibility for prayer and ministering the Word (Acts 6:4). The senior pastor, as the top leader, holds ultimate authority and responsibility under God for all that goes on. His or her authority is not only from God but affirmed by an organization (whether a denomination or local congregation) through ordination. This position, therefore, contains important human dimensions.

The position of pastor also involves leaders in an activity that carries great impact in the spiritual realm. The authority granted at the human level through ordination is taken seriously by the spirit world, whether or not the pastor has the proper gifting to fill that office. And pastors are the spiritual authorities under God over their churches, just as men are the spiritual authorities over their homes. Although some pas-

The authority granted at the human level through ordination is taken seriously by the spirit world.

tors (like some husbands and fathers) would rather not bear this enormous responsibility, there is no way out. It is theirs, assigned by God Himself.

This spiritual authority means the senior pastor is the gateway into and out of the church, just as the father is the gateway into and out of the family. What the pastor allows into the church, or allows to stay once there, has a right to be there. And sin allowed brings dire results to churches and their leaders, just as it did to Israel and her leaders throughout the Old Testament (recall Achan in Joshua 7 and the kings of Judah and Israel in 1 Kings 12 through 2 Kings 25). God has not changed His attitude toward sin or His requirements for those in authority.

The pastor must also lead the congregation in asserting its authority over whatever territory the Lord has given it responsibility for. (See the section "The Pastor's Commitment to the Church" in the next chapter for a discussion of this.)

I heard a sad story about a pastor who used his authority badly. He was accustomed, like most pastors, to being in complete control of Sunday services. One Sunday, however, a member of his church manifested a demon during the sermon. This disruption so upset the pastor that he went to his study after the service and made a pact with Satan: "If you'll promise never to do that again, I promise never to preach about you!" So for the sake of orderliness, this pastor compromised himself and his church.

The story, I hope, is unusual, but there are many pastors who either do not know what is really going on in their churches, or else they simply choose not to get involved in circumstances that require them to take authority. This latter situation seems to be the case in the following true account (in which I have changed details to preserve anonymity).

A Hornet's Nest

A young man I will call Henry took a position as associate pastor in a small-town church. He was excited about the prospect of working with the young, dynamic senior pastor who had a vision for spiritual renewal. Soon after Henry arrived, however, he realized that the senior pastor was very discouraged. Henry and his wife, who had some experience with spiritual warfare, prayed fervently about the senior pastor's discouragement and sensed that the enemy was trying to destroy his ministry, probably because the pastor had attempted to bring renewal to the church. Seven months later the senior pastor resigned and left, broken and beaten down.

Henry and his wife escalated their efforts in warfare prayer, asserting his authority as associate pastor against the enemy's activities, some of which seemed related to the fact that several leaders in the church were Freemasons. Soon a replacement senior pastor took over. Henry tried to share with him what he and his wife were discovering about the spiritual warfare going on in and around the church. But far from agreeing or even understanding, the new man explained all their concerns away in human terms. It became clear to Henry that the new senior pastor was not going to exercise his God-given authority over the congregation.

Henry had been asserting his own authority over the church in as many ways as he could. Among other things, he had begun going into the sanctuary weekly to pray over the space, the pulpits, the choir loft, the instruments, the pews, the classrooms and anything else he could think of. Church members began to remark that they sensed God at work during worship in a new way. Some were given new hope and expectancy for spiritual renewal.

Then Henry had a discussion with the senior pastor and made his position clear. All hell seemed to break loose! It was as if a hornet's nest had been struck by a stick. Bizarre things began happening to Henry at the church: Attacks started coming from fellow staff people, from church members, even from the senior pastor himself. It began to look as though the enemy had mounted a vicious counterattack, starting after the discussion with the senior pastor. Six months later that pastor persuaded the elders that the church could not afford two pastors, and Henry was asked to leave.

As soon as he did, the spiritual decay and apathy he had fought in the church exerted new strength on the congregation. The last word I had on the church was that it is a shadow of its former self and has continued to slide rapidly downhill.

When Pastors Do Not Take Authority

Sad to say, situations in which a pastor sides with the enemy, either consciously or unconsciously, are not uncommon. If the pastor does not exercise his or her authority on behalf of God's Kingdom, it will be exploited by Satan, as seems to have been the case in this situation. A major part of the problem in this and many similar circumstances is that the senior pastor has little or no sensitivity to spiritual issues, but rather a naturalistic, secular approach to ministry, more attuned to secular organizational and business practices than to the Holy Spirit and the spiritual warfare raging in and through the congregation.

A situation that, on the surface, looks a bit more manageable is referred to in Philippians 4:2–3. This is a brief plea from the apostle Paul that two women, Euodia and Syntyche, make peace with one another. He even urged the rest of the church to aid them in the process. Why would a disagreement between two women be of such consequence that Paul would take the time (while in prison yet!) to plead with them to make amends? As an apostle, church planter and pastor to many, Paul knew a disagreement between two women who had "contended at [his] side in the cause of the gospel" (verse 3, NIV) could destroy the entire church. If leaders and founders could cause division within a church, there is little chance that those who knew of it would not also be affected. Furthermore, people new to the faith could lose heart and turn away.

Gossip, disagreement, jockeying for higher position, sin in people's lives, critical spirits and bitterness are just a few of the problems many of us have seen and experienced within a church.

How Satan rejoices to see us fight one another rather than unite against him! It is the pastor's duty, as Paul's example shows, to ensure that such matters are dealt with swiftly, so that the enemy cannot gain a foothold in the entire church.

The Issue of Control

The control issue is a big one for pastors, elders, deacons, teachers, worship leaders and others used to being in charge. We often forget that the authority we have been given is a delegated authority. But ask yourself this: When in our church services might the Holy Spirit have a chance to break in if He wanted to do something? We usually schedule things so tightly that we leave Him no opportunity. We are ordinarily guided more by the bulletin than by the Spirit.

One evening in Sydney, Australia, I learned how hard it is—but ultimately how good it is—to give up control. I was speaking at a Pentecostal church with about four hundred in attendance. I delivered my sermon, then told the people that we were going to invite the Holy Spirit to come and do whatever He wanted. Then I prayed, asking the Holy Spirit to come.

And we waited . . . and waited . . . and waited. I was determined that whatever happened was to be controlled by Him rather than me.

After what seemed an eternity, but was probably only five or ten minutes, a man toward the back raised his hand to say that he sensed someone in the congregation had a chest problem. I asked the group who that might be, and a man to my right in front raised a hand. I asked the man with the word of knowledge to come forward and pray with the man who had raised his hand. Then someone got another impression, and I was able to connect that person with another hurting person; and so on. The result was a marvelous ministry time, *out of my control.*

On another occasion I was leading a seminar of about 250 pastors and their wives on the South Pacific island of Truk.

When would the Holy Spirit be able to do anything He wanted to do?

One evening, in order to demonstrate how to go about using the authority of Christ to minister healing, I decided to invite someone forward to be prayed for. God healed him dramatically in front of the group. Then I was at a loss as to what to do next. I did not want to call any more attention to myself, but I felt there were many there whom God wanted to heal. So I asked the people to put their hands where it hurt and simply asked the Holy Spirit to come and do whatever He wanted. The result was far beyond anything I could have imagined. Probably more than one hundred people received healing that night. And again, *things were out of my control.*

In the average church, when would the Holy Spirit be able to do anything He wanted to do? How would He be able to work His way into the series of carefully scheduled events?

I asked a Presbyterian pastor this once, and he agreed that the schedule as written up in their weekly bulletin allowed no time for the Holy Spirit. "What should I do?" he asked.

I suggested that he appear in the pulpit some Sunday with nothing prepared and simply tell the people he was going to turn things over to the Holy Spirit, and then wait until He did something.

"Oh, I couldn't do that," he replied.

Then I asked if he could relinquish his authority for ten or even five minutes. He thought that over, and he actually did give the Holy Spirit five minutes the next Sunday. The report I heard was that the time was well used by the Holy Spirit—but the pastor has not done it since.

We need to give Jesus not only the people and building and its contents but also the time and schedule. *He likes to be in control.* But so do we. So we seldom risk allowing the Holy Spirit to take charge. We need to learn to trust Him to take over, especially during ministry times. Unfortunately, we are afraid of silence, and He often allows a period of silence before He starts doing things. But it is worth the wait to see Him work when we take our hands off.

❦ Personnel

Under the pastors/elders stand another group often called deacons. The apostles delegated authority to these leaders, according to Acts 6:2–3, in areas of service to the needy, the handling of finances and like matters. Such leaders today may or may not be called deacons, depending on church polity. Their functions, however, require the delegation of authority by the pastors/elders.

Then there are other staff members to whom are delegated various responsibilities. Each is accountable to both the head pastor and God for the area over which he or she is given authority. The spirit world will respond to them according to the authority assigned them within the church polity and the responsibility vested in them by their leaders.

Given the low level of understanding of the spiritual implications of the positions people hold within church structures, it is good to hold training courses to increase awareness in this area. The enemy is vigilant to find and take advantage of those who do not know their authority.

Beyond the staff and church leaders, every church needs a core of *intercessors*. These are members of the congregation gifted in intercession whose job it is to pray regularly for the church, as God leads, and for specific requests coming from staff and members. Pastors should place a high priority on enlisting, training and making continual use of intercessors. To them can be delegated great authority for protection and stopping enemy activity within the congregation.

Intercessors should also be involved in backing up prayer ministries of church members who attack the enemy in areas like deliverance, healing and challenging territorial rights. In addition, each staff member should have personal intercessors as described in chapter 7. Many of the people who intercede for the church as a whole can double as personal intercessors.

The Sacraments in Spiritual Warfare

There is powerful authority, as we have seen, in obeying God. When He is obeyed, the enemy kingdom is put to flight. Carrying out the sacraments and other forms of dedication and initiation (for example, weddings, confirmations and dedications of buildings and hymnbooks) by those with God's authority to perform them can be powerful weapons in spiritual warfare. Although most church leaders value these rituals for their benefits at the human level, we often overlook the fact that the enemy takes hits when we conduct them.

We are commanded to initiate people through baptism (Matthew 28:19). Baptism was a ritual used by the Jews to initiate Gentile converts into Judaism. Then John the Baptist used it to initiate fellow Jews (including Jesus) into the faith renewal movement he led. Baptism was also used commonly in the Greek mystery religions as an initiation ritual. Like the Lord's Supper, building dedications, weddings or any other ritual, baptismal rites can be empowered by those in authority who perform them, or they can be performed simply as meaningless rituals without empowerment.

All churches believe that some church ritual is appropriate for children soon after birth. Some churches perform dedications, some perform baptisms. Whatever the ritual, the influence on the child can be powerful when the pastor or priest uses his or her authority to dedicate the child to God and speak appropriate, God-revealed blessings over the child and family. The authority to speak powerfully comes from God and is delegated by the parents. We can be certain that such use of spiritual authority is taken seriously in the satanic kingdom. Though most pastors do bless as they dedicate babies, the ritual often seems to be merely a human coming-out party rather than an intensely spiritual event.

Dedications and blessings ought to be conducted with greater seriousness than is often the case, and only after the pastor has been careful to receive from the Lord just which blessings to pass on to the child. He or she should also spend some time explaining to the congregation what the ritual means and where the power comes from. Dedications and blessings should be prophetic, as was that of Jesus (Luke 2:22–38), perhaps involving words from others besides the pastor. Under the Holy Spirit's guidance, dedications might relate to life goals or occupation, and little ones might be blessed with such things as protection, early turning to Christ, faithfulness, long life and freedom from serious illness or accident.

Though we should not rely heavily on information gotten from demons, there is an interesting consistency to their statements concerning when they were forced to vacate a Christian's spirit (the central part of a human being where the Holy Spirit comes to live at conversion). I have asked many demons when they were forced out, expecting the usual answer: at the time the person came to Christ. On several occasions, however, demons have pointed to infant baptism or dedication as the time they had to leave.

At the time of a person's conversion, most churches believe some public ritual is again appropriate. Some baptize at this point. Others use a ceremony of confirmation or simply a testimony. Once again, a pastor should use his or her authority to challenge the enemy kingdom through prophetic utterances and blessings relating to the person's dedication. In addition, at both infant and adult dedications, the water used can be blessed and thus empowered to convey further blessing to the person.

Communion services can also be times when powerful blessings are conveyed to the participants. I have seen people fall under the power of the Holy Spirit when the elements have been consecrated with the power to heal or bring blessing at the deepest level of need. Several times, when I have not felt up to par (often for emotional reasons) while participating in a Communion service, I have blessed the elements myself with the ability to bring *me* peace. And it has happened.

The Jews practiced circumcision to obey God's command on the one hand and to enable authority figures to bless the child on the other. Blessing was also practiced at weddings, and it was taken seriously. Genesis 48 and 49 record the way Jacob used his authority just before he died to make predictions in which he included blessings for his sons and grandsons—an event showing the prophetic dimension that such blessings can bear.

> *Communion services can also be times when powerful blessings are conveyed to the participants.*

Liturgical churches often perform the Eucharist (or Communion) for purposes other than blessing those present. We who are Low Church might well learn from them to use our authority to do the same, for special purposes such as breaking satanic strongholds or hindering or helping certain causes. I believe using such a ritual applies the power of God to a situation in a special way.

A spectacular example of the use of Communion to change circumstances is recorded by Kenneth McAll in *Healing the Family Tree* (1984). McAll and his wife were shipwrecked in 1972, just after experiencing a heavy storm while passing through the Bermuda Triangle. They found themselves "silently drifting" due to a burst boiler on the "banana boat" on which they were sailing.

McAll reports that as they drifted, both he and his wife heard a steady droning sound "which continued throughout the day and night." Knowing the area was famous for the number of ships and aircraft that have been destroyed there, often under mysterious circumstances, McAll began, after their rescue, to search for the reasons. He discovered that nearly two million slaves had been drowned in that area, cast overboard because the slavers felt they could not sell them. In response, McAll arranged for several "Jubilee Eucharists" to be performed by Anglican bishops and priests, both in England and in Bermuda, beginning in July 1977. These Eucharists were celebrated "for the specific release of all those who had met their untimely deaths in the Bermuda Triangle."

Though I believe McAll's assumption is wrong that they were releasing the souls of the dead, it seems clear that these empowered rituals have been effective in breaking demonic power over the area, since to my knowledge there have been no unexplainable accidents in the area since that time. I believe what happened was that the demons who stayed after their hosts had drowned were banished.

The sacraments and other dedication and initiation rituals are empowered by God in response to our obedience. In addition (as we have seen), church leaders have the authority to bless physical objects, such as the Communion elements and the water of baptism, to convey spiritual power to the recipients. Leaders can, therefore, claim authority to further empower the elements for special purposes. These purposes may be to meet a specific need, such as for healing, to bring peace, or for some other blessing. Or they may be prophetic. Such an increase in empowerment can bring about major defeat of the enemy in the participants' lives.

✧ Functions of a Church's Authority

In the life of any church, there are three major functions of authority. Let's look at each one.

To Prevent and Protect

This first function of a church's authority—preventing things from happening—is a protective function and has internal and external dimensions. Internally the authority needs to be exercised to prevent the enemy from carrying out his schemes among the members of the congregation. Prayer for protection is an important vehicle for this purpose. So is blessing. The members of the congregation should be blessed with protection regularly by their leaders.

Another important component of prevention and protection is teaching and prayer ministry (deep-level healing) to members and those applying for membership. Members of our congregations need to learn how to use their own authority to protect themselves. But before they learn this, they must get cleaned up spiritually. I am disturbed that we allow people to join our churches without checking to see if they are carrying crippling wounds or demons. We prepare them for membership by asking about their conversion experience or past church affiliation and by feeding them information about Christianity and the church. But many are hurting and many are carrying demons.

Membership classes should include deep-level healing and, if necessary, deliverance. Historians tell us that the early Church required a preparation period of up to two or three years during which converts were instructed, healed from emotional wounds and delivered from demons. Imagine what a church would be like if people got cleaned up on the way in!

In addition, leaders and followers both should be putting on the armor of God (Ephesians 6:13–18) daily. A pastor friend of mine was feeling led to put on the spiritual armor regularly.

288

As he prayed about it, he asked God how often he should put it on. The Lord answered, *As often as you put on your clothes.* So he does it daily.

One of my associates reports that he once asked a demon, "Where is the client's spiritual armor?" The demon replied, "It's on the floor at his feet. We never let him put it on. We hide it sometimes, or distract him to make sure he doesn't put it on. That's why he's so easy to control."

To Stop Enemy Attacks

The second function of church authority is stopping any attacks the enemy launches. Every congregation contains those vulnerable to satanic attack, especially since they do not usually get cleaned up on the way into church membership. So every church should function as a spiritual hospital, seeking out those who need prayer ministry (including deliverance) and taking the initiative to bring healing to them. Such an approach can prevent further attack since it reduces vulnerability.

In addition, leaders and intercessors should be on the lookout for enemy attacks and use their authority to put out whatever fires develop in the lives of their parishioners. As with prevention, so with stopping attacks. Instruction in how parishioners can assert their own authority is also a must.

To Mount Spiritual Attacks

In addition to ministering to individuals, churches need to mount corporate attacks on spiritual problems, both within the congregation and in the community. There may be times the enemy attacks a whole congregation, or substantial parts of it, with a problem. Often it seems that a wave of depression or unemployment or divorce has swept over a congregation. Such problems should be attacked by church leaders taking authority over the problem on behalf of those in the congregation suffering from it.

Usually, though, a church is so little threat to the enemy that he does little on any scale that might be noticed. He certainly does not want churches to wake up to his presence and activity, so he limits his work to individuals who have no idea that what is happening is not their own fault or the result of chance. Churches awakened to Satan's presence and activity, on the other hand, are attacked in big ways, at least until the leaders and membership get cleaned up spiritually to the point that they are not so vulnerable.

Each congregation should also tackle community problems. Once the leaders of a congregation have found out from the Lord the extent of the community they are responsible for (see next chapter), they should take authority over any satanic stronghold within that territory. Churches can put out of business "adult" bookstores, prostitution rings, abortion clinics, homosexual activities, gambling operations, dope peddling, alcoholism, thievery and other sinful activities being carried on within their sphere of responsibility. And when all the churches in a city band together to assert their joint spiritual authority (as they have in Cincinnati and in other cities in banning pornography), they can clean up whole cities.

Satan certainly does not want churches to wake up to his presence and activity.

17

Commitment

The Pastor's Commitment to the Church

There is a direct relationship between the commitment of a pastor (or any leader) and the authority he or she wields in the spirit world. Pastors who are committed to something other than their churches are vulnerable to enemy influence. Though serving the church, their primary commitment may really be to their own advancement or something else (such as money, prestige or an easy life). We cannot expect the spirit world to take them seriously when they assert their authority over the church people and places, or over the community they purport to serve.

This is an important lesson learned a few years ago by Pastor Bob Beckett of The Dwelling Place in Hemet, California. In the book *Breaking Strongholds in Your City* (edited by C. Peter Wagner, 1993), Beckett records how he had seen his position in Hemet as a stepping-stone to a more prestigious position elsewhere. This lack of commitment affected Beckett's spiritual authority, both inside the church he planted—which was riddled with divisions, church splits, and other "normal" problems—and within the community.

The turning point came when he heard the Lord asking him, *What is your commitment to Hemet?* This stunned Bob. He thought, *What a question! Who in his right mind commits himself to a place like Hemet?* But he realized,

> I could never begin to bring deliverance of any real and lasting significance to my own area if I was living here with my emotional and spiritual bags packed, always waiting for the day when the Lord would call me to a larger community with greater influence and significance.

> pp. 162–163

As he and his wife finally committed themselves to lifelong ministry in Hemet, even purchasing cemetery plots in the town, their authority was finally established within the congregation. This resulted in significant effects at the church level: conversions, healings, deliverances and exciting church growth. But they still felt their church was unable to make the same impact in their community.

So, calling lay leaders and other churches to join them in their *territorial commitment* to Hemet, they took "long-term territorial responsibility for the land [we] are living in." This eventually led to a Strategic Warfare Conference, during which they "put into practice this concept of repentance over our city, seeking God's forgiveness for social sins." Whites repented for their sins against Native Americans; Methodist and Pentecostal pastors apologized for their attitudes toward each other; a representative of the water company, whose major miscalculations years earlier had financially ruined the valley, repented for the company's mistakes. In this ground-level move toward reconciliation, "years of division and hatred were broken in the spiritual realm [and] the principalities and powers received serious setbacks." The conference was followed by establishing a prayer canopy over the city, symbolized by actually driving stakes into the ground.

From that day there has been a noticeable difference in the authority Beckett and the other pastors in town have been able to exercise, both in their churches and in their community. About 35 ministers freely cooperate in the work of evangelism. They also helped a church built on the site of an Indian massacre identify the spiritual authority of the enemy in their congregation, resulting in such things as violent deaths in the families of nearly all the pastors and the church's neighborhood becoming the "geographical center for gang violence in the whole area." Beckett writes,

> When the pastor learned about the Indian bloodshed and the history of violent deaths among pastors, he called a meeting of his elders and intercessors. They engaged in a time of sincere intercession and deep repentance for their land and their church.
>
> What happened? Less than two months later, gang members began to come to the Lord. At least one walked into the church during the Sunday service and said, "I want to be saved!" Another gang leader, his mother, and then the entire family came to Christ. Gang violence in the area has dropped since then, although it has not yet disappeared entirely.

p. 160

How many pastors sacrifice much of their spiritual authority, as Beckett did, by not being fully committed to the churches they serve? It is common for pastors to hold the same attitude as many employees in other occupations: giving preference to the desire to get ahead. In denomination after denomination, pastors serving smaller churches envy pastors with larger ones, and they work hard and pray for the day when they will "get promoted" to a larger church. Like Beckett, they have their emotional bags packed and are ready to move as soon as possible. Meanwhile, pastors with larger churches look down on those with smaller ones, since they consider the size of the church a badge of success and a mark of their approval by the Lord. Such attitudes delight Satan, who can poke holes in any church and in any pastor's authority when that pastor is committed more to getting ahead than to serving the Lord.

✺ Responsibility of the Church

It is important for a congregation and its leaders to discover, as Beckett did, what they have authority over. One obvious answer is the congregation itself. Such authority (as we noted earlier) involves preventing/protecting, stopping and attacking. The pastor and church leaders are responsible for asserting their authority in the spirit world to prevent or stop whatever the enemy is doing in the lives of their members.

And we can be sure the enemy is working any way he can to hinder and harass those who have committed themselves to Christ. A major concern of the leaders, then, should be to prevent and stop enemy activity among the flock. To be maximally effective in protecting the congregation and stopping attacks, leaders and those with intercessory gifts should be praying constantly with authority for their members.

The responsibility for leaders and members of churches to clean up whatever the enemy is doing within their circles is implicit in the letters to the seven churches in Revelation 2 and 3. The letters were written to the angels, or perhaps the pastors, of these churches, pointing out strengths and weaknesses and encouraging them to persevere to the end to receive the rewards the Lord wanted to give them.

We learn from these letters the kinds of problems to watch out for. In Ephesus the problem the leaders needed to take authority over was the loss of their first love, apparently due to the presence of sin in their midst (Revelation 2:4–5). In Pergamum the problems were eating food offered to idols, immorality and following a cult (2:14–15). In Thyatira the leaders tolerated a woman who called herself a messenger of God but was misleading people by teaching immorality and the eating of food offered to idols (2:20–23). The Lord called the church in Sardis dead, in spite of their reputation for being alive (3:1). And in Laodicea the problem was lukewarmness in spiritual matters, with an accompanying materialistic way of life that deluded them into feeling they were rich, in spite of the fact that they were really "miserable and pitiful" spiritually (3:15–17).

A major concern of church leaders should be to prevent and stop enemy activity among the flock.

Combining these messages gives a warning to look out for sin, compromising with idolatry, immorality, membership in cults, spiritual deadness, lukewarmness and loss of first love, misleading teaching within the church and materialism.

These first-century congregations were commended, on the other hand, for hard work, patience, discernment and perseverance in suffering (Ephesus, Revelation 2:2–3); for spiritual richness and steadfastness in the face of gossip and persecution (Smyrna, 2:9–10); for faithfulness in persecution (Pergamum, 2:13); for love, faithfulness, service, patience, growth in works and refusal to follow evil teaching (Thyatira, 2:19, 24); and for maintaining a little power, faithfulness to Jesus' teaching and endurance (Philadelphia, 3:8, 10). These are the traits leaders and intercessors in our churches today need to be concerned with, asserting their authority to protect against evil, to stop it and to bring about the characteristics for which the Lord commended the churches of Revelation.

Geographic Responsibility

A pastor called me several years ago and described some trouble his congregation was experiencing. In addition to more or less "normal" problems like divorce and bickering, a cult had arisen among the young people in his church, committed to the pagan god Dagon (1 Samuel 5). We decided to tackle this problem by conducting a seminar in which we taught on idolatry and ministered freedom to several people. Circumstances began to change in the church as the pastor and intercessors started to take seriously the satanic activity among their people and to assert their authority over the enemy.

In addition to the internal authority church leaders are to exert, God has made churches the spiritual gatekeepers for the communities they serve. This means each church is responsible for the geographic or social territory God has assigned it. Church leaders are to assert their authority in the spirit world over this territory to cancel whatever authority the enemy claims within that space.

In order to fulfill our responsibility in this area, we must learn first what territory we have authority over. If we do not already know, we need to spend time in prayer to find out. God wants to reveal to us just what He holds us responsible for. I believe for most churches this involves a certain geographical area near the church building, plus some social space defined in terms of the personal relationships of its members. The authority to be wielded over these territories consists of the same prevention/protection, stopping and attacking activities we have been emphasizing. The primary means is intercession.

> *God has made churches the spiritual gatekeepers for the communities they serve.*

Another major factor, however, is *understanding*. Over and over, as we deal with demons, we find that a major source of their power is the ignorance of the person they live in. Likewise, as long as church leaders are unaware of their authority and responsibility over a specific geographic territory, the enemy can work without hindrance.

God's Commissioning

Once during a lull in a seminar, a pastor I will call Bill asked me how I thought his church should proceed in escalating its involvement in spiritual warfare. His was a small church, the only Protestant congregation for perhaps a square mile of their city. Both of us wondered if the fact that they had not been active in spiritual warfare might have something to do with their small size. As Bill's eyes were opened to the spiritual dimensions of the position of his church in the community, he began to look for ways they could move responsibly in the direction of becoming a greater threat to the enemy.

What came to me, as I asked the Lord for guidance in answering Bill's question, was that his small church was the gateway through which or around which any spiritual enemy must go to gain access to that community. So I asked him what was going on in his community. Bill indicated that the enemy had a pretty good foothold. My next question to him was this: "Do you think your church bears any responsibility for the present situation? Could it be that whatever the enemy is able to do in your church's backyard can be done only with your permission? Or because your church is ignoring it?"

I told Bill the story I recounted in chapter 9 of Steve Nicholson, the pastor in Evanston, Illinois, who felt led to claim certain territory for the Lord. According to C. Peter Wagner in *Engaging the Enemy*, Nicholson identified a certain street on the north, another on the south, and streets on the east and west as defining the territory he was claiming responsibility for and challenging enemy spirits over. As he prayed and fasted, a high-level demon identifying itself as a spirit of witchcraft appeared to him, saying he was in charge of that area and would not give Steve that much territory. Steve replied something like "Sorry, but I'm taking it," and was able to break the spirit's grip—evidenced by the fact that immediately after this confrontation his church began to grow, largely through a steady flow of converts from witchcraft (most of whom, by the way, needed deliverance from demons).

My conclusion is that every congregation is commissioned by God to take, protect and commit itself to the spiritual cleansing of the territory in which it functions, as Beckett did. My suggestion to Bill was that their church find out from the Lord what territory He holds them accountable for, attack sinful establishments within this territory through authority praying and run them out of business. We have the authority and responsibility to participate in the cleansing of our communities, and the experiments going on in Argentina, Hemet and elsewhere predict our success if we go about our attacks in the right way.

✎ Authority over the History

Congregations can experience various kinds of dysfunction stemming from the fact that the enemy, at some time in the past, has been able to obtain rights in the church. This situation parallels the rats-and-garbage condition in individuals whereby, because of agreements made with the enemy by their ancestors, demons have the right to live in them. It also parallels the situation when a person buys a new home in which past inhabitants gave the enemy rights.

To deal with such dysfunction, leaders in a church need to take authority over its past, just as the new owner of a home does, to cancel all past activities or agreements that gave the enemy rights. As with a home, those wielding God's authority in the present have the right to cancel any authority given to the enemy by past occupants. When problems like divisions, immorality, dissatisfaction and criticism flourish in a church, there may be a satanic grip there with roots in the past.

As we investigate the history of a congregation, we often find such problems as bickering, fighting, immorality on the part of pastors, dominance by certain families and other indications that

Satan has been getting the best of the members and staff for generation after generation. When such problems have occurred in the history of a congregation, the first step toward breaking the enemy's power is for the congregation, led by its leaders, to engage in identificational repentance. In this way they assume responsibility for the sins of the past members of the congregation and repent for them, as Nehemiah and Daniel did (Nehemiah 1; Daniel 9). The next step is for the leaders and intercessors to direct the congregation in authority praying to cancel the devil's rights over the congregation and

Leaders in a church need to take authority over its past.

its property. (John Dawson's book *Taking Our Cities for God*, although it deals specifically with cities, provides useful guidance for dealing with the historical influences on our churches.)

While Betsy Runkle-Edens was serving as associate pastor of a church in Ohio, she and her husband, Gary, became interested in discovering why their church and the one across the street (of the same denomination) had separated. They found that the one they served, Second Church, although it had experienced numerical growth during the 1950s and 1960s, had never achieved spiritual vitality. The other one, First Church, had experienced some spiritual health but had remained small in numbers. Then they discovered that way back in 1836, a huge debate had surfaced at First Church over slavery and whether infants who die are damned. In anger, some of the members decided to leave and start their own church.

Although this bit of history appeared merely interesting and harmless at first, there was more to the story. Apparently from the day of the split onward, members of the two churches continued in animosity toward one another. The churches stereotyped each other, competed for members and refused to cooperate down through the generations in reaching their community for Christ.

In praying about this, Gary and Betsy felt they heard the Holy Spirit saying that corporate healing was necessary before these churches could experience God's blessing. So they urged the senior pastors to consult with their respective elders about the possibility of mutual forgiveness and healing for the sins of their forefathers.

So far nothing has been done about the matter. Both churches continue to struggle, and I believe they will remain ineffective until they take such spiritual issues seriously and do something about them. The enemy has legitimate rights in these churches until they repent and use their authority to take those rights away from him.

Contrast the condition of these churches with several situations, mediated by Ed Silvoso, in which numbers of churches have agreed to pray together and repent to each other for past sins and competitiveness. They have also agreed to learn how to conduct spiritual warfare against the enemy—to fight the real enemy instead of each other. In Resistencia, Argentina, the results—in terms of conversions, church growth, mutual affection among church leaders and cooperation among the leaders to break the enemy's power due to sinful establishments—have been phenomenal. The results have been similar with the churches in a California county and in several other places in Argentina and the United States where Silvoso has taught this approach (see the article by Silvoso listed in the bibliography and in my book *Behind Enemy Lines*, as well as books and DVDs by Silvoso listed on the Internet). When churches repent, cooperate and exercise their authority in concert, the Kingdom of God is enhanced in major ways, both within the churches and within the communities they serve.

A serious problem that affects many churches—which Betsy Runkle-Edens discovered while she was pastoring in Ohio—is that Freemasons have participated in planning and building churches and leading congregations. They especially like to lay the cornerstones and dedicate the buildings. Since this organization is committed to Satan (although without the knowledge of many, both inside and outside the organization), the enemy is able to gain considerable authority over a church through such dedications. In addition, many churches have several members, some in leadership positions, who belong to Masonic lodges.

It is no surprise, then, that many such churches are dying or have for years been spiritually ineffective. The power of the enemy gained through Masonic dedications can be canceled if leaders in the church use their authority to do so, but most pastors neither understand the problem nor know what to do about it. Until pastors and lay leaders gain understanding and act on it in their God-given authority, they can expect no renewal and little spiritual life.

Authority over the Property

We have mentioned the need for a pastor to take authority over a congregation, including its buildings. But once satanic power over the history has been broken, it is important to keep asserting our authority, since demons are opportunistic, seeking and finding every opportunity to infect church buildings, their environs and furnishings. I do not know what all the rules are, but apparently it is necessary to claim authority over places regularly to assure that they are spiritually clean.

It is necessary to claim authority over places regularly to assure that they are spiritually clean.

Several years ago several participants in a seminar and I were asked to check out a bell tower in the church building where we were meeting. Some felt there might be demonic influence in a room in that tower. And as we entered the room, even I, who do not usually feel such presences, felt something evil. Then we received two pieces of information that tended to confirm that the room needed spiritual cleansing. First, a runaway teenager had found a way to get into the church and had lived in that room for several weeks. Also, a musical and drama group that had experienced much dissension had used the room for practice and storing their instruments.

With these facts in mind, we asked the Holy Spirit what to do and began authority praying according to His leading. We dealt with the history of the church and, with the authority of one of the pastors, claimed the room for Jesus Christ alone. Soon we all sensed the spiritual heaviness lift and the room take on a completely different feel.

During a seminar in a different place, one of the young women assisting in ministry had a disturbing experience when she left us. We were working to release someone from a demon, and this woman had to leave to go to another engagement. As she left the church, she experienced a powerful attack from the evil one, such that she could hardly move. She came running back into the church building, asking for someone to pray over her. Someone did, claiming protection for her as she left. We found out later that before we had arrived to start our seminar, the church's prayer team had prayed earnestly, taking authority over the inside of the church but paying no attention to the parking lot outside. When this woman left the church, then, she was apparently hit by some angry demons who could not get into the church building but had rights to the parking lot by virtue of the fact that they had not been commanded to leave.

In another congregation, some unpleasant things began happening shortly after they received a carpet donated by a funeral home. The presence of the carpet was not considered until in prayer someone sensed the Lord revealing that this was the cause. Thankfully the church had not yet installed the carpet. They disposed of it and the strange events stopped. They might have taken authority over the carpet and found they could thus cancel the enemy's power, but they chose to get rid of it because they felt God telling them to.

In another situation that I mentioned in chapter 9, a series of tragedies was probably averted when a pastor called me to ask whether I thought his church should rent a Masonic lodge on Sunday mornings for worship. I strongly advised against it, reasoning that although the Christians might be able to do spiritual housecleaning each Sunday, the fact that the Masons met there between Sundays, rededicating it regularly to Satan, meant they would re-infect it every week. And given the nature of that organization, such infection would be at a high level, making it risky for the church to meet there. They might find, for example, that they had failed to clean out a room completely of all evil presences—a room in which worship took place or a choir practiced or nursery children were tended to. This would put any vulnerable people in those groups at great risk.

I have mentioned teachers who experienced dramatic changes in their students when they started to take authority over their classrooms in Jesus' name. The same applies to Sunday school teachers. If church buildings are prayed over properly, there should be no problem. But church buildings are primary targets for demons, since by infecting them, demons can cause disruption in God's camp. So we find that individuals, often young people, submit to temptation to sin on church property, thus giving the enemy rights to the places where they sinned. Earlier I mentioned the pastor's son who confessed to having had sexual relations in the balcony of his father's church. This incident, although unknown to the pastor, marked the start of a nosedive in his ministry. Sin committed by an individual in secret, as we learn from the story of Achan (Joshua 7), can have disastrous effects on the nation or congregation of which he or she is part.

It is important, therefore, for us to cleanse the rooms spiritually whenever we use them, even if they are on church property, to protect against any possible interference. Church buildings should be cleansed regularly in case people have carried in demons on their persons, or if demons have gained the right to enter by some other means. It is possible the enemy sends his agents with street people who come for help during the week. And, of course, in most churches a fair number of those who attend are carrying demons.

When demons get into churches, there are certain places they seem to congregate more than others. A friend with the gift of discernment, who has been involved in cleansing several churches, finds that the three greatest concentrations of demons are in the nursery, in the part of the church office where the records and offerings are processed and in the musical instruments. Demons are also frequently present in the library and around the pulpit. At one church powerful demons of depression were found working at every entrance to the building. In attempting to rid at least one church of these demons, my friend found they would not budge when he commanded them to leave. They would leave only when the pastor asserted his authority over them.

To counteract the influence of demons in a newly built church in Fairbanks, Alaska, the pastors called for the members to gather one Sunday afternoon with paintbrushes. The church supplied the paint and the people were invited to write blessings, Scripture and whatever else God brought to their minds on the walls and ceiling before they were painted. The painters then painted over the words, and the blessings were painted into the building.

In addition to contaminating church buildings, demons can also infest the furnishings of a church. In churches for which families have purchased pews or windows, enemy agents can be given rights to those items by virtue of their rights in the families—unless, of course, the authority of Jesus has been used to cleanse them. I have already suggested the possibility of a carpet being infested, and we have noted that musical instruments are a likely place for demons to hang out. So are the seats of disgruntled choir members—or, for that matter, discontented members of the congregation. At one of my seminars, the leader of a Christian musical group reported a dramatic change in the results of their concerts when they started blessing their instruments. The blessings probably broke any enemy power that was there and added God's power.

Being Alert

Two things should be clear by now concerning church leadership and the other aspects of authority we have dealt with: First, *we are at war*; and second, *we have great authority* to win regularly in confrontations with the enemy. Since Satan's main weapon is our ignorance, I hope and pray that the kind of information we have been discussing will awaken us to wield the weapons God has given us. There is much we do not know about spiritual warfare. But I hope this presentation will alert us to some of the principles that seem to be at work, as well as to what we can do by way of experimentation to find success.

We who are in church leadership should not be frantic or fearful about the challenges of the enemy. We should, rather, take care to exercise our authority regularly over both our people and our property and furnishings. We must recognize that enemy spirits have a job to do—to mess us up—and that they are at it full-time. We need to walk in authority day in and day out, therefore, always mindful of the enemy's schemes (2 Corinthians 2:11). Our awareness of the warfare we are in should make it as natural as breathing to assert our authority by claiming God's presence and power, in and over us and our surroundings.

Now we will wrap up our discussion by turning to a few more general matters, including the relationship of authority-focused thinking to the kind of Christianity Jesus intends to be normal.

18

Our Authority Is Great

❧ He Never Got Frantic

Once there was a Man who came into the world sent by God the Father to bring freedom from captivity (Luke 4:18) and to be lifted up so He could draw all the peoples of the world to Himself (John 12:32). This was an incredible assignment; there were so many people to help. The enemy was so active and effective. Those in power were so uncaring, and in the habit of misusing their power to benefit themselves alone. And Jesus felt such compassion for those who were hurting (Matthew 9:36; 14:14).

Where was truth? Where was honesty? Where were those who cared for the oppressed? Who cared at all to do God's will?

The situation was enough to keep the anxiety level of the strongest caring person very high; enough to lead to impatience, frustration, anger and even violence if people did not see things His way and get on board His program.

But Jesus knew who He was, where He had come from and where He was going. Knowing these things, He was secure in Himself and able to exercise the authority granted Him by the Father in spite of criticism and opposition. With this knowledge to undergird Him, Jesus went about His Father's business with an admirable singleness of purpose.

He was disappointed at times, especially with the disciples, and angry, especially at the religious leaders who oppressed rather than helped the hurting. He got tired, especially on days when the crowds would not let Him alone, and lonely for the presence of the Father. And He hurt with compassion for the sheep wandering without a shepherd (Matthew 9:36).

But with a world to win, and only three years to do His job, He never got frantic! He did what the Father showed Him to do. He healed many but walked right past many others. He cast out demons from many, but there must have been many more He never helped. He spoke gladly to the crowds at times but at other times ran away from them.

And He is our model. What better message could this book convey than to challenge us to be what Jesus was and do what He did? Oh, that we would have the security He had, knowing who we are and why we are here! And the commitment to do the will of the Father, whatever opposition and misunderstanding we have to put up with. And the ability to feel His compassion for those around us in enemy captivity.

> *Jesus was secure in Himself and able to exercise the authority granted Him by the Father in spite of criticism and opposition.*

❧ We Are at War

We have seen clearly that we are at war against "the wicked spiritual forces in the heavenly world" (Ephesians 6:12). It is also clear by now that the context in which we are to operate authoritatively is one of warfare between the kingdoms. Jesus has put uniforms on us, given us weapons and commissioned us to fight. We know who gets to win. But for reasons we do not understand, although Jesus has won the victory, the war is not yet over. Many battles still need to be fought. Many prisoners who have been taken need to be set free (Luke 4:18–19).

But we have at least two enemies, not one. Satan and his demonic helpers, of course, constitute an ever-present challenge. The other enemy is his chief weapon: *ignorance*. Although Paul said, "We are not unaware of [Satan's] schemes" (2 Corinthians 2:11, NIV), most American Christians today, even those who know their Bibles best, are almost totally unaware of his schemes, as well as the authority we have been given to thwart them.

Such widespread ignorance makes us sad, but we can be happy about the fact that we see at least the beginnings of a movement toward greater spiritual awareness. Some are even speaking of a worldwide movement of the Holy Spirit. Incredible things are occurring around the globe, even as I write, and some of them are happening in the United States. Signs and wonders, healings and deliverances—often accompanied by people turning to Christ in numbers unprecedented in human history—are being reported from China and the Muslim world.

And in the United States, certain churches are discovering the importance of the Holy Spirit, intercessory prayer, contemporary worship, healing, spiritual warfare and even fasting. As I write, I have just come back from an incredible weekend seminar in an Episcopal church that is becoming biblically normal. And I get to conduct a dozen or more such seminars per year in Presbyterian, Methodist, Baptist, independent, even Nazarene church contexts in the United States as well as in Switzerland, Korea, Australia, Hong Kong, Norway and other places. It is unlikely that such non- or even anticharismatic groups would have been open to people working overtly in the power of the Holy Spirit a generation ago. But God seems to be "breaking loose" these days in many interesting and unpredictable places.

A hunger for spiritual vitality on the part of many Christian leaders and ordinary Christian followers seems to be coinciding with the willingness of God to work in power anywhere He is invited.

One indication of this outpouring of the Spirit in our day is the rise of movements of Christian men toward *reclaiming their rightful authority*, at least at the human level. Organizations such as Promise Keepers have led the way. In a country where women have outnumbered men in churches for decades and, by default, have had to take the leadership God expects men to take, this is a breath of fresh air. Christian men and women alike are realizing that if God is to come and heal our land, we must exercise our God-given authority over homes, families, churches, communities and beyond. The Promise Keepers movement is a start in the right direction; they paved the way for numerous other smaller movements with male-oriented emphases.

We should pray that both men's and women's movements will carry their members all the way past the spiritual ignorance that has characterized American Christianity.

Normal Christianity

As I began to move in the authority Jesus gives us, I recognized that the Christianity I had been living was sub-biblical and, therefore, subnormal. As Christians we are not intended to live the way most of us have been functioning—with little or no recognition of what is going on in the invisible spiritual world. As this dimension was opened up to me, I began to become more what a normal, biblical Christian ought to be.

I have tried in these pages to suggest various aspects of what I think normal Christianity should look like. By way of summary, then, along with some amplification, let me suggest three major components of normalcy.

Staying Close to Jesus

I have emphasized throughout this volume that if we are to be normal Christians, *we must stay close to Jesus in the same way He stayed close to the Father.* Our aim in our relationship with God should be nothing short of total intimacy—the kind Jesus practiced. He received His power from being filled with the Holy Spirit. His authority, however, sprang from His intimacy with the Father. He spent hours and hours in prayer, keeping in close contact with the Father. In this way He kept His will lined up with the Father's, seeing to it that He never did anything except on the Father's authority (John 5:19; 7:16–18).

Jesus is the Vine, we are branches. As with grapevines, both vine and branches are important to the bearing of fruit. Neither can function by itself. Branches in particular cannot function or even live by themselves. As Jesus said,

> Remain united to me, and I will remain united to you. A branch cannot bear fruit by itself; it can do so only if it remains in the vine. In the same way you cannot bear fruit unless you remain in me . . . for you can do nothing without me.
>
> John 15:4–5

This means spending time with Jesus in prayer. It also means listening constantly for His voice, whether through Scripture, through people, through reading or directly. We need to keep on good terms with Him, growing in our commitment and staying close to Him. Just as it was necessary for my son to keep on good terms with me if he wanted to continue having permission to use my credit card, so it is with us and Jesus. We should be in constant conversation with our Lord, friend to friend (John 15:15), as those chosen to be with Him. For He seeks to relate to us as He did to the apostles, to whom He said, "I have chosen you *to be with me.* . . . I will also send you out to preach, and you will have authority to drive out demons" (Mark 3:14–15).

Note the order of the reasons Jesus gave for choosing the Twelve: first, *to be with Him,* and only then to preach and drive out demons. Relationship first, ministry second. As in the beginning we were made for a close relationship with God, so Jesus chose twelve to be closely related to Him, to be His friends. They would walk and talk with Him, not as servants but as those who shared the Kingdom with Him. *That Kingdom would be theirs as well as His.* Jesus would share with them all the knowledge the Father shared with Him (John 15:15). And they could ask Him for anything so long as they stuck close to Him (John 15:7), since their relationship was more His choice than theirs (John 15:16).

Relationship first, ministry second.

God's power is there for us through the filling of the Holy Spirit. But keeping our wills lined up with God's can be another matter. This comes for us, as with Jesus, from spending time with God in private and listening to Him as we seek to represent Him in ministry and in all other facets of our lives. Jesus' success rate in ministry was 100 percent since He always lined up His will with that of the Father. Our record is considerably less than His. The difference, I believe, lies in our ability to hear and follow the Father's voice. For me the biggest challenge in healing ministry is not in the area of power but in the area of intimacy in my relationship with the Father—a relationship that is essential if we are to be successful in coordinating our wills with His.

The major external fruit of our intimate relationship with the Father is love. As we mature in intimacy, we mature in love— love for God and love for all whom God loves. Loving God has been a constant theme in these pages as we have dealt with our authority under Christ. What we have not emphasized so far is that this intimacy requirement mandates that we also practice an intense love toward God's people, our brothers and sisters.

Reminding us of this requirement and its relationship to the ability of God to flow His power through us, Jack Deere writes in *Surprised by the Power of the Spirit*:

> Spiritually mature Christians love God and his people passionately, and they hate anything that takes them away from God. Only in the context of such love will Bible knowledge and the gifts of the Spirit ever achieve their divine purposes. The power of the Spirit can flow unhindered through passionate love for God and his children.
>
> p. 206

There is one aspect of the relationship of intimacy to authority that I find quite puzzling. People who seem to have gone off track in their spiritual lives retain what looks like the same amount of power and authority they had when they were faithful and better motivated. Could it be that Romans 11:29—translated in the NIV as "God's gifts and his call are irrevocable"—applies here? If so, those who once were given spectacular gifts get to keep them even though they are no longer faithful to the Master. Perhaps, though, these are the ones Jesus says will not make it:

> Not everyone who calls me Lord, Lord will enter the Kingdom of heaven, but only those who do what my Father in heaven wants them to do. When the Judgment Day comes, many will say to me, Lord, Lord! In your name we spoke God's message, by your name we drove out many demons and performed many miracles! Then I will say to them, I never knew you. Get away from me, you wicked people!
>
> Matthew 7:21–23

With this as a warning, it behooves us to do our best to keep close to Jesus so we can participate in His life and work as God intended us to work—on His terms rather than ours.

Knowing Who We Are

Second, we need to underline what we have said throughout this book: *We must know who we are and the authority that entails.* We are children of the King! Royal blood flows in our veins. We have the authority to come boldly and confidently into His presence (Hebrews 4:16) and call God "Abba," Dad. We do not have to fear Him as Isaiah did (Isaiah 6:5). Further, we know we are loved by God because of who we are, not because of anything we may accomplish. As John says, "See how much the Father has loved us! His love is so great that we are called God's children—and so, in fact, we are" (1 John 3:1).

One mind-blowing aspect of our status is the *trust* God puts in us by granting us this position and the authority inherent in it. When Jesus gave His disciples authority and power and then sent them out to minister, He trusted them. (Would you have trusted the disciples with anything, especially with authority and power?) When Jesus reinstated Peter, He trusted him and gave him authority to look after His sheep (John 21:15–19). When Jesus left the earth, He entrusted us with the Holy Spirit and the authority that goes along with His presence in us, predicting that with Him we "will do what [Jesus did]—yes, [we] will do even greater things" than He did (John 14:12).

Jesus trusted the disciples and us so much that He authorizes us to be called *His friends*, not slaves, because He has entrusted us with "everything I heard from my Father" (John 15:15). It is, therefore, our Kingdom as well as His (Luke 12:32; 22:29–30).

Knowing We Are at War

A third element crucial to Christian normalcy is that *we must recognize we are at war and behave accordingly.* We are to put on the armor of God (Ephesians 6:13–18) and join the ranks of God's shock troops, fighting on His behalf behind enemy lines. For, according to 1 John 5:19, "The whole world is under the rule of the Evil One." As soldiers we are to be obedient to our Leader and disciplined in our personal lives. We should not be running or hiding, trying to avoid the war; we must enter it actively, seeking victories for our Master in His war with our enemy.

In warfare we risk the possibility of defeat. Even in our war, not all battles are won, although ultimate victory is sure. But even when we are bested in battle, we are fighting. I have confessed that, during nearly forty years of my Christian life, God wanted me to fight the enemy but I was unprepared and hiding. For years I barely knew a war was being waged. I was probably more of a hindrance than a help to the war effort.

Biblically normal Christianity requires that we wake up to the reality of the war and learn to use the weapons God has given us to fight the real enemy. Our churches are largely secular, living and working at the natural or human level. Some have been doing a good job at that level. But normal, biblical Christianity demands that we live and work at both natural and supernatural levels. Only when we fight at both levels can we effectively fight our enemy who lives and works at both. For, in addition to the human level,

> The weapons we use in our fight are not the world's weapons but God's powerful weapons, which we use to destroy strongholds. We destroy false arguments; we pull down every proud obstacle that is raised against the knowledge of God; we take every thought captive and make it obey Christ.
>
> 2 Corinthians 10:4–5

These verses speak of a different level of warfare than we are used to fighting on, and a different caliber of weapons than we are used to wielding. But we have the authority to fight at that level and use that kind of weapon. Now let's learn how—and become normal.

✣ Allegiance/Relationship, Truth/Knowledge and Spiritual Power

There are at least three crucial dimensions to Christian life and witness: relationship, truth and power.

Allegiance Leading to Relationship with Christ

Allegiance to Christ, in contrast with any other allegiance, is the starting point for the *relationship* with Jesus that saves us and facilitates the authority we have been discussing. This relationship assures us of the quality of life Jesus promised when He said, "I have come in order that you might have life—life in all its fullness" (John 10:10). We have the authority to be part of God's family (John 1:12), in close relationship with the God of the universe, and to live this abundant life even while living in enemy territory. And when Jesus returns, we have the right to enjoy this relationship forever with Him.

Jesus put this relationship with Himself first and considered the intimacy with Him that flows from it in choosing His closest followers. Mark 3:14–15 records that Jesus "chose twelve, whom he named apostles. I have chosen you *to be with me,* he told them. I will also send you out to preach, and you will have authority to drive out demons." Once again, note the order: These men were chosen first to be close to Him, and only then to preach and work in authority in relation to demons. So authority starts with allegiance/commitment that leads to closeness in a relationship with Jesus.

Allegiance to Christ ———— leads to ————▶ Relationship with Christ

The relationship flowing from our allegiance to Christ is foundational to the authority in which we walk as we seek to live the fruits of the Spirit (Galatians 5:22–23). This relationship provides us with the authority to love the unlovable, to be joyful in the midst of gloom, to be peaceful when things are falling apart, to be patient when things look hopeless, and all in all to live righteous lives in an evil world. In short, *our relationship with Christ provides us with the authority to live as He did.*

In addition, our authority to win victories over the enemy is calibrated to the strength of our commitment to our Master. The enemy spirit world knows just how committed we are and is able to work in and around us wherever there is a weakness. Our level of commitment speaks eloquently to the evil spirit world, granting us great authority if our commitment is great and less authority if our commitment is weak.

Our allegiance to Christ also gives us the authority to challenge other allegiances, both in ourselves and in others. There are many possible allegiances or commitments; some are weak (like commitment to a brand of soap or toothpaste), but a few are strong (like those to Jesus, family or job). If we are pressured to change something to which we are weakly committed, we change. On the other hand, we would rather die than break some of our strong allegiances. We need to challenge all lesser allegiances to make sure our commitment to Jesus is at the top.

Our relationship with Christ provides us with the authority to live as He did.

Allegiance to Christ	—— confronts ——→	Other allegiances

One of the enemy's priorities is getting us to use our faculties to commit ourselves more to other allegiances than to Jesus Christ. (The temptation in American society might be to make our job our primary allegiance.) This weakens our authority. In the society in which Jesus worked, the primary allegiance of most people was family. So in His teaching He appealed for people to make Him their primary allegiance (Matthew 8:21–22; Luke 14:26), even to the point of suffering and dying for Him.

Truth/Knowledge Leading to Understanding

The second crucial dimension of our Christian life and witness is *truth leading to understanding*. God's truth provides the knowledge and understanding we need to operate in the authority we have been given. Jesus taught truth with authority (Matthew 7:29) and truth about authority. With Him we have the authority to handle God's truth, to experience it, to speak it, to teach it.

One fact we dare not miss in a discussion of truth, however, is that the Greek words for *truth* and *knowledge* imply that these have been *learned by experience*. Scripture is not talking about intellectual or theoretical truth and knowledge. It advocates an understanding of truth that has been gained by experience. It is the truth experienced, not simply thought, that will set us free (John 8:32). And as the preceding verse says, the basis of this experience is obedience. We can count on the Holy Spirit to lead us in this quest for understanding (John 16:13).

Truth (experienced)	—— leads to ——>	Understanding

Like Jesus, we are to *confront ignorance and error with God's truth*. We cannot effectively confront an allegiance with truth. One allegiance can be confronted only with another allegiance. Nor can we confront power with truth. Power can be challenged effectively only with power. Whenever there is ignorance concerning any issue, however, including ignorance about allegiances or power, we are to learn and speak truth, as Jesus did. Learning the truth about false allegiances or counterfeit power can be a meaningful start toward confronting them in kind.

In Jesus' ministry, teaching truth was what He spent the most time doing, combating the ignorance and error around Him. Likewise in this book I have attempted to teach truth to supplant the ignorance and error in most of our churches concerning the subject of authority.

Truth ———— combats ————➤ Ignorance and error

The fact that our authority is grounded in truth is not to be taken lightly. It is the authority granted by the True One who frees people, in contrast with the domination and captivity our enemy brings about through deceit and lies. Much of what the world believes and practices is based on lies, such as the most important goals in life being material and temporal; or that God and spiritual things are not important, since only what we can see and touch is real; or that we, not God, are the masters of our fate, and so on. *The right to be connected to the Source of truth, and to speak and live that truth in a world like this, is an inestimable privilege.*

That privilege carries with it a great responsibility, however—the responsibility that goes with all authority: to use what we are given rightly. As 2 Timothy 2:15 instructs us, we are to win God's approval of our use of His authority by being those "who correctly [teach] the message of God's truth."

Authority to Use God's Power to Bring Freedom

The third of our crucial dimensions, the *authority to use God's power* for God's purposes, is our major concern in this book. A primary function of spiritual authority is to enable us to work in God's power in a variety of ways here on earth. These ways are prominent throughout the chapters of this book. The aim of spiritual power used in the authority of Jesus Christ is *freedom.* Our enemy holds countless people of God, not to mention those outside the Kingdom, in captivity, but we have the authority to free them.

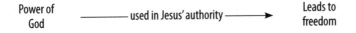

Power of God ———— used in Jesus' authority ————➤ Leads to freedom

When we use our authority to bring physical healing or inner healing to people, we are setting captives free and taking people out of Satan's hands. When we bless people, we are conveying God's power to enable them to work toward freedom. The apostle Paul writes in Galatians 5:1, "Freedom is what we have—Christ has set us free!" This is the aim of the authority we have been given. Jesus wants us free from the enemy's enslavement, free to be what both He and we want us to be. The authority and power is not for us to show off; it is to be used to bring freedom so that we can be in a proper relationship with Jesus.

The following summary chart puts these three dimensions together; the most important dimension is pictured as a tabletop and the others as legs, supporting the allegiance/relationship dimension.

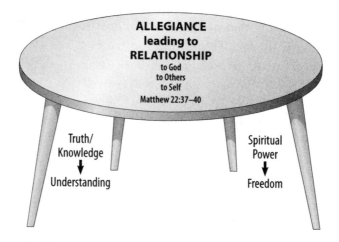

All Three Elements in Balance

Although each of these dimensions—allegiance feeding relationship, truth leading to understanding, and power bringing freedom—is distinct, Jesus interrelated them constantly as He ministered to those around Him. When He taught, He taught truth about both allegiance and power. When He healed, He used the true power of the true God to whom He was totally committed (allegiance) and with whom He had a close relationship. When He appealed for allegiance (for example, in Matthew 11:28), it was on the basis of God's truth and in God's power.

The interrelationship among these elements formed the basis for Jesus' authority, and it forms the basis for ours. If our authority to work in the power of Christ is authentic, it must be conditioned by wholehearted commitment to Him and a total concern for His truth. Thus, allegiance and truth serve as the backdrop to the proper use of spiritual authority and power.

But we need to guard against the tendency to become unbalanced or deficient, either by overemphasizing or by ignoring any of these three focal elements of our Christian experience. Evangelicals have often concentrated on truth, assuming that a proper allegiance will develop as a by-product if the person has enough truth. The power dimension is often completely neglected. Thus, we evangelicals keep two strong arrows in our quiver but ignore the third. We have gone a long way with the two arrows, but without the freedom that comes only by confronting the enemy's power with God's, our approach has suffered.

In reaction, Pentecostals and charismatics have so often focused on power that for many, the importance of truth and allegiance has gotten lost in the shuffle. Not that these groups have ignored allegiance and truth; they have not. But power, especially when surrounded by a lot of emotion, can distract from other important emphases. And it has often been allowed to distract.

Either approach is off balance and unbiblical. A fully biblical expression of Christianity emphasizes all three crucial dimensions in balance. We should make sure to use all that God has given us in each of these important areas, as Jesus and well-balanced charismatics do. Remember, the only kind of Christianity in Scripture is well-balanced charismatic.

✺ We Must Continue to Experiment

I have pointed out that there is a lot about the spirit world we do not understand. It used to be that, although many had ideas and practices in this arena that worked, they kept them secret or shared them only within a limited circle of acquaintances. But today more and more people are venturing into this realm and learning and writing about it. And whenever people begin sharing ideas, theories and experiments more openly, the process of learning escalates. Someone advances an idea and someone else critiques it, offering what he or she considers a better approach. Then someone else comes along with a radically different suggestion, and different traditions develop, each practicing its own approach and conducting experiments based on its own theories. In this way new ideas and techniques get developed, less effective ones get dropped and science moves forward.

If the same regularity exists in the interactions between the spirit and human worlds that exists in the physical world (and I believe it does), we can speak of developing a science of the spirit realm by means of the same process described above. Thus, I make no excuses for experimentation. As with the physical and human worlds, where God has left much for us to discover on our own (that is, without the benefit of special revelation), so in the spirit world. We must start with whatever the Bible shows us, but there is much more to discover through practice, theorizing and experimentation.

We know from the gospels, for example, that Jesus gives His followers authority and power. We read in the scriptural casebook some of what Jesus and the apostles did with that authority and power, but the descriptions of those events are simply outlines of what happened. We are told few details of what they did as they healed or delivered people from demons. Nor are we given such information as how long it took or whether they or others did any follow-up to bring the freed people to complete wholeness.

What we learn from our personal experience, then, are insights like these:

Often authority prayer events take quite a bit of time.

Often healings are not immediate.

Often the use of visualization helps bring about healing that seems to come in no other way.

Often getting information from demons helps to assist in deliverance.

Often the person who has been freed needs to work hard and have considerable support to consolidate the gains made during the prayer ministry time.

Scripture does not answer all our questions as we assert the authority Jesus has trusted us with. So we experiment, praying all the while that we are not going beyond what pleases God, and we develop practices that are not explicit in Scripture but that work consistently to set captives free. Often we are criticized by those who feel we go too far. Usually these people have little or no experience and would never launch out themselves to use the authority and power Jesus gives us.

A typical critique was leveled at me and several others recently by some well-meaning, thoughtful people who accused us of being unbiblical in our use of God's authority (Priest, Campbell, and Mullen 1995). It is all right to critique ministries like ours, for, as I said, that is how we learn and how a science of the spirit realm will be developed. But these people had zero experience in most of the areas in which they found our approaches off base. And, as nearly as I can tell, they do not plan to tackle these areas in practice, only in theory.

In a meeting with one of these critics, I suggested that it was difficult to take his criticisms seriously, given that he has never faced most of the problems we deal with regularly in this ministry. When we face them, we soon run out of biblical information concerning what Jesus or the apostles did in such situations. So we are forced to use our own creativity under the guidance of the Holy Spirit, and we do. "When you have worked with twenty-five demonized people," I said to this critic, "and discover that you, too, must go beyond approaches specifically indicated in the Bible, let's talk again."

I will not stop working in Jesus' authority merely because people do not like what I am doing.

If he ever does what I suggest, our conversation and relationship will be considerably different.

I continue to take critiques like his seriously, but I will not stop working in Jesus' authority merely because people do not like what I am doing. If I must choose between helping a person to freedom by using approaches not found in Scripture (though not antiscriptural) or else allowing that person to remain in bondage because my approach is not specifically taught in Scripture, I choose to help.

The fact that God blesses our efforts so regularly, using them to bring freedom to people in amazing ways, encourages us to continue both ministering and experimenting to find better ways to help people, in spite of the criticism. I take the approach of D. L. Moody, who said, I understand, in response to a person criticizing his evangelistic methods, "I like the way I do it better than the way you don't do it."

Putting These Ideas into Practice

When I teach on the subject of spiritual authority, those who buy what I have to say often ask, "How do I get started?" They have usually been unaware that they are living in enemy territory and are being harassed by Satan. When these facts are pointed out, however, they can often identify circumstances in their lives that they suspect are the result of enemy activity. So what do they do now?

Be Aware

The first issue is awareness. Like almost everything else we do, awareness is a matter of habit. We have learned as part of our Western worldview to assume that things we cannot see cannot hurt us. So we are habitually unaware of the invisible world. This habit must be changed if the material in this book is to be of any use. We have noted the assumption of the apostle Paul, articulated in 2 Corinthians 2:11, that we are aware of the enemy's schemes. But, in fact, we in our day and culture are ignorant of them unless we force ourselves to become aware of that dimension of our human condition.

In considering the matter of awareness, some refer to those who have gone too far, saying, "I don't want to be one of those who believe there's a demon under every rock and behind every bush." Nor do I. But I think it is important to find out which rocks and bushes demons *are* hiding behind. It is not wise to turn aside from the whole matter just because some carry it too far. Satan loves us to go to one extreme or the other.

So let me suggest that we risk overdoing things for a while, in order to school ourselves to the fact that there are malevolent beings out there working full-time to try to mess up our lives. I have found it helpful to go through a little ritual each morning that on the one hand brings protection and on the other hand keeps me alert to the presence of the demonic world and its devices. I suggest saying something like this:

> In the name of Jesus, I claim protection from any enemy spirits that seek to hurt or harass me or my family today. I forbid them to affect me or any of my family spiritually, emotionally, physically or in any other way.

Claim What Is Yours

As our awareness grows, we need to learn to claim what is rightfully ours. By this I mean that we should claim such things as protection from harm and freedom from harassment. Throughout the day I try to increase my consciousness of the fact that I live in a hostile world by calmly claiming God's protection as I take my daily walk, when I get into my car and at any other times there might be danger or risk.

Claiming our rights does not mean we have to remain continually conscious of the threat of the spirit world. I claim protection as I get into my car, for instance (or soon after), and then I go about my business without further concern unless I perceive danger, like a dangerous intersection or being crowded by another car. Then I claim protection again—usually saying something like "In Jesus' name I claim safety and protection"—knowing that both God and the enemy spirit world are listening, and that angels are carrying out God's orders.

When it seems that I am being harassed or interfered with in some way, I use the expression I recommended earlier: "If this is the enemy, stop it!" This helps not only to diffuse impending arguments but to minimize disruptions of public meetings, and even headaches or occasional physical problems, if they are caused by demons. (Some are, many are not.) People tell me that sometimes when they experience emotional downs, they are able to get over them by breaking the enemy's power in this way. Even lustful thoughts or thoughts of anger and bitterness can be banished by commanding the enemy to stop feeding them into one's mind.

Assert Your Authority to Change Things

Building on our awareness and the claiming of our rights, we can move to asserting our authority to change things. I have spoken of the authority God has given us to bless, bring healing, deliver from demons and forgive. I have also mentioned the canceling of enemy rights to places, property, artifacts, music and other things that have been dedicated to him. And we have discussed the authority to cancel rights obtained through curses, vows, sin and in other ways. All these bring about changes as we assert our authority.

Jesus used His authority at least once to change the weather. Maybe we can, too. I have experimented with this use of our authority. On two occasions the weather changed soon (one immediately, one later) after I commanded it to. I do not know if my command did it or not. On numerous other occasions, I have commanded weather to change and it has not!

Jesus also used His authority to multiply food. I have heard of at least three instances in recent years of the multiplication of food. One occurred in Colombia when some missionaries had prepared food in individual portions for a gathering of low-income people. If I remember correctly, about twice as many showed up as they had planned for, but each received an individual portion.

One of the major purposes of this book has been to alert us to the many areas of life in which I believe Jesus wants us to assert our authority. Let me remind us that we are continually to use the credit card Jesus has given us in our day-to-day activities. Although we must be careful to use that authority responsibly— not arrogantly, pridefully, emotionally or obtrusively—we are to use it at all times.

We are also to assert this authority in our families. Whatever our status in the family, we have others to be concerned about. The enemy is fond of attacking the weakest and least protected. We are responsible to use our authority to protect whoever is under our authority, and probably others as well, at least on occasion. We have considered suggestions as to how heads of households can protect those under their authority. And we have pointed out that there seem to be counter-rules by which those with lesser authority can protect themselves and even have influence on those with greater authority. For the many women who find themselves in disadvantageous positions with respect to authority, the use of 1 Corinthians 7:14 as the basis for asserting authority can be very effective.

I hope chapters 16 and 17 have been helpful in applying an understanding of spiritual authority to the Church. I tried to raise certain issues that most pastors seem not to recognize concerning their authority and its use. And finally I have commented on our need to claim the authority of our Lord and Master in the places where we work. Circumstances change in the classroom, in the office, even in places where we enjoy coffee breaks, when someone takes the authority Jesus gives us to kick out whatever enemy spirits may be infecting the place.

We have spoken of the use of authority in ministry. I have not gone into the detail I might have in this area because I have written seven other books on the subject (all available on Amazon.com):

Christianity with Power offers a general treatment of worldview and the use of authority in ministry.

Deep Wounds, Deep Healing explores ways to use our authority in a ministry of deep-level healing that gets at problems of an emotional or spiritual nature.

Defeating Dark Angels speaks of our use of Jesus' authority in dealing with demonization.

Confronting Powerless Christianity continues the theme of attempting to awaken evangelical Christian leaders to the present use of spiritual power.

A broader use of authority in dealing with various matters, including territorial spirits, is treated in the compilation *Behind Enemy Lines*.

A quest for a science behind the relationship between the spirit world and the human world is found in *The Rules of Engagement*.

A quick approach to inner healing is the subject of *Two Hours to Freedom*.

❧ Do We Know the Enemy's Schemes?

I am concerned that we know what our enemy is up to. Awareness is crucial: No army goes into battle without studying their enemy thoroughly. And from what Paul said in 2 Corinthians 2:11, it looks as though God expects us to be onto our enemy and his devices. Since he works 24/7 to thwart what God is doing in, with and through us, no weak-kneed, mild-mannered approach to defeating him will work. Though we are to be gentle toward people, in relation to the enemy of our souls we are to conduct all-out warfare.

No army goes into battle without studying their enemy thoroughly.

Let's learn his schemes and how to use the authority God gives us to speak God's power when and wherever we can, to squelch what the enemy is doing or wants to do. In our hands is the credit card of *In Jesus' name*, backed by the authority of Jesus' resurrection defeat of Satan and all his followers. Let's use it.

I pray that this book will be effective in challenging you to be and do all that God wants you to be and do, in and with His authority. I bless you to that end.

Bibliography

Beckett, Bob, with Rebecca Wagner Sytsema. 1997. *Commitment to Conquer.* Grand Rapids, Mich.: Chosen Books.

Bubeck, Mark L. 1975. *The Adversary.* Chicago: Moody.

Cho, Paul Y. 1984. *Prayer: Key to Revival.* Dallas: Word.

Clinton, J. Robert. 1988. *The Making of a Leader.* Colorado Springs: NavPress.

———. 1989. *Leadership Emergence Theory.* Altadena, Calif.: Barnabas Publishers.

Crow, D. Michael. 1996. "Spiritual Authority: Theoretical, Biblical, Historical." Doctoral tutorial paper, Fuller Seminary.

Dawson, John. 1989. *Taking Our Cities for God.* Lake Mary, Fla.: Creation House.

Deere, Jack. 1993. *Surprised by the Power of the Spirit.* Grand Rapids, Mich.: Zondervan.

Foerster, W. 1985. "Exousia." In *Theological Dictionary of the New Testament: Abridged in One Volume,* edited by Gerhard Kittel and Gerhard Friedrich, translated by G. W. Bromiley. Grand Rapids, Mich.: Eerdmans.

Foster, Richard J. 1978. *Celebration of Discipline.* New York: Harper and Row.

Hibbert, Albert. 1982. *The Secret of His Power.* Tulsa, Okla.: Harrison House.

Kraft, Charles H. 1989. *Christianity with Power.* Portland, Ore.: Wipf and Stock.

———. 1994. *Behind Enemy Lines.* Portland, Ore.: Wipf and Stock.

———. 1995. "Christian Animism or God-Given Authority." In *Spiritual Power and Missions,* edited by E. Rommen. Pasadena, Calif.: William Carey Library.

———. 2005a. *Appropriate Christianity.* Pasadena, Calif.: William Carey Library.

———. 2005b. *Christianity in Culture.* Rev. ed. Maryknoll, N.Y.: Orbis Books.

———. 2010a. *Deep Wounds, Deep Healing.* Rev. ed. Ventura, Calif.: Regal.

———. 2010b. *Two Hours to Freedom.* Grand Rapids, Mich.: Chosen Books.

———. 2011. *Defeating Dark Angels.* Rev. ed. Ventura, Calif.: Regal.

Kraft, Charles, and David DeBord. 2000. *The Rules of Engagement*. Portland, Ore.: Wipf and Stock.

MacNutt, Francis, and Judith MacNutt. 1988. *Praying for Your Unborn Child*. New York: Doubleday.

McAll, Kenneth. 1984. *Healing the Family Tree*. Rev. ed. London: Sheldon Press.

Merriam-Webster's Collegiate Dictionary. 2008. 11th ed. Springfield, Mass.: G & C Merriam.

Murphy, Ed. 1990. "From My Experience: My Daughter Demonized?" *Equipping the Saints* 4, no. 1 (Winter).

Nee, Watchman. 1972. *Spiritual Authority*. New York: Christian Fellowship Publishers.

Otis, George Jr. 1999. *Informed Intercession*. Ventura, Calif.: Renew.

Priest, Robert J., Thomas Campbell, and Bradford A. Mullen. 1995. "Missiological Syncretism: The New Animistic Paradigm." In *Spiritual Power and Missions,* edited by Edward Rommen. Pasadena, Calif.: William Carey Library.

Pytches, David. 1985. *Spiritual Gifts in the Local Church*. Minneapolis: Bethany House.

Sandford, John and Paula Sandford. 1985. *Healing the Wounded Spirit*. Tulsa, Okla.: Victory House.

Sherman, Dean. 1990. *Spiritual Warfare for Every Christian*. Seattle: Frontline Communications (YWAM).

Silvoso, Edgardo. 1991. "Prayer Power in Argentina." In *Engaging the Enemy*, edited by C. Peter Wagner. Ventura, Calif.: Regal.

Strong, James. 1981. *Strong's Exhaustive Concordance: Compact Edition*. Grand Rapids, Mich.: Baker.

Verny, Thomas, and John Kelly. 1981. *The Secret Life of the Unborn Child*. New York: Dell.

Von Campenhausen, Hans. 1969. *Ecclesiastical Authority and Spiritual Power in the Church of the First Three Centuries*. Translated by J. A. Baker. Stanford, Calif.: Stanford University Press.

Waetjen, Herman C. 1984. "Binding and Loosing." In *Evangelical Dictionary of Theology*, edited by Walter A. Elwell. Grand Rapids, Mich.: Baker.

Wagner, C. Peter, ed. 1988. *How to Have a Healing Ministry*. Ventura, Calif.: Regal.

———. 1990. "Territorial Spirits." In *Wrestling with Dark Angels*, edited by C. Peter Wagner and Douglas Pennoyer. Ventura, Calif.: Regal.

———. 1991. *Engaging the Enemy*. Ventura, Calif.: Regal.

———. 1992. *Prayer Shield*. Ventura, Calif.: Regal.

———. 1993. *Breaking Strongholds in Your City*. Ventura, Calif.: Regal.

Wimber, John. 1987. *Power Healing*. San Francisco: Harper and Row.

Wink, Walter. 1986. *Unmasking the Powers*. Philadelphia: Fortress.

Wright, Nigel. 1990. *The Satan Syndrome*. Grand Rapids, Mich.: Zondervan.

Subject Index

Scripture Index

21:14   90
21:23   11
22:37–39   34
23:3   111
23:13   40
23:16–21   108
25:14–15   99
25:26   99
25:30   99
27:25   179
27:51–53   139
28:9   242
28:18   42, 51, 72
28:19   284
28:19–20   42, 51
28:20   54, 238

Mark

1:22   40
1:25   86
1:27   11
1:32   32
1:41   86
3:14–15   311, 316
4:35–41   28
5:1–13   270
5:1–20   33
5:6–8   259–60
6:1–6   40
6:34   86
8:11–12   76, 86
10:16   239
10:42–45   146
11:28   40
12:40   104

Luke

1:19   21, 140
1:42   239
2:22–38   285
2:34–35   239
3:21–22   40, 166, 237
3:22   118
4:1–13   166, 190, 270
4:5–6   39
4:6   23, 24, 143, 146, 155

4:18   53, 232, 307
4:18–19   309
4:28–30   167
4:33–35   90
4:35   86
4:36   40
4:38–39   90
4:39   56, 253
4:40   90
5:12   90
5:12–14   90
5:13   56, 253
5:15   90
5:17   237
5:17–26   254
5:18–20   90
5:24   56
6:6–10   90
6:10   56
6:19   90
6:28   64, 239
7:1–10   63
7:2–10   90
7:6–10   56
7:11–15   267
7:13   86
7:13–15   90
7:14   56
7:21   90
8:22–25   28, 112, 167
8:25   110
8:26–39   90
8:41–42   267
8:43–48   90
8:44   56
8:49–56   267
8:51–56   90
9   54, 79, 238, 258
9:1   42, 54, 73, 110, 150, 253, 258
9:1–2   72
9:1–6   45, 110
9:2   165
9:4–5   152
9:10–17   112
9:11   90
9:13   90, 111

9:16   242
9:42–43   90
9:51–55   111
10   54, 79, 258
10:1–12   110
10:5   64, 238
10:5–6   152, 242
10:6   64
10:9   42, 165, 253
10:10–11   64
10:17   42, 54, 79, 111
10:19   72, 166
10:20   79
10:21   238
11:13   119, 126
11:16   76
11:19   40
12:32   47, 314
12:41–48   100
12:42–48   197
13:10–13   90
13:34   107
14:1–4   90
14:26   317
15:7   133
16:1–8   100
18:35–43   90
19:11–27   197
20:2   40
21:36   59
22:29–30   47, 314
22:31–32   167
22:40   59
22:42   232
22:50–51   90
23:8–9   86
24:30–31   242
24:36   242
24:49   52, 73, 118, 122
24:50–51   242

John

1:12   147, 316
2:4   167
4:34   94
5   255
5:2–9   91

Charles H. (Chuck) Kraft is retired from the faculty of the School of Intercultural Studies at Fuller Seminary (formerly the School of World Mission) after forty years as professor of anthropology and intercultural communication. He taught anthropology, communication, contextualization and spiritual dynamics (inner healing, deliverance and spiritual warfare) to missionaries and prospective missionaries.

He holds degrees from Wheaton College (B.A., anthropology), Ashland Theological Seminary (B.D., theology) and Hartford Seminary Foundation (Ph.D., anthropological linguistics). He served as a pioneer missionary among a tribal group (Kamwe/ Higi) in northeastern Nigeria for three years, followed by five years each on the faculties of Michigan State University and UCLA teaching linguistics and African languages.

Chuck is the author of thirty books and numerous articles in the fields of his expertise. He spends most of his time now ministering to those with emotional and spiritual problems and conducting deep healing (inner healing) seminars in churches worldwide. God has used him to lead thousands to spiritual and emotional freedom in Jesus Christ.

Those who would like ministry or a seminar may contact him at ckraft@fuller.edu.